The Challenges
Leadership

MW00562052

Despite the rising interest in school districts, there are relatively few comprehensive resources available for graduate students in educational leadership programs. *The Challenges of School District Leadership* takes the position that the best way to prepare the next generation of school district leaders is to make certain that they are prepared to address the unending challenges that characterize public education today. Drawing on the latest research as well as actual examples, the book spotlights ten of the perennial challenges facing superintendents and school boards. Among the challenges discussed in detail are balancing equity and excellence, accommodating demographic change, coping with the increasing politicization of district leadership, deciding how to organize (or reorganize) a school system, and meeting the demands of educational accountability. Key features of this exciting new text include the following:

- **Problem Oriented**—Books on school district leadership typically address the functions of the central office, not the complex problems with which district leaders must grapple. This is the only book to date that focuses on what leaders need to do in order to understand and address strategic and operational challenges.
- **Organizing Themes**—The book asserts the following: 1) challenges derive from both external and internal sources; 2) because school districts function within a highly politicized context, ignoring these challenges is normally not an option; 3) every response to a challenge involves costs as well as benefits; and 4) district responses to challenges often generate additional challenges.
- **Chapter Structure**—Each chapter opens with a brief, illustrative case which is followed by a discussion regarding the nature of the challenge and the circumstances in which it may arise. Sections following that deal with the different ways that school district leaders are addressing the challenge and the costs and benefits of those responses.

This text is appropriate for graduate students in educational leadership, education policy, and the politics of education as well as school district leaders.

Daniel L. Duke is Professor of Educational Leadership in the Curry School of Education at the University of Virginia. He is also a member of the Partnership for Leaders in Education, a unique collaboration between the Curry School and the Darden Graduate School of Business Administration.

The Challenges of School District Leadership

Daniel L. Duke

University of Virginia

Routledge
Taylor & Francis Group

NEW YORK AND LONDON

First published 2010
by Routledge
270 Madison Avenue New York, NY 10016

Simultaneously published in the UK
by Routledge
2 Park Square, Milton Park, Abingdon, Oxon OX14 4RN

Routledge is an imprint of the Taylor & Francis Group, an informa business

Typeset in Minion by EvS Communication Networx, Inc.
Printed and bound in the United States of America on acid-free paper by Walsworth Publishing Company, Marceline, MO.

Library of Congress Cataloging in Publication Data
Duke, Daniel Linden.
The challenges of school district leadership / Daniel L. Duke.
p. cm.
Includes bibliographical references and index.
School districts. 2. School boards. 3. School superintendents. 4. Educational leadership. I. Title.
LB2817.D85 2010
379.1'535—dc22
2009041818

ISBN 10: 0-415-99622-8 (hbk)
ISBN 10: 0-415-99623-6 (pbk)
ISBN 10: 0-203-85427-6 (ebk)

ISBN 13: 978-0-415-99622-8 (hbk)
ISBN 13: 978-0-415-99623-5 (pbk)
ISBN 13: 978-0-203-85427-3 (ebk)

To Yvonne Brandon, Tom DeBolt, Deborah Jewell-Sherman,
Dennis Lauro, Pam Moran, and Eleanor Smalley:
Superintendents with the capacity to care and the courage to lead.

CONTENTS

PREFACE

What causes some school systems to thrive while others struggle? The difference, according to many observers, is leadership. School systems that consistently perform well seem to be blessed with capable leaders at all levels, from the school board and the central office to individual schools and classrooms. But what, exactly, do these capable leaders contribute that their less successful counterparts do not? What, in other words, is the "leadership difference?"

All school systems face challenges. School district leaders function, for example, in environments characterized by uncertainty and ambiguity. They never know for certain when resources will disappear, enrollments will fluctuate, and new mandates will be promulgated from above. Law suits and lobbying by special interest groups are always possibilities. Widespread agreement regarding the mission of public education can never be taken for granted. Superintendents rarely know for certain when they will be able to fill key positions with highly qualified professionals.

The difference between more successful and less successful school systems often boils down to the ability of leaders to anticipate and address the unending challenges that arise to threaten performance. In this book we shall examine many of these challenges, especially ones that impact instructional effectiveness and student achievement. We will see how district leaders vary in their responses to challenges and consider which responses tend to be more and less effective.

Some of the challenges that face school district leaders can be found in any bureaucratic organization. All organizations, for instance, need to organize to accomplish their missions. Other challenges are relatively unique to the world of education; interpreting the results of student testing and making the necessary adjustments when test results are disappointing come to mind.

Some of the challenges that face school district leaders are perennial. Year in and year out, securing the resources and personnel needed to operate tests the wits and political skills of a good many superintendents and school board members. Other challenges only may arise once in the tenure of a particular leader. Such a challenge may involve a fight for control with a disgruntled mayor or an unexpected influx of refugees from a foreign country.

The only thing that these challenges have in common is the expectation that school district leaders will address them in a manner that minimizes the negative impact on teaching and learning. This book is intended for those who exercise, or hope one day to exercise, leadership at the district level. These individuals range from superintendents and school board members to deputies, associates, and assistants charged with programmatic responsibilities. While what goes on in schools and classrooms is of great salience to the discussions that follow, this is not a book that focuses on the leadership exercised by principals and teachers.

A disclaimer is also in order. This is not a book of recipes that guarantee the successful resolution of daunting problems. The complex nature of the challenges facing contemporary school district leaders and the political world in which these challenges must be addressed preclude standardized solutions. In some cases, the problems are not problems at all. Rather, they are dilemmas with no solution. This is not to say that school district leaders can afford to ignore dilemmas. They must act. Unlike a problem, a dilemma cannot be "fixed" because every effort to address one aspect of the dilemma creates other issues.

Instead of recipes, this book offers road maps. By mapping the terrain that contemporary school district leaders must traverse and describing the potholes and detours that stand between them and high performance, the book can serve as a useful guide. Readers also can benefit from the experiences of fellow "travelers." While no school district leader's journey is ever quite the same, there are often enough similarities to provide valuable advice and insight.

INTRODUCTION

In every community there is one individual, more so than any other, on whose shoulders rests the burden of future generations' hopes and dreams. This individual is not a physician, not a cleric, not a business leader, not even a politician. The individual is a school district superintendent. Superintendents are entrusted with ensuring that the youth of every community receive the education necessary to achieve their aspirations and become contributing members of society. Such an awesome responsibility is not to be taken for granted. At every turn contemporary superintendents face an array of challenges. This book explores many of these challenges and the various ways that superintendents and their associates are addressing them. The central assumption supporting this work is that school district leaders typically have choices regarding how to respond to challenges. Where there are choices, there is the potential for more effective and less effective responses. It is hoped that this book will assist school district leaders and those who aspire to school district leadership to identify and assess the range of possible responses to some of public education's most pressing challenges.

GROWING INTEREST IN SCHOOL DISTRICTS

If superintendents several decades ago had sought guidance concerning a particular problem or issue, they would have found relatively little systematic research on school districts. Most of the available scholarship focused on schools and classrooms. Why school districts were neglected is unclear. Perhaps educational researchers found the "front lines" inherently more interesting than the "headquarters." Teaching and learning, of course, take place at the "chalkface." School district offices conjure up images of red tape, regulations, and bureaucracy. Many people, including veteran educators, are unsure what actually goes on at the school district level. Uncertainty begets suspicion and wariness. Central offices are associated with constraints and compliance, not cooperation and capacity building.

Recent inquiry has resulted in a dramatic shift in our understanding of school districts and the role they can play in promoting good education. Thanks to comprehensive histories of high-performing school districts (Duke, 2005; Ouchi, 2003), investigations of dramatic school district turnarounds (Duke, 2008; Reville, 2007; Simmons, 2006; Supovitz, 2006) in-depth studies of particular challenges facing school districts (Hill, Campbell, & Harvey, 2000; Hightower, Knapp, Marsh, &McLaughlin, 2002), case studies of school districts by the University of Virginia's Partnership for Leaders in Education and Harvard University's Public Education Leadership Project, and incisive reports by the Council of the Great City Schools, the Wallace Foundation, and other organizations committed to improving public education, contemporary school district leaders have a wealth of information and insight from which to draw. The education community now realizes that school districts play a crucial role in determining what happens in schools and classrooms. As one analysis of five innovative school districts concluded:

> *Districts can make a difference.* If as a nation we are serious about improving achievement for all students, we cannot expect the staff of each of the nation's approximately 95,000 public schools to figure out how to do this work on their own...school districts play an essential role in providing a coherent instructional framework to help schools, particularly low-performing schools, succeed. (Togneri & Anderson, 2003, p. 49)

Central office bureaucracies are capable of being truly supportive of principals and teachers. Visionary superintendents and their associates are demonstrating that low-performing school systems can be transformed and good school systems can get even better.

School district success, regrettably, is not universal. The continued existence of low-performing and under-performing school systems provides part of the justification for this book. All school districts confront challenges that can distract leaders from their core missions. It is not the case that outstanding school districts avoid such challenges. The difference between good school districts and struggling school districts lies in how they choose to address their challenges. While there may not be one best way to respond to particular challenges, there clearly are inadequate and ineffective responses. By drawing on the growing body of knowledge concerning school districts, this book seeks to understand the kinds of challenges school district leaders are likely to face, how they are addressing them, and the ways these challenges can be prevented from impeding performance in schools and classrooms.

KEY ASSUMPTIONS ABOUT SCHOOL DISTRICTS

To set the stage for the book, it is necessary to discuss several aspects of the environments in which school district leaders work. One of the first words that comes to mind when thinking about contemporary school districts is *complexity*. When school district experts speak of organizational complexity, they can be referring to many things. Complexity may characterize school districts with missions that are complicated, controversial, or ambiguous. It would be difficult, in fact, to locate a school district where the focus of operations is solely "reading, writing, and 'rithmetic." Today's public schools are expected to address a variety of concerns, ranging from keeping the nation economically competitive to serving the health, mental health, and welfare needs of disadvantaged youth. As the breadth of their mission grows, school districts predictably experience uncertainty regarding priorities and how best to allocate limited resources.

Complexity also is associated with the proliferation of special programs designed to address various aspects of a school district's mission. School districts support programs to improve reading achievement for at-risk students, programs for after-school tutoring and daycare, programs for the professional development of staff members, programs to adjust resources for low-performing schools, and programs devoted to school safety and security. No sooner does a troubling issue such as childhood obesity or school bullying surface in the media than pressure builds for school districts to create a new program to address it. Programs may result from federal, state, and local initiatives, but every program, regardless of its origin, shares certain common features with other programs. Programs must be supported with resources, managed, and monitored for effectiveness. These functions require additional personnel, thereby adding to the size of central offices and promoting the impression of an every-expanding bureaucracy. Special programs also are associated with new rules and regulations governing such matters as eligibility to receive program benefits, program staffing, and program delivery.

Rules and regulations, in fact, constitute another dimension of complexity. The term *formalization* is used by organization theorists to describe the extent to which organization members are constrained by rules and regulations. To appreciate the high degree of formalization found in many school districts, one need only refer to the district policy manual. Virtually every action that school district personnel undertake is governed by a policy of some kind along with related rules and regulations.

Keeping track of all the policies, rules, and regulations becomes a major challenge in and of itself, in the process contributing to the perception of inexorable school district complexity.

This is a book about the challenges faced by school district leaders. Organizational complexity surely must be considered one of the most daunting challenges. Complexity, however, is not only a challenge. It also is a response to challenges. Every addition to a school district's mission, every new program, every new policy and regulation is a response to a challenge of some kind. The point is this. School districts continually confront challenges; yet in the very act of responding to these challenges, new challenges may be generated.

Consider the case of a school district that must address a sharp drop in funding. To respond to this challenge, the superintendent decides to reduce expenses by eliminating music teachers. She instead sub-contracts with a national firm that provides music training. The firm sends a music instructor for several hours every week to each elementary school in the district. This arrangement saves a considerable amount of money, but it creates new challenges. To ensure compliance, the contract with the national firm must be managed. Who will mange the contract becomes an issue. Principals already have more than they can handle. So, too, do central office supervisors. Another issue arises when parents begin to complain about the quality of the instruction provided by the national firm's music instructors. Some parents claim the instructors are too demanding. Others point out that their children are not receiving as good instruction as they did from the fulltime music teachers that previously ran the elementary music programs.

Questions eventually are raised about the wisdom of cutting fulltime music teachers. Why didn't the superintendent try to reduce the budget in other ways? Parents point to aspects of school district operations that they would have preferred to see reduced. They begin to lobby school board members to reinstate fulltime music teachers.

The efforts of these parents to alter the course of action chosen by the superintendent is another illustration of school district complexity. School districts exist in environments characterized by scarce resources, lobbying, politics, and conflicting opinions about what should be done. Decisions made in such environments invariably are perceived to benefit some individuals and groups more than others. Pleasing everyone seems to be virtually impossible. Every victory comes at a price.

In a perfect world, there would be agreement that the most practical course of action is also the most effective course of action. Consensus would exist that what school districts are required to do by law also reflects what people believe to be the ethically correct course of action. We, of course, do not live in a perfect world. School district leaders frequently feel that, by obeying the laws governing education, they are not doing what is ethically or morally right. They make decisions for politically expedient reasons that they know are not educationally sound. Every decision made by a school district leader can be a questionable decision under particular circumstances. Ultimately, it is this pervasive sense of uncertainty that makes the job of leading a school district so challenging.

A WORD ON THE NATURE OF CHALLENGES

Critics of public education seem to suggest at times that all the problems faced by school district leaders are of their own creation. Apologists for public education, on the other hand, suggest that school districts are helpless victims of changing demographics, government mandates, economic ups and downs, and other forces beyond the control of educators. This book adopts a balanced position in line with Edgar Schein's (1985) contention that all organizations, public and private, face both internal and external challenges. To be effective, they must address both types of challenge successfully.

Schein contends that one set of challenges fits under the rubric of *external adaptation*. Educators, for the most part, exert little control over these challenges. Failure to adapt to the environment, according to Schein, can threaten the continued existence of the organization. This warning may not have been as applicable to schools and school districts in years past, but the No Child Left Behind Act and various state accountability measures are dramatically changing the landscape of public education. Perennially low-performing schools now can be reconstituted or closed, and failing school districts may be subject to state takeover.

To adapt to their environments, school districts must understand the needs of their students. Achieving such understanding can be quite challenging when a locality is subject to demographic shifts, immigration, and changes in the economy. School districts function in a political as well as a social context. Most of the resources upon which school district leaders rely are derived from politically based sources, including local voters, state legislators, and the federal government. Failure to read the political tea leaves correctly can be very costly to school districts. Individuals who are dissatisfied with public education have become adept at organizing political action groups and lobbying for their causes. School district leaders frequently feel they are lodged between a rock and hard place when efforts to address one group's concerns are sure to threaten another group's interests.

The economic sphere constitutes another dimension of every school district's external environment. Local businesses count on their schools to provide them with skilled employees. When skilled employees are not forthcoming, businesses become highly critical of the schools and their leaders. They question how their tax dollars are being spent. But school districts do not exist only in a local environment. They are part of an increasingly global economy. Today, when China or India sneezes, the United States catches cold. School districts are expected to prepare young people who can compete with their counterparts in Singapore and South Korea. When the U.S. economy experiences a decline, the public invariably points a finger at their schools.

As if the challenges resulting form school districts' social, political, and economic contexts were not daunting enough, school districts also function within a cultural context. It is not unusual for school districts to face challenges to their programs, policies, and practices because they are deemed incompatible with local values and beliefs. Just because a state policy requires schools to teach evolution and sex education is no guarantee that local residents will accept such dictates. Insensitivity to community norms has cost more than one school district leader their job.

Clearly, then, the effectiveness of every school district depends to a great extent on how well district leaders are able to understand and adapt to the external environment. At the same time, however, every school district must negotiate the challenges associated with what Schein calls *internal integration*. Internal integration depends on school district personnel being committed to achieving a common mission using approved practices and programs. There is considerable evidence that such a commitment cannot be taken for granted. The "urban legends" of public education suggest that some teachers insist on following their own compass once the classroom door is shut. Other stories describe renegade principals who selectively enforce school district policies. Then there are accounts of the failure of school boards and superintendents to see eye-to-eye. The key to internal integration is *aligned leadership* where leaders at every level of a school district agree on the direction in which the district is headed and the means by which to get there.

This book examines a variety of challenges facing contemporary school district leaders. Some challenges are more closely associated with external adaptation; others are more representative of internal integration. In every instance, though, the challenges have implications for *both* external adaptation and internal integration. Consider the challenge of educational accountability. Pressure for greater educational accountability originally derived from the external environment, especially the federal government and state legislatures. These entities wanted a thorough accounting of how tax dollars were being spent and to what effect. Over time, efforts by school districts to respond to demands for greater accountability generated a variety of internal challenges. Principals complained that additional paperwork prevented them from functioning as instructional leaders. Teachers resented evaluations of their performance based on student test scores. Parents disliked the heavy emphasis on the standardized testing of their children. As will be seen throughout the discussion to follow, efforts by school district leaders to address one challenge frequently give rise to other challenges.

So what is a "challenge?" Why is the term *challenge* used instead of *problem*? For the purposes of this book, a challenge is any development that poses a potential threat to the ability of a school district to provide effective teaching and learning. Effective teaching and learning is teaching and learning that achieves the specified objectives of the school district's academic program. These objectives typically are based, in the post-No Child Left Behind world, on state curriculum guidelines and, in some cases, on local school-board-adopted content standards.

The term *challenge* is preferred over *problem* because of the belief that only challenges that are inadequately addressed become problems. The position taken in this book is that challenges are a normal by-product of complex organizations operating in complex environments. Some school districts from time to time, of course, face more challenges than other school districts, but no school district is blessed with challenge-free operations. The important difference between school districts is not the number of challenges that they face, but how well challenges are addressed. The grail for every school district leader is to address a challenge so effectively that it does not grow into a problem. A challenge becomes a problem when efforts by school district leaders to address the challenge fail to prevent a negative impact on teaching and learning.

CHALLENGES ADDRESSED IN THIS BOOK

Three sections make up the organization of *The Challenges of School District Leadership*. The first section covers strategic challenges—challenges that relate directly to the mission of school districts. Chapter 1 addresses two outstanding priority concerns—educational equity and educational excellence—and the possibility that they may constitute competing priorities under certain circumstances, especially when school districts experience changing demographics. Chapter 2 considers some of the specific challenges that result from shifts in the student population. These challenges range from fluctuating enrollments to changes in the make-up of the student body. The third chapter is devoted to challenges related to school district governance. When it comes to making decisions regarding the mission of public education and how that mission should be achieved, school district leaders must contend with a variety of opinions about what is best for children from a multiplicity of groups seeking to influence the education process.

The second section of the book deals with a variety of operational challenges. These are challenges that arise as school district leaders attempt to achieve their districts' missions. Chapter 4 focuses on school district structure and the challenges that result from trying to get organized for teaching and learning. Educational accountability, the demands it places on school district leaders, and the mechanisms for achieving it are discussed in the fifth chapter. As a result of the No Child Left Behind Act and other accountability measures, considerable attention has been given to groups of students that are not experiencing success in school. Chapter 6 addresses the challenges associated with improving instruction so that all students can achieve at high levels. The likelihood of improving instruction is greatly reduced when teachers and administrators are unable to ensure that students learn in safe and orderly environments. Chapter 7 is concerned with various challenges that threaten the orderly operation of schools and classrooms. Instructional improvement is hard to imagine without capable teachers and instructional leaders. Chapter 8 examines a variety of challenges related to staffing schools, including recruitment and retention of highly qualified teachers and principals and ensuring that school-based personnel focus on student achievement.

The third section of the book is devoted to what might be regarded as two fundamental challenges of school district leadership. Each involves achieving a reasonably high level of understanding of a complex phenomenon. Such understanding is a crucial ingredient in meeting the strategic and operational challenges of school district leadership. Chapter 9 discusses the challenges of understanding the complexities of the change process. The final chapter is devoted to understanding perhaps the most elusive phenomenon of all—leadership.

In an effort to present these challenges in a reasonably coherent and consistent manner, each chapter opens with a brief case study that illustrates a key dimension of the particular set of challenges under discussion. An analysis of various aspects of these challenges follows. The chapter then uses a set of reflective questions to organize a discussion of the ways that school district leaders are addressing the challenges. The strengths and weaknesses of particular responses are identified along with research findings related to the actions of school district leaders. Each chapter ends with an "executive conclusion" summarizing the key points made in the chapter.

In his path-breaking examination of the collapse of entire societies, Jared Diamond (2005) notes that disaster can result from failure to anticipate challenges. A similar warning holds for school district leaders. The history of public education suggests that sooner or later school districts will confront most, if not all, of the challenges addressed in this book. For school district leaders, there is no substitute for being prepared. It is hoped that this book will help with that preparation.

REFERENCES

Diamond, J. (2005). *Collapse*. New York: Viking.

Duke, D.L. (2005). *Education Empire: The Evolution of an Excellent Suburban School System*. Albany: State University of New York Press.

Duke, D.L. (2008). *The Little School System That Could: Transforming a City School District*. Albany: State University of New York Press.

Hightower, A.M., Knapp, M.S., Marsh, J.A., & McLaughlin, M.W. (eds.). (2002). *School Districts and Instructional Renewal*. New York: Teachers College Press.

Hill, P.T., Campbell, C., & Harvey, J. (2000). *It Takes a City: Getting Serious about Urban School Reform*. Washington, D.C.: Brookings Institute Press.

Ouchi, W.G. (2003). *Making Schools Work*. New York: Simon & Schuster.

Reville, S.P. (ed.). (2007). *A Decade of Urban School Reform*. Cambridge, MA: Harvard Education Press.

Schein, E.H. (1985). *Organizational Culture and Leadership*. San Francisco: Jossey-Bass.

Simmons, J. (2006). *Breaking Through: Transforming Urban School Districts*. New York: Teachers College Press.

Supovitz, J.A. (2006). *The Case for District-based Reform*. Cambridge, MA: Harvard Education Press.

Togneri, W., & Anderson, S.E. (2003). *Beyond Islands of Excellence: What Districts Can Do to Improve Instruction and Achievement in All Schools — A Leadership Brief*. Alexandria, VA: Association for Supervision and Curriculum Development.

1

Strategic Challenges

1

THE CHALLENGE OF COMPETING PRIORITIES

ACCESS TO EXCELLENCE

Thomas Jefferson High School for Science and Technology is arguably the finest public school in the United States. Opened in 1985 by Fairfax County Public Schools in northern Virginia, the high school offers a learning environment and a curriculum designed for high-achievers. Courses frequently are taught in laboratory settings created through the generosity of local corporations. AT&T, for example, helped set up a Telecommunications Laboratory. The Life Sciences and Biotechnology Laboratory was initiated by Hazleton Laboratories, Inc. Honeywell, Inc. provided support for the Computer Systems Laboratory. Jefferson students benefit from state-of-the-art technology and instructors with advanced degrees.

The success of Thomas Jefferson High School for Science and Technology can be ascertained from the performance of its students in academic competitions and on various standardized tests. Jefferson students annually win more National Merit Scholarships and take more Advanced Placement tests than students from any other high school. Graduates of Jefferson go on to attend the most prestigious colleges and universities in the nation.

There is only one problem with Thomas Jefferson High School for Science and Technology. It cannot accommodate all the students who want to enroll. Knowing that admission to Jefferson almost ensures academic success, parents in Fairfax County begin grooming their children for the entrance examination in middle school. Expensive private programs to

3

prepare students for the examination flourish in Fairfax County. Parents realize that there are 420 openings for ninth graders each year and that the number of students seeking admission far exceeds 420. In 2001, for example, 2,884 eighth graders sat for the entrance examination.

Fairfax superintendents have learned to be on their guard at the beginning of every school year because the racial and ethnic make-up of Jefferson's entering class invariably becomes a public issue. When Dan Domenech learned that the entering class of 2001 contained only 2 African-American and 7 Hispanic students out of 420 rising ninth graders, he decided that the admissions process had to be revised. Born in Cuba, Domenech was well aware of the importance of a high quality education for all groups of students.

Domenech considered several options. Slots at Jefferson could be allocated by geographic region. Given the residential patterns in Fairfax, such a policy would produce more minority representation. Alternatively, each racial and ethnic group could be guaranteed a specified number of slots at Jefferson. The problem was that Fairfax County was comprised of dozens of racial and ethnic groups with substantial populations. Neither of these policies was received well by parents of white and Asian parents whose children typically filled most of the slots at Jefferson.

Eventually Domenech decided on a compromise of sorts. The traditional selection criteria, which included the admission examination results and teacher recommendations, were to be used for 400 ninth grade slots. The remaining 20 slots were reserved for under-represented neighborhoods. Domenech understood that few people would be pleased with this compromise, but at least it represented a step in the right direction.

✳✳✳✳✳

As superintendent of a large and highly diverse school system, Dan Domenech faced an important challenge. The reputation of Fairfax County Public Schools depended, to a great extent, on its ability to offer programs of academic excellence, programs epitomized by Thomas Jefferson High School for Science and Technology. At the same time, he was obligated to do everything in his power to promote educational equity. How could every student who sought admission to Jefferson be guaranteed access? Was such an outcome even desirable? Could a top quality program be sustained if enrollments increased? Would it be better to shut down Jefferson than to continue to operate the school and deny access to hundreds of students? Such questions go to the very heart of every high-performing school district's mission.

WHAT IS THE MISSION OF A PUBLIC SCHOOL DISTRICT?

When the U.S. economy began to struggle in the face of growing foreign competition in the late 1970s and early 1980s, corporations were accused of trying to do too many things. The key to success, according to business gurus like the authors of *In Search of Excellence* (Peters & Waterman, 1982), was to "stick to the knitting." Corporations, in other words, should decide what they were best at producing and concentrate on producing it. Using excess capital to acquire unrelated businesses was no substitute for continuously improving the core business.

Should public school districts heed such advice? Is it possible for a public school district to develop a truly focused set of priorities? U.S. history reveals a tendency for virtually every social problem eventually to produce a plea for public schools to get involved. Americans' expectations for public education over the past century have been ambitious, diverse, and often controversial. When the United States fell behind the Soviet Union in the space race, public schools were called on to produce more scientists and engineers. When policy makers finally acknowledged that minorities were victims of discrimination, public schools were called on to lead the march to an integrated society where all people would be treated fairly. In his history of Hamilton High, Grant (1988) describes one incarnation of the high school in which the focus of attention shifted from academics to a host of social services. To address the needs of its changing student body, Hamilton High initiated "free breakfast and lunch programs for children on welfare, sex education programs, drug counseling, suicide prevention programs, medical advice and counseling for pregnant teenagers, an in-school nursery for children of students, and after-school child care" (p. 66).

It is impossible to understand the mission of public schools and school districts without understanding the social and temporal contexts in which they function. Priorities are formed in the crucible of contemporary culture. Contexts change, and with change come new problems for educators to confront. Some of these problems have no precedent. The pressures on schools in the aftermath of the September 11 terrorist attacks and Hurricane Katrina come to mind. Other problems are all too familiar for veteran school district leaders. Of this second set of problems, perhaps no two are more familiar than the demands for educational equity and educational excellence. When it comes to determining school district priorities, this pair of concerns typically are at, or near, the top of the list.

From Brown to No Child Left Behind

A quick survey of the educational issues that have dominated the agendas of policy makers since the end of World War II reveals the persistence of equity and excellence. Having fought and died to protect American democracy, African Americans returned form World War II to a society where they were denied the full benefits of democracy. Their insistence on freedom from racial discrimination led to the landmark *Brown v. Board of Education* in 1954 (Imber & Van Geel, 2000, pp. 189–191). The foundation for the case derived from the equal protection clause of the Fourteenth Amendment, which forbids any state from denying citizens the equal protection of the laws. The Supreme Court agreed with the plaintiff in *Brown* that segregated schools for blacks were inherently unequal. The path to school integration thereby was paved.

Before substantial numbers of black students could travel that path, however, another educational priority interceded. One month after federal troops were sent to Little Rock, Arkansas, to ensure the peaceful integration of Central High School in September of 1957, the Soviet Union successfully launched a satellite that orbited the Earth. Americans grew concerned that their nation had fallen behind in science and technology. Demands were made to increase the rigor of high school education. Only by raising the quality of instruction in key courses such as mathematics and physics would the United States be able to match the achievements of its Cold War rival. James Bryant Conant (1959), former president of Harvard University, called for small high schools to be consolidated, thereby creating large enough pools of high-achieving students to enable teachers to group students by ability. To challenge these students, a variety of accelerated courses, including Advanced Placement courses, were developed, and high school tracking became institutionalized in public high schools. Eminent scientists displaced teachers as curriculum developers, and teachers spent their summers attending workshops and institutes in order to be able to implement the rigorous new curriculums.

As school districts around the country geared up to address the need for higher educational expectations, attention began to shift back to matters of equal opportunity. The intent of the *Brown* decision remained unrealized, as states in the South either openly resisted desegregation or pursued policies of token desegregation. In the first of a series of initiatives that marked the beginning of a much more active role in public education, the federal government pressed for passage of the Civil Rights Act of 1964, which enabled the Attorney General of the United States to initiate lawsuits to compel school districts to desegregate. The law also made it possible for federal funds to be withheld from segregated school systems. A year later, Congress passed the Elementary and Secondary Education Act, the most comprehensive education bill up to that time. The primary focus of the bill, especially its Title I, was to provide greater access to educational opportunities for disadvantaged children. All poor children, not just poor black children, stood to benefit from the federal government's expanding role in public education.

The federal focus on expanding educational opportunities continued for nearly two decades. New groups of students received protection under the Fourteenth Amendment. In 1972 Congress passed Title IX of the Education Amendments Act, thereby enabling females to enjoy the same educational benefits as males. The needs of non-English-speaking students received similar attention as a result of a court decision in 1974. The ruling in *Lau v. Nichols* compelled school districts to abandon the sink-or-swim practice of assigning non-English-speaking students to regular classrooms where many were unlikely to learn what they needed to progress in school. A year after *Lau*, Congress passed Public Law 94-142, the Education of All Handicapped Children Act. The bill guaranteed procedural due process for all children identified as having special needs based on physical, cognitive, and emotional handicaps. In little over ten years, considerably more than half of the students attending public schools in the United States were placed under the protective umbrella of federal law. In the process, the principle of equal educational opportunity, which had driven initial efforts to assist black students and poor students, was joined by another important principle—*educational equity*.

While interpretations of the meaning of educational equity continue to vary, a fairly common understanding of its implications holds that the term is an acknowledgment that, under certain circumstances, providing unequal treatment may be necessitated in order to redress the prior effects of discrimination and educational inequities. Equal opportunity, in other words, may be insufficient to make up for the accumulated effects of poverty, racial bias, and other social hurdles.

As the United States began to experience economic problems, first in the mid-1970s with sharply rising prices for petroleum and then with stiff competition from industrial powers Japan and Germany, fears surfaced that all the attention being devoted to educational entitlements had eroded the academic rigor of public schools. As a result, young American workers were perceived to lack the preparation needed to sustain traditionally high levels of productivity. To make matters worse, too few Americans were opting for careers in science, engineering, and technology. National concern culminated in the 1983 blue-ribbon commission report entitled *A Nation at Risk* (National Commission on Excellence in Education, 1983).

The authors of *A Nation at Risk* indicated that the very security of the American way of life had been jeopardized by declining student achievement, watered-down curriculums, and low academic expectations. Embarrassing comparisons were drawn between the achievement of U.S. students and students in other countries. Among the report's recommendations was that all students should undertake a rigorous program of study and that expectations for acceptable performance must be raised substantially. When educational excellence had been called for previously, identifying the brightest students and providing them with accelerated coursework had been the preferred prescription of policy makers. *A Nation at Risk* proclaimed that nothing short of educational excellence for *all* students would ensure that the United States remained competitive in an increasingly global economy.

As states and school districts busied themselves with raising graduation requirements, increasing expectations in core areas such as mathematics and science, eliminating unchallenging electives, and developing common curriculum standards, concerns once again surfaced regarding students who struggled academically. Drawing on the title of the report issued by the National Commission on Excellence in Education, educators and advocates expressed their fear that the push for more rigor would have an adverse impact on "at-risk" students. Warnings of rising dropout and retention rates were sounded.

To raise academic standards without disadvantaging large numbers of students, policy makers insisted on greater accountability on the part of school districts and their leaders. States began developing curriculum standards and standardized tests aligned to the standards. Students were required to take external standardized tests to determine whether they had learned the required content, and the test results often were published in school and district "report cards." No longer was it possible for low-performing schools and school districts to fly under the radar.

The move for greater educational accountability reached its zenith with the passage in 2002 of the No Child Left Behind Act. According to Hess and Petrilli (2006, p. 27),

> The No Child Left Behind Act sought to shift federal education policy from its historic emphasis on redistributing money and regulating how that money was spent to a focus on the performance of students, schools, and school districts.

Guidelines were developed for establishing standards of learning, measuring academic performance, prescribing strategies to correct low performance, and sanctioning schools and districts that continually performed below benchmarks. Data on student achievement, for the first time, had to be reported by sub-groups—African American students, Hispanic students, poor students, female students, special education students, and so on. No longer would schools and school districts be able to offset low performance by one sub-group with test scores from a high-achieving sub-group. To make adequate yearly progress under No Child Left Behind, all sub-groups had to attain established targets on standardized tests.

Six years after the passage of the No Child Left Behind Act, concerns persisted that children still were being left behind. To persuade presidential candidates to keep educational equity on the "front burner," members of a new group, The Education Equity Project, went to Washington, D.C. Speaking for the group, which included school district leaders, New York City Schools Chancellor Joel Klein reminded the candidates that, as long as black high school students continued to lag an average of four years behind their white peers in reading and math, the promise of equal educational opportunity embodied in the *Brown* decision remained an empty one (Turque, 2008).

The preceding overview of educational policy initiatives illustrates the periodic ascendance of concerns for educational equity and educational excellence. When equity rises to the top of policy makers' agendas, it typically results from concerns that the nation is failing to live up to the promise of a democratic society. When excellence becomes the focus of attention, the issue is whether the United States can retain its position of pre-eminence internationally. Interestingly, educational equity is rarely linked to international pre-eminence, and educational excellence is seldom associated with fulfilling the promise of a democratic society.

The world is characterized by limited resources. There is rarely enough time, energy, and funding to permit the pursuit of every ideal. Is it possible for school districts to achieve both educational equity and educational excellence? Are some of the measures that districts take to ensure equity likely to undermine efforts to promote excellence? These and related questions are addressed in the following sections.

The Pursuit of Equity

No school district leader can afford to ignore concerns about educational equity. Initiatives related to equity are regularly found among lists of district priorities. When Superintendent Dan Domenech and the Fairfax County School Board developed a strategic plan to guide the giant school system into the 21st century, most of the ten goal priorities involved some aspect of educational equity:

- All students will be reading at grade level by the end of second grade; goals will be established for students with limited English proficiency and for students who have disabilities that affect reading achievement.
- The percentage of juniors and seniors enrolled in Advanced Placement (AP) or International Baccalaureate (IB) courses will be maintained or increased, with at least two-thirds of students scoring a three or higher on an AP exam or a four or higher on an IB exam. Enrollment for Black and Hispanic students will increase by ten percent.
- The percentage of students scoring above the national average on the verbal and on the mathematics sections of the SAT will exceed the previous year's percentage, and the gap between minority and majority students' scores will narrow by ten percent.
- By better identifying all children who are entitled to receive gifted and talented (GT) services and by making those services readily available to all eligible students, the number of Black and Hispanic students in the gifted and talented program will increase annually and, over a five-year period, move toward the percentage of Black and Hispanic students in the general population.
- The minority student achievement gap for Black and Hispanic students taking the eighth grade SOL tests in reading and math will narrow by ten percent.
- … student behavior will improve as measured by…a ten percent reduction in the disparity of suspensions between minority and majority students. (*Strategic Plan*, Fairfax County Public Schools)

Noteworthy with regard to Fairfax's strategic goals is the concern for narrowing the achievement gap between minority and majority students and reducing disparities in suspensions and participation in advanced academic programs. Developers of the strategic plan realized that educational equity and educational excellence are connected. This realization is apparent in the school district's vision statement:

The vision for Fairfax County Public Schools is to provide a gifted-quality education for every child in an instructional setting appropriate for his or her need. (*Strategic Plan*, Fairfax County Public Schools)

Three questions related to the pursuit of educational equity are addressed in the remainder of the chapter. School district leaders should be prepared to explore each of these queries in their efforts to increase opportunities for all students.

The Challenge of Educational Equity

1. What obstacles must school districts overcome in order to move toward greater educational equity.

2. What is the school district's role in reducing the achievement gap between groups of students?

3. Is it possible for school districts to achieve both educational equity and educational excellence?

OBSTACLES TO EQUITY

In the contentious world of educational policy, there is one matter on which agreement is virtually universal. The greatest hurdle to be overcome on the road to educational equity is the wide gap in achievement between groups of students. Two groups that receive considerable attention are African American and Hispanic students. In all but a handful of schools, these students' academic achievement falls significantly below the level of their white peers. Achievement gaps, however, also have been found between poor children and more advantaged children (Pianta, Belsky, Vandergrift, Houts, & Morrison, 2008), English-language learners and English-speakers (*Policy Notes*, 2005), and students with disabilities and non-disabled students (Ogbu, 2003).

For every under-performing group, there are a variety of indicators of differential achievement, numerous "causal stories" to account for the gaps, and multiple strategies for narrowing the gaps. This section zeroes in on one group—African American students—to illustrate some of the complex challenges that differential achievement presents for school district leaders.

Every year every school district in the United States administers a variety of standardized tests, and every year since the advent of the No Child Left Behind Act, local newspapers publish the results. In communities where African Americans live, African American parents scan the results to see how their students are performing. While individual black students frequently perform well, the average pass rates and average scores almost always reveal a double-digit difference between African American and white students (Chubb & Loveless, 2002; Ogbu, 2003). Even in affluent communities like Fairfax County, Virginia, and Shaker Heights, Ohio, black students tend to perform well below their white peers (Duke, 2005; Ogbu, 2003). There are indications that the achievement gap widens the longer students are in school, suggesting that schools contribute in some way to the gap (Reardon, 2008).

The achievement gap is not limited to performance on standardized tests. Black students on average have lower grade point averages than white students (Ferguson, 2001). Graduation rates for white students exceed rates for black students, sometimes by as much as 30 percent or more (Diplomas Count, *Education Week*, 2008). Other gaps have been noted in course level enrollment, performance in specific courses, and rates of participation in gifted programs (Ford, Grantham, & Whiting, 2008; Ogbu, 2003). Black students are more likely than white students to be retained at grade level, to be placed in special education, to drop out of school, and to be suspended and expelled (Chubb & Loveless, 2002; Ogbu, 2003).

Few people dispute the fact that African American students as a group are not benefitting as much from public education as are their white counterparts. Why this is the case is another matter altogether. Opinions vary widely concerning the reasons for the achievement gap. Such opinions, referred to by Stone (1989) as "causal stories," grow into narratives used by policy makers and special interest groups to justify particular prescriptions for narrowing the gap. Stone notes that individuals and groups that succeed in getting their causal stories accepted are in a strong position to dictate how to correct the situation.

School district leaders must understand and reflect on the various causal stories offered to account for the black-white achievement gap. Furthermore, they should be able to express a reasoned opinion regarding the existence and persistence of the achievement gap. Every effort by a school district to address the achievement gap needs to be grounded in an informed causal story. Explanations for the achievement gap between African American and white students can be divided roughly into two groups—causes linked to what goes on in schools and causes derived from sources outside of schools.

School-Based Explanations   Suggesting to educators that they may wittingly or unwittingly contribute to the achievement gap is almost certain to spark defensiveness and controversy. Most educators believe that they are doing what is best for their students. Research, however, reveals several ways that educators can be part of the problem. It is these school-based causes to which school district leaders must attend before addressing causes that reside largely beyond educators' control.

The "soft bigotry of low expectations" is a school-based cause that receives considerable attention (Noddings, 2007, p. 34). Researchers have noted that teachers, especially white teachers, frequently have lower academic expectations for black students (Weinstein, 2002). Lower expectations are manifested in the classroom in various ways. Teachers may not call on black students as often as they do on white students. When they do call on black students, they may ask them easier questions and provide them less time to respond. Black students may be given simpler assignments and graded less rigorously than white students. Weinstein (2002) has demonstrated that students are aware of differential expectations. The confidence and self-esteem of black students is undermined by the knowledge that their teachers perceive them to be less capable than white students.

Closely related to the problem of low expectations are the practices of homogeneous grouping and tracking. As Weinstein (2002, p. 104) points out, "In children's eyes, how students are grouped for instruction within their classroom provides clues about their relative smartness." Students are well aware of which groups contain the students that teachers regard as brighter and which groups contain the students considered less capable. Over time students assigned to the latter groups come to accept their fate. Homogeneous grouping, in other words, can become a self-fulfilling prophecy when the groups are perceived to be permanent.

When students reach secondary school, they often encounter tracking. Tracking is the logical follow-up to homogeneous grouping in elementary school. Students deemed less capable are counseled, or sometimes required, to take less rigorous coursework. Research fails to find benefits in the creation of classes with high concentrations of low-achieving students (Mickelson, 2001, pp. 221–222). What starts out as a "track" eventually becomes a "rut." There is little escaping a low track once a student begins taking less challenging classes. Weinstein (2002, p. 224) and her colleagues tried to improve the quality of instruction in one California high school's low track classes, but the results were discouraging:

> By the end of the first year, we were frustrated: high expectations… shared responsibility, calls to parents were not enough. Classes limited to low achieving students did not work: our students needed student models of scholarship and good behavior.

Tracking and homogeneous grouping would be causes for concern regardless of the students involved, but when a disproportionate number of the students in low tracks and low within-class groups are students of one race or ethnic group, these practices may constitute a form of unintended—or sometimes intentional—discrimination (Mickelson, 2001, p. 221). In many school systems with African American students, it is, in fact, the case that these students are over-represented in low tracks and low within-class groups.

The negative effects of grouping and tracking practices often are related to how schools are staffed. Low-track classes, for example, often are taught by teachers who lack experience and adequate credentials (Michelson, 2001, p. 237). Schools with large percentages of African American students also are more likely to be staffed by larger percentages of less qualified teachers. Part of the staffing problem, of course, is tied to resources. Schools with large percentages of African American students typically are located in communities where the funds available for public education are limited (Odden & Busch, 1998, pp. 8–13). Inadequate funding, of course, is ultimately a function of forces largely beyond the control of local educators.

Local educational leaders, however, have an obligation to raise public awareness of revenue-related disparities and their likely consequences for students. School district leaders frequently raise their voices to express concern for inadequate funding. They may be less willing, however, to engage in open discussions of the black-white achievement gap and its school-based causes. When Grogan and Sherman (2003) interviewed a sample of Virginia superintendents, for example, they were surprised to discover that most superintendents were reluctant to raise the achievement gap issue in public. It goes without saying that failure to raise public awareness of an issue like the achievement gap reduces a school district's ability to enlist external support in addressing the issue.

Other Explanations   Besides the explanations for the black-white achievement gap that derive from the actions, or inaction, of educators, there are a number of causal stories involving factors largely beyond educators' control. In his effort to understand why an achievement gap existed in affluent Shaker Heights, Ohio, Ogbu (2003, pp. 33–44) reviewed many traditional explanations, including school-based practices and policies, genetic deficits, lower socioeconomic status, discrimination and racial segregation, cultural differences, and language-dialect differences. While he acknowledged the validity of some of these explanations, he also argued that the black-white achievement gap cannot be fully understood without an in-depth knowledge of the educational beliefs and behaviors of African Americans themselves. To gather this information, he and his colleagues actually spent time in the homes of Shaker Heights black families. Ogbu reported that black students had high academic aspirations, and they were proud of the excellent reputation of Shaker Heights schools. He was surprised to discover, therefore, that these students "did not work hard [in school], admitted that they did not work hard, and believed that they could have made better grades if they worked as hard as they could and should" (p. 260).

Ogbu (2003) offered no simplistic explanation for his disturbing findings, instead presenting a variety of possible contributing factors. Some black students, for example, perceived that American society continued to be characterized by unequal opportunity. They doubted whether hard work in school would yield the same rewards for black students as for white students. Ogbu found that some black students also associated success in school with "acting white." They experienced a certain degree of peer pressure not to excel in academic work, work that was regarded as a product of the dominant society. Ogbu characterized this problem as an issue of "oppositional culture." Another reason for the lack of hard work in school, according to Ogbu, derived from parents' low level of involvement in their children's schooling. Parents "did not supervise their children's homework closely; neither did they teach their children appropriate use of their time" (p. 261).

Ogbu's conclusions generated considerable controversy. After conducting his own research with students in Shaker Heights, Ferguson (2001) supported some of Ogbu's findings and challenged others. When seventh to eleventh graders were surveyed, they indicated completing less homework on average than whites, participating less in class discussions, and enrolling in fewer Advanced Placement and honors classes. They also reported being more inclined to act tough and get into fights than their white counterparts. These findings, to Ferguson, seemed to support the notion of an oppositional culture on the part of black students.

Once Ferguson (2001) controlled for socioeconomic status, however, some of his findings had to be reinterpreted. Middle- to upper-class blacks and whites were similar in their propensity to participate in class discussions. Black makes actually reported being more interested in their studies than white males. The survey also indicated that black students spend more time on their homework than white students. Since black students, regardless of socioeconomic status, tended to complete their homework less often, Ferguson conjectured that they may lack certain academic skills and receive less help at home. Finally, Ferguson found that black and white students are equally pleased with their teachers, and both groups feel they are treated fairly by teachers.

Ferguson is not alone in his contention that the black-white achievement gap is likely to be confounded by socioeconomic factors. Noguera (2008, p. 150) found that high school students with the lowest grade point averages reside in the poorest neighborhoods. A disproportionate number of these students are African American and Hispanic. Rothstein (2004) pointed out that parents' low income alone may be less of an issue than the overall financial assets to which black families have access:

> ... black families who earned a low income in one specific year
> are likely to have been poorer for longer than white families who

earned a similar income that year... [which] helps explain why black students, on average, score lower than white students with the same family incomes. (p. 42)

Rothstein went on to note several other contributors to the achievement gap that are beyond the control of educators. Related to socioeconomic status and, subsequently, to race and ethnicity are health needs and mobility. Children from low-income families are less likely to receive preventive health care and more likely to develop health problems that cause them to miss school. The shortage of affordable housing for low-income families results in frequent moves. Educators find it difficult to provide consistent instruction when students are constantly switching schools.

The preceding discussion highlights some of the challenges facing school district leaders who are committed to promoting greater educational equity. While they can do little to reduce disparities in income and change certain aspects of minority culture, school district leaders are in a position to create conditions conducive to narrowing the achievement gap between various groups of students.

The School District's Role in Reducing the Achievement Gap

What actions can school district leaders take to narrow the achievement gap between various groups of students and promote greater educational equity? The literature provides abundant evidence of effective district-based initiatives. Six will be highlighted in this section, but there are many more actions that could have been cited. Some of these will be discussed in subsequent chapters.

Equity: What Can School District Leaders Do?

Raise awareness of achievement gaps.

Increase expectations and set targets.

Identify and investigate proven policies, programs, and practices.

Develop a strategic plan that focuses on literacy, order, and instruction.

Allocate extra resources to schools where achievement gaps are greatest.

Continuously monitor, evaluate, and fine tune policies, programs, and practices.

Raise Awareness of Achievement Gaps   It goes without saying that educators and community members are unlikely to address achievement gaps if they are unaware that such gaps exist. As a result of requirements under the No Child Left Behind Act for reporting disaggregated student achievement data, lack of awareness of achievement gaps should no longer be an issue. Besides the black-white gap, differences in achievement can be determined annually for other minority groups, poor students, male and female students, non-English-speaking students, and special education students. Student achievement data also can be tracked over time so that school district leaders can see whether gaps are narrowing or getting wider.

Kotter (1996) points out that the first act of change leadership is creating a sense of urgency regarding what needs to be changed. The continued existence of achievement gaps is indisputably a condition that demands change. Equally indisputable is the fact that educators alone are unlikely to eliminate the gaps. Effective teaching and other interventions are capable of narrowing gaps in achievement, but significant reductions in differential achievement also require the active involvement of parents and community members (Noguera, 2008, p. 154; Ogbu, 2003, pp. 274–281). These groups can reinforce the value of working hard in school, provide role models of academic success, establish supplementary educational programs, and advocate for children.

Engaging parents and community members requires leadership. That leadership, in the case of Fairfax County Public Schools, came initially from an African American school board member who relentlessly insisted that something had to be done to address the black-white achievement gap. In other instances, leadership may be provided by a superintendent committed to educational equity or a local civic organization. At any given time, there are a number of troubling conditions that compete for the attention of politicians and the public. It is the responsibility of school district leaders to keep concerns regarding educational equity at the top of the public's agenda for action.

Increase Expectations and Set Targets   "You get what you expect" is one of those often-repeated warnings that is particularly applicable to public education. In an effort to raise expectations, the No Child Left Behind Act introduced adequate yearly progress (AYP) as a yardstick by which to determine the progress of schools and school districts. States have done their part by raising graduation requirements and the scores required to pass state tests. Ultimately, however, the issue of expectations plays out between individual teachers and students at the classroom level. Weinstein (2002, p. 103) identifies the six features of classroom life that influence expectations. These include:

1. The ways in which students are grouped for instruction.
2. The materials and activities through which the curriculum is taught.
3. The evaluation system that teachers use to assess student learning.
4. The motivational system that teachers use to engage student learning.
5. The responsibility that students have in directing and evaluating their learning, and
6. The climate of relationships within the class, with parents, and with the school.

School district leaders may not directly influence classroom expectations, but they can create the organizational conditions that support high expectations for all students. One dimension of these conditions may entail "opportunity-to-learn" standards that define the availability of rigorous programs, qualified staff, academic assistance, and other resources for *all* students (Ravitch, 1995, p. 13). Another dimension may involve the standards by which school administrators and teachers are evaluated. Establishing high expectations for students means little if they are not coupled with high expectations for educators.

One of the most important contributions to high expectations that school district leaders can make is to set specific annual targets for academic improvement to guide teachers and principals. A good example are the goals that Dan Domenech set for Fairfax County Public Schools (see pp. 14–15). The targets are aimed at reducing achievement gaps, but not only for state standardized tests. They also address gaps in student enrollment in AP and IB courses, student representation in gifted and talented programs, and scores on the SAT tests as well as disparities in suspensions between minority and majority students. By setting specific targets for the school district, district leaders provide guidance for the school-based developers of improvement plans. The success of district efforts to promote greater educational equity across schools ultimately depends on the alignment of school targets with district targets.

Identify and Investigate Proven Policies, Programs, and Practices   As important as it is to raise awareness of achievement gaps, it is equally important to let people know that achievement gaps can be and are being narrowed. It is hard to imagine a more crucial function of school district leadership than fostering hope that inequities can be corrected. A crucial strategy for generating hope involves the identification of policies, programs, and practices that have been demonstrated to be effective at raising the performance of low-achievers. While school district leaders may not personally undertake this process, they should see to it that members of their staffs monitor research on and evaluations of interventions aimed at narrowing the achievement gap.

Many professional organizations and think tanks make it their business to collect and disseminate information on promising policies, programs, and practices, so the task is not as daunting as it might seem. Among the sources of information are the Association for Supervision and Curriculum Development, the American Association of School Administrators, the American Educational Research Association, the National Association of Elementary School Principals, the National Association of Secondary School Principals, the National Education Association, the American Federation of Teachers, the Council of the Great City Schools, and the Council of Chief State School Officers. These groups share information through publications, conferences, and training programs.

While a thorough review of promising interventions is beyond the scope of this chapter, subsequent chapters will identify a variety of policies, programs, and practices that have proven effective. School district leaders must see that care is exercised when adopting approaches to raising achievement. It is unconscionable to risk victimizing low achievers by resorting to interventions that lack evidence of effectiveness. Struggling students are not guinea pigs on whom untested policies, programs, and practices can be tried.

Fortunately, examples of effective interventions abound. They range from early childhood education programs such as the High/Scope Perry Preschool Program (Nores, Belfield, Barnett, & Schweinhart, 2005) to comprehensive school improvement programs such as Success for All (Slavin & Madden, 2002). A proven program that engages community members and parents as well as an array of health and mental health specialists is the School Development Program of James Comer (2004). Some schools have opted to develop their own initiatives rather than adopt or adapt an external model. Examples of highly successful schools that enroll high numbers of poor and minority students are available from a variety of sources (Chenoweth, 2007; Johnson & Asera, 1999; McGee, 2004; Picucci, Brownson, Kahlert, & Sobel, 2002).

Identifying proven interventions not only can give hope to students and parents, it can inspire confidence in the teachers who must undertake the "heavy lifting" of raising student achievement. Though hard to measure, hope and confidence in the long run may prove to be the most consequential outcomes of effective school district leadership.

Develop a Strategic Plan that Focuses on Literacy, Order, and Instruction   When it comes to raising the academic performance of underachieving groups, less may be more. Trying to focus on a wide variety of different initiatives is no focus at all. One of the primary responsibilities of school district leaders faced with educational inequities is to set priorities to guide the allocation of time, energy, and resources. When achievement gaps are present, three areas of concern frequently are identified: literacy, order, and instruction. It is hard to imagine any narrowing of achievement gaps without attention to these areas. Fortunately, these are areas over which school district leaders can exercise considerable influence. Accounts of school districts that have experienced success in raising the achievement of under-achieving groups indicate that these areas serve as key priorities and that strategic plans can be constructed around improving each (Hightower, 2002; Reville, 2007; Supovitz, 2006).

Problems with literacy, especially reading, constitute the basis for most low achievement. Schools that fail to meet adequate yearly progress typically are characterized by low scores in reading and English (Allington, 2006; Duke, Tucker, Salmonowicz, & Levy, 2007). The problem is especially pronounced in schools with large numbers of recent immigrants from non-English-speaking countries. It is difficult to find a subject in the curriculum that does not require students to read, write, listen, and communicate. When Thomas Payzant became superintendent of Boston Public Schools, he recognized the centrality of literacy and saw to it that a system-wide instructional model was adopted that focused on getting all students to read, write, talk, and explore topics with teachers and classmates (Reville, 2007, p. 21). When Alan Bersin and Anthony Alvarado assumed the executive and instructional leadership of San Diego City Schools, they quickly implemented a common Literacy Framework to guide elementary instruction (Hightower, 2002, p. 82). When Deborah Jewell-Sherman launched her campaign to turn around Richmond Public Schools, she zeroed in on raising reading scores in Richmond's lowest achieving schools. She insisted that each of these schools adopt the Voyager reading program, and she negotiated a partnership with Voyager to provide systematic professional development for teachers.

Providing instruction in literacy is challenging under the best of circumstances. When classrooms are characterized by disorder and indiscipline, the task becomes even more difficult. Many schools with large numbers of low-achieving students also report high rates of violence and discipline referrals. Such conditions undermine parent confidence and lead to an exodus of students whose parents have the means to find alternatives. When school district leaders develop strategic plans to address achievement gaps, they need to consider setting targets for promoting safe and orderly schools and classrooms. Specific measures that school districts can take in this regard will be addressed in Chapter 7.

No effort to raise student achievement can afford to ignore the quality of instruction, especially instruction for struggling students. When the Learning First Alliance studied five school districts that managed to raise student achievement across all races and ethnicities for three consecutive years, it reported that all five districts established a focus on instruction (Togneri & Anderson, 2003). Further, the investigation revealed the fact that instructional improvement depended on a coherent, systemwide approach. Leaving instructional improvement up to individual schools was simply too risky. John Fryer understood the need for a systemic approach to instructional improvement when he became superintendent of Duval County (Florida) Public Schools (Supovitz, 2006). Much of the credit for Duval's systemwide turnaround can be credited to Fryer's insistence on the development of a common vision of good instruction. When researchers analyzed data from the Early Childhood Longitudinal Study, they concluded that relying on teacher background qualifications was insufficient to ensure effective instruction (Palardy & Rumberger, 2008). They recommended that policy makers promulgate policies that focus on continuous instructional improvement for all teachers. The issue of instructional improvement will be taken up in greater detail in Chapter 6.

Allocate Extra Resources to Schools where Achievement Gaps are Greatest Reducing achievement gaps depends on priorities and planning, but without sufficient funding, priorities and plans may go unrealized. In the past, school district leaders who turned to educational researchers for support in their efforts to justify greater funding for low-achieving schools found little compelling evidence. Since the mid-1990s, however, the impact of additional resources on student achievement has been well-established (Darling-Hammond, 1997; Flanagan & Grissmer, 2002). The impact appears to be greatest for disadvantaged and minority students.

School district leaders are helping to raise student achievement by channeling additional resources to low-achieving schools. Jerry Weast, superintendent of Montgomery County (Maryland) Public Schools, saw to it that Broad Acres Elementary School, the poorest school in the district and a candidate for state takeover, received extra funds for teacher training, reduced class size, a full-day Head Start program, full-day kindergarten, and special intervention for low achievers. The result was a dramatic increase in student achievement, especially for minority students (de Vise, 2008a). When Jim Pughsley led the Charlotte-Mecklenburg school system, he pursued a similar tack for all low-achieving schools. These "Equity Plus" schools received 30 percent greater funding than other schools. The additional money was used to lower teacher-student ratios and hire reading and math specialists, among other things. The result, once again, was increased student achievement.

School district leaders obviously are in a better position to re-allocate resources within their districts than to address funding disparities across school districts. In *Savage Inequalities*, Jonathan Kozol (1991) described in disturbing detail the enormous gap in educational finances between urban school districts with large percentages of disadvantaged students and affluent suburban school districts. To reduce these disparities, school district leaders have become politically active and enlisted the assistance of sympathetic legislators. When relief is not forthcoming from the political process, the court of last resort is the court system. Working with educational organizations and concerned citizens, school district leaders have brought suit on behalf of their students. Without equitable educational funding, the dream of comparable access to educational benefits is unlikely to become reality.

Continuously Monitor, Evaluate, and Fine Tune Policies, Programs, and Practices   The need for school district leadership does not diminish once awareness of inequities has been raised, expectations have been increased, proven interventions have been identified, priorities have been set, and resources have been secured. School district leaders must continue to supervise efforts to reduce achievement gaps and increase the distribution of educational benefits to all students. Doing so requires monitoring, evaluating, and finetuning policies, programs, and practices intended to reduce inequities.

There is no guarantee that policies designed to improve the quality of schooling necessarily benefit all students. Duke and Canady (1991, p. 7) have offered the following definition of a good school policy in order to guide school district leaders in their assessment of policies:

> A *good school policy* is one that increases the likelihood that school goals will be achieved without adversely affecting any particular group of students.

Policies may not please all parties, but they should avoid discriminating against or placing at a disadvantage sub-groups of students. Duke and Canady (1991) identify a variety of policies related to grading, grouping, homework, and discipline that have been shown to adversely affect particular groups of students. Policies that require teachers to assign and grade homework, for example, may place poor students at a disadvantage if they lack home environments conducive to completing homework and the school does not provide settings in which homework can be completed. Perhaps no area of school policy has generated more concern among minority advocates than discipline. Minority students, and particularly African American students, are more likely to receive disciplinary referrals than their white peers and also more likely to be suspended and expelled (Fenning & Rose, 2007). The likelihood of meeting academic expectations and advancing to the next grade are greatly reduced when students miss large amounts of time due to exclusionary discipline. School district leaders should see to it that policies are reviewed on a regular basis to ensure that they are administered fairly and contribute to the education of all students.

Similar reviews are needed for programs and practices intended to assist struggling students. Good intentions are not enough, especially when resources are limited. If certain programs and practices fail to yield desired outcomes, they should be revised or replaced. A case in point involves out-of-class assistance for low-achieving students. There is some evidence that external tutoring programs and programs that provide undifferentiated assistance may be less effective than *targeted* assistance—in other words, assistance that addresses each student's particular problems (Duke, 2008a; Glod, 2008).

Monitoring, evaluating, and finetuning school district policies, programs, and practices are all dimensions of educational accountability. Accountability is more than reporting test scores. It entails assurances that efforts to achieve equity are having the intended effect. To ensure that these functions are performed on a continuing basis, some school districts such as San Diego and Fairfax County have created central office accountability units. In the case of Fairfax County, the Department of Educational Accountability includes the Office of Minority Student Achievement, an operation devoted to monitoring the performance of minority students in all schools in the district, and the Office of Program Evaluation, which is charged with regularly evaluating the effectiveness of nearly a hundred district intervention programs (Duke, 2005, pp. 152–156). The challenge of educational accountability will be taken up in greater depth in Chapter 5.

MUST EQUITY AND EXCELLENCE
BE COMPETING PRIORITIES?

This chapter's third question for school district leaders asks whether it is possible to achieve both educational equity and educational excellence. Must these two goals necessarily represent competing priorities?

Doubtless the point is obvious, but it still needs to be underscored. It is hard to achieve what cannot be envisioned. Do school district leaders possess a clear vision of what educational equity and educational excellence would look like if they were achieved? Are they able to communicate these visions to others? Only by comparing visions of equity and excellence can a determination be made of their compatibility.

If, for example, educational equity means having virtually all students achieve relatively modest levels of "adequate" performance on standardized tests, then efforts to realize educational equity may undermine the pursuit of educational excellence. Alternatively, if educational equity entails providing virtually all students with opportunities to stretch themselves to the boundaries of their abilities, then the pursuit of equity actually can reinforce the quest for excellence. It is worth noting that the National Commission on Excellence in Education (1983, p. 12) defined excellence at the level of the individual student as performance "on the boundary of individual ability in ways that test and push back personal limits."

What of the meaning of educational excellence? If educational excellence means focusing on one dimension of human ability and identifying a small number of students who surpass their peers in this ability, then efforts to achieve excellence are likely to undermine the cause of educational equity. But, if excellence is associated with introducing all students to multiple models of excellence in various areas of human endeavor, then the pursuit of educational excellence can complement the quest for educational equity.

When school district leaders think about educational excellence, what often comes to mind are gifted and talented programs, honors tracks, Advanced Placement and International Baccalaureate classes, magnet programs, and specialty schools with entrance requirements. Access to such opportunities typically is limited. Savvy parents understand this fact and begin grooming their children early. In elementary school they lobby principals for the best teachers for their children and insist on getting their children into gifted and talented programs. In one school system with which the author is familiar, parents "in the know" make certain that their children learn to play a musical instrument in elementary school. These parents understand that if their children are involved in band and orchestra when they get to high school, they will be scheduled together for most of the school day (in order to attend band or orchestra class). The band and orchestra students, in effect, form a separate track, one which caters to the needs of the college-bound. Children whose parents fail to understand how the system works are left to fend for themselves in regular courses. It comes as no surprise that most band and orchestra students are white, despite the fact that half of the high school population is African American.

Assuming that educational equity and educational excellence should be compatible, not competing, priorities, what can school district leaders do to promote a convergence of interests? Among the initiatives that have the potential to promote both equity and excellence are reducing low-level middle school courses, increasing access to challenging courses in high school, developing programs of gifts and talents, and exposing students to multiple models of excellence. Let us briefly examine each.

Promoting Equity Through Excellence

- Reduce low-level middle school courses
- Increase access to challenging courses in high school
- Develop programs of gifts and talents
- Expose students to multiple models of excellence

REDUCE LOW-LEVEL COURSES IN MIDDLE SCHOOL

Middle school has been a perennial trouble spot in the American public school experience, especially for minority students. The black-white achievement gap widens in middle school, suggesting schools may be contributing to the problem (Reardon, 2008; Viadero, 2008). Behavior and attendance problems increase in middle school, along with suspensions. One causal story to account for the minority middle school malaise concerns the sharp contrast to elementary school presented by the middle school experience. Because neighborhoods continue to be racially segregated in many parts of the United States, black and Hispanic students often attend elementary schools that are predominantly minority. In these settings, minority students frequently flourish, earning good grades and building solid self-esteem. Then comes middle school. Because middle schools often draw from a wider area than a single neighborhood, minority students are more likely to encounter white students in middle school. For the first time, they become aware of the achievement gap. The good feelings associated with elementary school evaporate, replaced by growing frustration with academic work. It does not help the self-esteem of minority students to be assigned to low-level and remedial classes made up largely of other minority students.

When Eric Smith was superintendent of the Charlotte-Mecklenburg School District, he confronted the middle school challenge head-on (Johnson, 2002). Committed to both reducing the achievement gap and promoting academic rigor, he was alarmed to discover that white students outnumbered black students three-to-one in advanced classes in middle school. Lagging behind in middle school was a virtual guarantee of lagging behind in high school. Smith told counselors to revise the schedules of

8,000 middle school students. Low-level courses were reduced, and black students were re-assigned to advanced courses. Many teachers and parents protested the dramatic move, but Smith insisted that black students were capable of doing advanced work. The function of a public school system, he maintained, was not to sort and select students, but to enable all students to reach their potential. When the number of black students taking college preparatory courses in high school climbed sharply and test scores of black students rose 20 percentage points, the wisdom of Smith's initiative was apparent. The interests of educational equity were well-served by promoting educational excellence.

INCREASE ACCESS TO CHALLENGING COURSES IN HIGH SCHOOL

Providing all students with access to more rigorous academic work in middle school means little if students are not exposed to challenging content in high school. Scholars like E. D. Hirsch note that many schools over-emphasize a narrow, skills-based curriculum (Manzo, 2008). Only contact with the foundational knowledge upon which the academic disciplines are based, they contend, can equip students to meet the demands of the Information Age. Much the same point was made in the famous New Jersey court case, *Abbott v. Burke 1990*. The case centered around the claim that poor urban school districts were essentially "basic skills districts," while more affluent districts provided a wealth of educational opportunities, including advanced courses, well-equipped laboratories, and the latest computer technology. The court declared that "the constitutional requirement of a thorough and efficient education encompasses more than instruction in the basic communications and computational skills, but also requires that 'students be given at least a modicum of variety and a chance to excel'" (Anyon, 1997, p. 140).

Eric Smith followed up his middle school initiative by increasing access to Advanced Placement and International Baccalaureate courses in Charlotte-Mecklenburg high schools. Minority students were encouraged to take a college preparatory curriculum. As a consequence, the number of African American students enrolled in college preparatory courses rose by 450 percent (Johnson, 2002). In Fairfax County, Dan Domenech promulgated a policy that allowed any student to enroll in an AP or IB course (Duke, 2005). Had he stopped at this point, his efforts would have been hailed by many as a bold step toward merging the pursuit of equity and the goal of excellence. But he went even further. He insisted that every student who was enrolled in an AP or IB course had to take the end-of-course external examination. Only in this way are teachers of advanced courses likely to work equally hard with all students. If teachers handpick students to take end-of-course exams, as is the case in many other districts that have opened access to AP and IB courses, they may give less attention to students who they judge to be unable to score well on the exams.

Another strategy designed to increase student participation in AP and IB courses involves cutting back or eliminating honors courses (de Vise, 2008b). Between 2003 and 2008, the Prince William, Virginia, school system eliminated the honors designation for high school courses and steered students into AP, IB, or Cambridge college preparatory programs.

For students who traditionally would not have had access to AP and IB course to thrive in these more challenging settings, special support is necessary. AP and IB teachers need staff development on strategies for helping students to adjust to higher expectations and more demanding assignments. The College Board has designed a training program for teachers called EXCELerator that has been tested with some success in Duval County Public Schools (Gewertz, 2008). The AVID (Advanced Via Individual Determination) program also holds promise for socializing students to more rigorous coursework. The key is not to encourage students to take challenging courses and then abandon them.

The importance of access to advanced courses for minority students cannot be over-stated. Attewell and Domina (2008) report that 12th-grade tests scores and probabilities of entry to and completion of college are directly related to access to a more rigorous curriculum. Ferguson (2001, p. 22) contends that the single greatest predictor of the black-white grade point average gap in high school is the proportion of courses taken at the honors and AP levels. While some of the variance in course-taking can be attributed to parental education and beliefs, school-based factors also play a role. Minority students are more likely to enroll in challenging high school courses if they have been exposed to challenging coursework in their previous school experiences and if they are counseled to tackle such courses. School district leaders must send unambiguous directives that schools are expected to provide all students with opportunities to take rigorous courses, the earlier the better.

The middle college movement represents another step that school district leaders are taking to push an agenda combining equity and excellence. Designed to provide a seamless link between high school and college, middle colleges cater to students who might be unlikely to consider college. By allowing students to complete high school and simultaneously begin work on a community college or college degree, middle colleges smooth the transition between high school and college. Middle colleges offer students a more serious learning environment than they might find in their regular high school. Opportunities for personalized guidance and assistance are greater because instructors are able to work with a relatively small number of students.

DEVELOP PROGRAMS OF GIFTS AND TALENTS

It is not a secret that many minority groups are under-represented in gifted and talented programs. When the Council of the Great City Schools conducted a review of the Pittsburgh Public Schools in 2006, for example, it found that only 29.7 percent of the students in gifted and talented programs were African American (*Focusing on Achievement in the Pittsburgh Public Schools*, 2006, p.65). African American students comprised almost 60 percent of district enrollment. Worth pointing out is the fact that the report also noted that African American students were over-represented in special education programs, making up 63.5 percent of the students identified as disabled.

School district leaders are unlikely to make much headway in eliminating gifted and talented programs, but they can mitigate some of the negative impact of such programs by creating programs of gifts and talents. The purpose of the latter programs is to identify areas of talent in every student. Faced with criticism of its highly selective gifted and talented programs, Fairfax County Public Schools, under Robert Spillane's leadership, piloted the Schoolwide Achievement Model (SAM). SAM was designed to identify and nurture talents in all students (Duke, 2005, pp. 91–92). The School Board, unfortunately, did not provide funding to continue the initiative.

Tom DeBolt, superintendent of the Manassas Park (Virginia) City Schools also saw a need to recognize and cultivate talent in all students, not just those designated as "gifted and talented." The result was a unique music program in which every fourth and fifth grade student is provided with a musical instrument and school-based music lessons (Duke, 2008b, p. 101). DeBolt reasoned that many of Manassas Park's students came from families that could not afford private music lessons. Unless the school district intervened, these students might never know if they possessed musical talent. Tom DeBolt clearly understood that equity and excellence go hand in hand.

EXPOSE STUDENTS TO MULTIPLE MODELS OF EXCELLENCE

The point is obvious, but it needs to be made nonetheless. Educational excellence is not about making every student an expert at taking tests. Nor is it a matter of having every student master calculus and physics. The viability of our society depends on many kinds of excellence. Too many schools, though, expose students to a very limited vision of excellence.

Schools alone are unlikely, of course, to make a student "excellent." That is not the point. What schools *can* do is expose students to multiple models of excellence. Not just excellence in one type of thinking, but excellence in various spheres of human endeavor—performing arts, visual arts, caretaking, writing, research, reasoning, advocacy, entrepreneurship, and so on. It goes without saying that students are less likely to attain excellence later in life if they cannot recognize excellence when they see it. As Mauritz Johnson (1982, p. 3) noted, the school's potential role in promoting excellence

> ... lies in its capacity to make students aware of the criteria for many forms of excellence, to show them models of such excellence, and to encourage them to imagine even higher levels of excellence. We cannot expect people to strive for something that they do not value and that those around them do not respect.

Johnson's last point should be emphasized. If their teachers have a limited view of excellence, students are less likely to appreciate the various forms of excellence in the world around them. Noddings (2007, p. 83) makes a similar point when she charges educators with restoring "genuine respect for the full range of human talents and occupations."

As in so many things, excellence begins at the top. School district leaders who are committed to promoting educational excellence should begin by understanding what it means to be an excellent leader. They then need to help teachers understand the meaning of excellence in teaching. Teachers, in turn, must encourage students to learn what constitutes excellence in different walks of life. In this way, students, if they so choose, can undertake their own pursuit of excellence. Perhaps it is the pursuit of excellence, not its actual achievement, that ultimately has the greatest potential for leveling the playing field and promoting true equity.

EXECUTIVE CONCLUSION

School districts are complex organizations, and complex organizations benefit from a clear focus and sense of direction. A clear focus depends on the willingness of leaders to designate priorities. When school district leaders attempt to address too broad a range of needs, they risk losing focus and creating confusion. If everything is a priority, nothing is a priority.

School district leaders probably have no choice but to make educational equity the highest priority. Public schools exist, after all, to provide young people with the knowledge necessary to become contributing members of society. Equity alone, however, is unlikely to satisfy the expectations of many parents or ensure that the nation remains competitive in an increasingly global economy. The challenge for school district leaders is to make certain that the twin priorities of educational equity and educational excellence compliment rather than compete with each other. To do so, they must monitor achievement gaps between various student sub-groups and be alert for points in the school experience where gaps widen. Such points may be indicators that the schools themselves are contributing to achievement differences. While school district leaders cannot control all the forces that produce educational inequity, there are many forces that they can influence. These include the general level of awareness of achievement gaps, school-based expectations and targets for improvement, the identification of proven programs and practices to help struggling students, the setting of priorities to guide the allocation of resources in ways that can narrow achievement gaps, and monitoring all efforts to raise student achievement to ensure that ineffective interventions are adjusted or eliminated.

School district leaders also should understand how they can promote greater equity by supporting a broader vision of educational excellence. Most students can benefit from greater access to challenging curriculum content and advanced coursework. But, many students will require considerable support in order to enjoy these benefits. They cannot simply be assigned to AP and IB courses and then be left to fend for themselves. Teachers will need a great deal of staff development to understand how to work with students who typically take regular courses. School district leaders also can promote the cause of educational excellence by initiating programs designed to identify and cultivate talents in all students and expose students to a wide variety of types of excellence.

REFERENCES

Abbott v. Burke 119 N.J. 287. (1990).

Allington, R.L. (2006). *What Really Matters for Struggling Readers*, second edition, Boston: Pearson.

Anyon, J. (1997). *Ghetto Schooling*. New York: Teachers College Press.

Attewell, P., & Domina, T. (2008). Raising the bar: Curricular intensity and academic performance. *Educational Evaluation and Policy Analysis*, 30(1), 51–71.

Chenoweth, K. (2007). *"It's Being Done:" Academic Success in Unexpected Schools*. Cambridge, MA: Harvard Education Press.

Chubb, J.E., & Loveless, T., eds. (2002). *Bridging the Achievement Gap*. Washington, D.C.: Brookings Institution Press.

Comer, J.P. (2004). *Leave No Child Behind*. New Haven, CT: Yale University Press.

Conant, J.B. (1959). *The American High School Today*. New York: McGaw-Hill.

Darling-Hammond, L. (1997). *The Right to Learn*. San Francisco: Jossey-Bass.

de Vise, D. (February 26, 2008a). Two Md. Schools separated by more than county lines. *The Washington Post*, B-5.

de Vise, D. (May 19, 2008b). Honors courses give way to AP rigor. *The Washington Post*, B-1,2.

Diplomas Count, *Education Week* (June 5, 2008).

Duke, D.L. (2008a). Diagnosing school decline. *Phi Delta Kappan*, 89(9), 667–671.

Duke, D.L. (2008b). *The Little School System That Could: Transforming a City School District.* Albany: State University of New York Press.

Duke, D.L. (2005). *Education Empire: The Evolution of an Excellent Suburban School System.* Albany: State University of New York Press.

Duke, D.L. (1955). What is the nature of educational excellence and should we try to measure it? *Phi Delta Kappan*, 66(10), 671–674.

Duke, D.L., & Canady, R.L. (1991). *School Policy*, New York: McGraw-Hill.

Duke, D.L., Tucker, P.D., Salmonowicz, M.J., & Levy, M.K. (2007). How comparable are the perceived challenges facing principals of low-achieving schools? *International Studies in Educational Administration*, 35(1), 3–21.

Fenning, P., & Rose, J. (2007). Overrepresentation of African American students in exclusionary discipline. *Urban Education*, 42(6), 536–559.

Ferguson, R.F. (2001). A diagnostic analysis of black-white GPA disparities in Shaker Heights, Ohio. In D. Ravitch (ed.), *Brookings Papers on Educational Policy 2001*. Washington, D.C.: Brookings Institution Press, 347–414.

Flanagan, A., & Grissmer, D. (2002). The role of federal resources in closing the achievement gap. In J.E. Chubb & T. Loveless (eds.), *Bridging the Achievement Gap*. Washington, D.C.: Brookings Institution Press, 199–225.

Focusing on Achievement in the Pittsburgh Public Schools. (2006). Washington, D.C.: The Council of the Great City Schools.

Ford, D.Y., Grantham, T.C., & Whiting, G.W. (2008). Another look at the achievement gap. *Urban Education*, 43(2), 216–239.

Gewertz, C. (March 12, 2008). Opening AP to all. *Education Week*, 23–25.

Glod, M. (June 13, 2008). Mandated tutoring not helping Va., Md. Scores. *The Washington Post*, B-1.

Grant, G. (1988). *The World We Created at Hamilton High*. Cambridge, MA: Harvard University Press.

Grogan, M., & Sherman, W.H. (2003). How superintendents in Virginia deal with issues surrounding the black-white test-score gap. *Educational Leadership in an Age of Accountability: The Virginia Experience*. Albany: State University of New York Press, 155–189.

Hess, F.M., & Petrilli, M.J. (2006). *No Child Left Behind*. New York: Peter Lang.

Hightower, A. (2002). San Diego's big boom: Systemic instructional change in the central office and schools. In Hightower, A., Knapp, M.S., Marsh, J.A., & McLaughlin, M.W. (eds.), *School Districts and Instructional Renewal*. New York: Teachers College Press, 76–93.

Imber, M., & Van Geel, T. (2000). *Education Law* (second ed.). Mahwah, NJ: Erlbaum.

Johnson, D. (May 5, 2002). School chief works fasts, furious. *The Washington Post*, C-5.

Johnson, J.F., & Asera, R., eds. (1999). *Hope for Urban Education: A Study of Nine High-performing, High-poverty, Urban Elementary Schools*. Austin: The Charles A. Dana Center, University of Texas.

Johnson, M. (1982). *The Continuing Quest for Educational Quality*. Albany: School of Education, State University of New York.

Kotter, J.P. (1996). *Leading Change*. Boston: Harvard Business School Press.

Kozol, J. (1991). *Savage Inequalities*. New York: Crown.

Lau v. Nichols, 414 U.S. 563 (1974).

Manzo, K.K. (May 21, 2008). Learning essentials. *Education Week*, 23.

McGee, G.W. (2004). Closing the achievement gap: lessons from Illinois' Golden Spike high-poverty high-performing schools. *Journal of Education for Students Placed at Risk*, 9(2), 97–125.

Mickelson, R.A. (2001). Subverting Swann: first- and second-generation segregation in the Charlotte-Mecklenburg schools. *American Educational Research Journal*, 38(2), 215–252.

National Commission on Excellence in Education. (1983). *A Nation at Risk*. Washington, D.C.: U.S. Department of Education.

Noddings, N. (2007). *When School Reform Goes Wrong*. New York: Teachers College press.

Noguera, P.A. (2008). *The Trouble with Black Boys*. San Francisco: Jossey-Bass.

Nores, M., Belfield, C.R.,Barnett, W.S, & Schweinhart, L. (2005). Updating the economic impacts of the High/Scope Perry Preschool Program. *Educational Evaluation and Policy Analysis*, 27(3), 245–261.

Odden, A., & Busch, C. (1998). *Financing Schools for High Performance*. San Francisco: Jossey-Bass.

Ogbu, J.U. (2003). *Black American Students in an Affluent Suburb*. Mahwah, NJ: Erlbaum.

Palardy, G.J., & Rumberger, R.W. (2008). Teacher effectiveness in first grade: the importance of background qualifications, attitudes, and instructional practices for student learning. *Educational Evaluation and Policy Analysis*, 30(2), 111–140.

Peters, T.J., & Waterman, R.H. (1982). *In Search of Excellence*. New York: Harper & Row.

Pianta, R.C., Belsky, J., Vandergrift, N., Houts, R., & Morrison, F.J. (2008). Classroom effects on children's achievement trajectories in elementary school. *American Educational Research Journal*, 45(2), 365–397.

Picucci, A.C., Brownson, A., Kahlert, R., & Sobel, A. (2002). *Driven to Succeed: High-performing, High-poverty Turnaround Middle Schools*. Austin: The Charles A. Dana Center, University of Texas.

Policy Notes. (2005). 13(1). Princeton, NJ: Educational Testing Service.

Ravitch, D. (1995). *National Standards in American Education*. Washington, D.C.: Brookings Institution Press.

Reardon, S.F. (2008). *Differential growth in the black-white achievement gap during elementary school among high- and low-scoring students*. Palo Alto, CA: Institute for Research on Education Policy & Practice, Stanford University.

Reville, S.P. (2007). *A Decade of Urban School Reform*. Cambridge, MA: Harvard Education Press.

Rothstein, R. (2004). The achievement gap: a broader picture. *Educational Leadership*, 62(3), 40–43.

Slavin, R.E., & Madden, N.A. (2002). "Success for All" and African American and Latino student achievement. In J.E. Chubb & T. Loveless, (eds), *Bridging the Achievement Gap*. Washington, D.C.: Brookings Institution Press, 74–90.

Stone, D. (1989). Causal stories and the formation of policy agendas. *Political Science Quarterly*, 104(2), 281–300.

Strategic Plan. (n.d.). Fairfax, VA: Fairfax County Public Schools.

Supovitz, J.A. (2006). *The Case for District-based Reform*. Cambridge, MA: Harvard Education Press.

Togneri, W., & Anderson, S.E. (2003). *Beyond Islands of Excellence: What Districts Can Do to Improve Instruction and Achievement in All Schools — A Leadership Brief.* Washington, D.C.: Learning First Alliance.

Turque, B. (June 12, 2008). Standing up for the children. *The Washington Post*, A-21.

Viadero, D. (April 16, 2008). Black-white gap widens faster for high achievers. *Education Week*, 13.

Weinstein, R.S. (2002). *Reaching Higher: The Power of Expectations in Schooling*. Cambridge, MA: Harvard University Press.

2

THE CHALLENGES OF CHANGING DEMOGRAPHICS

DIVERSITY COMES TO MANASSAS PARK

The city of Manassas Park became Virginia's newest city when it withdrew from Prince William County in 1975. A year later the City Council decided that the arrangement whereby Manassas Park students continued to attend Prince William schools no longer was satisfactory. A School Board was appointed, and Manassas Park went into the business of providing public education. The students who attended school in the new school system constituted a relatively homogeneous group of white students from working-class families. Manassas Park consisted primarily of modest homes, many constructed to house GIs returning from World War II.

The first demographic change to hit Manassas Park was one largely of its own creation. Lacking much commercial and industrial property, the cash-strapped school system managed to annex 404 acres of Prince William County in 1989. The city's intention was to go into the land development business and create a series of attractive sub-divisions that would lure more affluent residents to Manassas Park and generate greater property tax revenues. Members of City Council soon discovered, however, that families with school-age children were reluctant to move to Manassas Park until its outdated school facilities were upgraded.

With the hiring of a new superintendent in 1995, Manassas Park found the leader who would be able to mobilize the support needed to rebuild the city's schools. Tom DeBolt predicted that "if we build it, they will come." And come they did. Manassas Park soon attracted middle-class families looking to escape the heavy traffic and high costs of its neighbors. Revenues increased, and the school system's reputation for academic quality grew. School enrollment almost doubled from what it had been when the school system began.

The next demographic change to impact Manassas Park was a direct result of the affordability of its housing in comparison to that of its neighbors. Attracted by the availability of jobs in northern Virginia, Hispanic immigrants in large numbers moved to Manassas Park. By the fall of 2003, almost one in every three children enrolled in Manassas Park schools was Hispanic. Another 14 percent were African American and 7 percent were Asian/Pacific Islander. Two years later, the Hispanic enrollment had risen to 38 percent, while the percentage of other racial and ethnic groups dropped. With the influx of immigrants came new challenges for Manassas Park educators. Roughly one quarter of the students were classified as Limited English Proficient (LEP).

Some long-time residents of Manassas Park predicted that the city would soon pass the "tipping point" and become largely an Hispanic community. Meanwhile, neighboring communities began to take action to limit the number of people who could share a given residence and to apprehend undocumented immigrants. Amidst this growing concern, the red-hot local economy began to soften. Then the sub-prime mortgage crisis hit all of northern Virginia.

Overnight, homes in Manassas Park and elsewhere were vacated as owners found it impossible to meet balloon payments on their mortgages. The hardest hit segment of Manassas Park were low-income residents. In the summer of 2008 Superintendent DeBolt estimated that Manassas Park had 300 empty homes, many located in largely Hispanic neighborhoods.

*****

The job of leading a school district undoubtedly would be a lot simpler if enrollments and the make-up of the student body never fluctuated. The world in which today's educators live, however, is reflected in the experience of Manassas Park. It is a world characterized by rising and falling enrollments influenced by economic conditions and birth rates and by increasing diversity due to immigration and mobility. These demographic changes constitute a major source of the challenges associated with competing priorities that were addressed in the first chapter. But those challenges are just the tip of the proverbial iceberg. This chapter examines additional challenges associated with demographic changes, challenges that most school district leaders are facing and likely will continue to face.

DEMOGRAPHIC CHANGE IS COMPLEX

Before discussing the challenges of demographic change, it is necessary to review the multiple meanings of the term. Under the rubric of demographic change are clustered a variety of population shifts, each with the potential to disrupt standard operating procedures in schools and school systems.

The most obvious demographic change involves the overall number of students attending public schools. Following World War II, the United States experienced an unprecedented "Baby Boom." Approximately 78 million Americans were born between 1946 and 1964. Many school districts were forced to implement double shifts in order to accommodate increased enrollments. School buildings could not be constructed fast enough to keep up with the demand for space. Then the birth rate declined in the late 1960s, in part as a result of the availability of the birth control pill. The "Baby Bust" that followed left many of the recently constructed schools half full. In 2007 a new Baby Boom gained momentum, as 4.3 million future students were born. This "Echo Boom," as it was dubbed, promised new strains on school systems.

Fluctuations in school enrollments force school systems to hire and fire employees, close schools in certain neighborhoods while opening schools in other neighborhoods, and re-assign students. Shifting birth rates are not the only cause of enrollment fluctuations. They also may result from parents opting to send their children to private and parochial schools or to home school them. In 2007, 6.2 million out of 49.6 million students in the United States were enrolled in non-public schools. Charter schools constitute another challenge. Washington, D.C., school officials were surprised to discover in September, 2008, that public school enrollment had dropped by 8.7 percent from the previous year (Turque, 2008). The reason—over 4,000 students switched to charter schools. Changes in the local economy can have an impact on enrollments as well. The past century, for example, has seen a steady exodus of families from rural areas to cities and suburbs where employment opportunities are greater. The result has been dwindling enrollments, school district consolidation, and even the disappearance of some rural school systems.

School district leaders have little control over most sources of enrollment fluctuation. Only in the area of academic reputation can they have a demonstrable impact. Parents seek out school districts with reputations for academic excellence and avoid school districts perceived to be low-performing and troubled.

Another popular meaning of demographic change concerns the racial and ethnic make-up of the student body. During the late years of the 19th and early years of the 20th century, America's public schools enrolled and socialized millions of white immigrant children, primarily from Europe. The next major demographic change followed the *Brown* decision in 1954. School districts in the South and later in other parts of the United States desegregated, often under court order. While some communities embraced this change, others resisted. "White flight" resulted in many school systems resegregating.

The last decades of the 20th century found the United States experiencing a second wave of immigration, this time including large numbers of Latin Americans and Asians. During the 1990s, the annual number of legal and illegal immigrants into the United States was estimated to be 820,000 (Fowler, 2004). In 2007 the number of minority residents in the nation for the first time topped 100 million (U.S. Census Bureau News, 2007).

By the early 21st century, Hispanics had overtaken blacks as the largest minority group among public school students (Frankenberg, 2007, p. 8). Racial and ethnic-minority students are not evenly distributed across the nation's school districts, however. They make up a disproportionately large percentage of the 100 largest school districts. In 2005, for example, 71 percent of students in the 100 largest school districts in the United States were other than non-Hispanic white (Largest 100 Districts, 2008). For the nation as a whole, minority students made up just 43 percent of total enrollment. In Los Angeles, Chicago, and Dade County, Florida, more than nine out of every ten students was a minority student and many of them were recent immigrants (Garofano, Sable, & Hoffman, 2008, p. A-18). School district leaders in districts with large numbers of recent immigrants sometimes find themselves in the awkward position of being asked to identify undocumented newcomers. Such requests may lead to lawsuits when newcomers believe that their right to privacy has been violated (Schulte, 2008).

Yet another connotation of demographic change concerns the socioeconomic status of school district residents. Shifts in the financial circumstances of families sending students to public schools present daunting challenges for school district leaders. One increasingly common scenario finds relatively well-to-do suburban school systems enrolling growing numbers of students from poor families. Consider the experience of Virginia's Fairfax County Public Schools. Between 1990 and 1994, Fairfax County, one of the wealthiest counties in the nation, witnessed a 134 percent increase in the number of school-age children from households with earnings below the federal poverty line (Duke, 2005, pp. 71–72). This number represented eight percent of the giant school system's total enrollment. By 2003, the percentage had jumped to 23 percent. With poverty came increasing numbers of renters, and as the number of renters climbed, so too did the student mobility rate. It was not unusual for 30 percent of a school's student enrollment to change annually as a result of families needing to change residence.

Two other types of demographic change portend challenges for school district leaders. Shifts in the number of single residents and senior citizens can impact the financial circumstances of school systems. Both groups are less likely to support spending for public education than parents of school-aged children. It has been predicted that aging Baby Boomers will compete for public resources with their grandchildren and great grandchildren. School district leaders are well aware that the number of parents with school-age children typically is exceeded greatly by the number of adult residents who are either childless or who have grown children. Generating adequate revenue to operate schools in the face of such demographics can require substantial political skill.

THE CONSEQUENCES OF DEMOGRAPHIC CHANGE FOR SCHOOL DISTRICT LEADERS

As a result of various types of demographic change, school district leaders can expect to confront an array of challenges. This section explores several of the more obvious challenges, including the politics of fluctuating enrollments, racial and ethnic resegregation, the "urbanization" of suburban schools, and the special problems of non-English-speaking newcomers. These challenges have been converted to the following questions in order to focus discussion.

The Challenges of Demographic Change

1. What conflicts are enrollment fluctuations likely to generate for school district leaders?

2. Can school systems do anything to prevent racial and ethnic isolation and resegregation?

3. In what ways are suburban school systems beginning to resemble urban school systems?

4. With what issues must school district leaders grapple in order to accommodate English language learners?

Enrollment Politics

If anyone doubts that public education is a drama played out in the theater of politics, they need only attend a school board meeting where school re-districting or school consolidation is on the agenda. These contentious issues are to special interest groups what magnets are to metal. In both cases, the source of contention derives from enrollment fluctuation. Financial concerns typically prompt school district leaders to consider re-districting and school consolidation. Sometimes the number of students exceeds the available space in a school and it is believed to be cheaper to re-assign students to less crowded schools than to build a new school. Consolidation may be called for when enrollment drops to a level where continued operation of two separate schools is too expensive.

The fundamental question in politics is "Who benefits?" The assumption is that every important decision is likely to benefit certain individuals or groups more than others, or at least produce fewer adverse effects for some than for others.

Consider the situation that faced school district leaders in Fairfax County when they announced a plan to re-district thousands of students among five high schools and their feeder schools in February 2008. The move was prompted by concerns that one high school, South Lakes High School, was 780 students under capacity. South Lakes also enrolled a higher share of students living in poverty and English language learners (ELLs) than neighboring high schools. School district leaders assured parents of students already attending the affected high schools that they would not be moved. Only prospective students were scheduled for re-districting.

A month after the announcement, a parent group that was formed to protest the re-districting plan filed suit in Fairfax County Circuit Court (Chandler, 2008). The suit alleged that (1) the school board exceeded its authority when it sought to balance socioeconomic characteristics in the schools and (2) the school board was "arbitrary and capricious" because its members violated board policies by not sufficiently analyzing the impact of re-districting on transportation and costs. In July of 2008 a judge ruled that the re-districting plan was executed within the school board's authority. The judge's decision, however, did not put an end to the controversy. Parents took advantage of Fairfax's policy permitting student transfers for curricular reasons. Claiming that South Lakes High School did not offer certain Advanced Placement courses, a third of the re-districted rising freshmen assigned to South Lakes switched to another high school.

This was not the first time parents in Fairfax County organized to oppose a school board decision regarding student assignments. When student enrollments in the eastern part of the county dropped in the early

1980s, school district leaders proposed closing one of two high schools and consolidating the two student bodies (Duke, 2005, pp. 46–47). The ensuing battles between advocates for each high school pitted neighbor against neighbor and produced charges of racism and elitism. When the school board announced its decision to close Ft. Hunt High School, parents took out full-page ads in the local newspaper, organized a massive letter-writing campaign, and even produced a booklet recounting the school's glorious past.

School consolidation dates back to the mid-20th century when efforts were made to eliminate one-room schools. Between 1945 and 1980 the total enrollment in elementary and secondary schools mushroomed from 23 to 40 million, while the number of schools dropped from 185,000 to 86,000 (School Consolidation, 1985). The arguments for school consolidation typically involve financial, curricular, and diversity concerns.

Maintaining two or more small schools that are reasonably close geographically may entail unnecessary duplication of expenditures related to administration, staffing, and facilities operation. In some cases, consolidation may involve two small school districts. When researchers analyzed the financial benefits of school district consolidation in New York, they found that doubling a district's enrollment (by merging with another school district) cuts operating costs per student by 62 percent for a 300-student district and by 50 percent for a 1,500-student district (Duncombe & Yinger, 2007). In rural areas, where a large percentage of small schools and school districts are located, finding a sufficient number of qualified teachers and specialists also can be a challenge. Combining schools may permit better staffing and allow a greater range of courses and extra-curricular activities to be offered.

When neighborhood schools tend to be racially segregated, school consolidation also can be a vehicle for achieving some measure of integration. When citizens of Charlottesville, Virginia, complained that the city's two middle schools were racially segregated, the school board opted to create one school for all fifth and sixth graders and another school for all seventh and eighth graders, thereby integrating Charlottesville's middle-level programs.

School district leaders should be aware that the supposed benefits of school consolidation have been challenged on a variety of counts. Parents often express concern about the long bus rides that may be required to attend a consolidated school. Rural residents fear that closing a school can lead to the erosion of community identity and have adverse effects on the social and economic health of small towns. Critics of consolidation note that savings in school administration and staffing may be offset by higher transportation costs.

Perhaps the most popular contemporary argument against school consolidation, however, concerns the perceived benefits of small schools. Small schools have been associated with reducing dropout rates, providing safer environments for students and teachers, increasing the likelihood that students receive personal attention from adults, and promoting teacher leadership (Duke & Trautvetter, 2001). School size also has been found to be a predictor of student achievement (Fowler & Walberg, 1991; Lee & Smith, 1997). As schools grow in size, overall student achievement, especially for minority students, tends to decline. When Wasley and her associates (2000) examined the impact of Chicago's efforts to downsize large schools, they reported evidence of improved student achievement, persistence, and attendance. Parents, teachers, students, and community members also indicated higher levels of satisfaction with small schools. These findings pose a significant challenge for school district leaders committed to school consolidation.

Just as school consolidation has its critics, so, too, does school re-districting. Many of the criticisms concern the process by which re-districting decisions are made. Claims are heard that enrollment projections are based on faulty assumptions and questionable data. Parents contend that they had no opportunity to express their reservations. Re-districting plans may be attacked for favoring particular groups. Groups citing discrimination often represent the parents of children who must travel the furthest to attend a newly assigned school. In other cases, re-districting has the effect of reifying patterns of racial and ethnic isolation.

Given all the potential problems with school re-districting and consolidation, what can school district leaders do to minimize controversy and conflict? The following steps may not prevent every affected individual from criticizing the results of re-districting and school consolidation, but they do constitute a conscientious approach to handling enrollment fluctuations that can reduce complaints of favoritism and insensitivity.

First, school district leaders should tap as many sources of local population estimates as possible in order to anticipate changes in school enrollments. The public should be kept apprised of possible increases and decreases in enrollment and their likely consequences for student assignments and facilities needs. Parents and taxpayers in general usually do not appreciate surprises. They need time to adjust to the prospect of re-districting and school consolidation.

Second, school district leaders should draft a clear and credible set of criteria for deciding when and how to re-district or consolidate. These criteria should be made public, citizens should have an opportunity to react to them *before* they are implemented, and the district's attorney should review them to make certain they meet all legal requirements. It is essential that the criteria do not appear to favor any particular neighborhood or group.

The following criteria were adopted in September 2001, by the Fulton County, Georgia, Board of Education to guide the re-districting process occasioned by demographic changes. There are three primary criteria, geographic proximity, school capacity, and projected enrollment, followed by four secondary criteria for use in cases where primary criteria provide several options. The criteria and how they should be applied were explained to local residents in a series of community forums.

Redistricting Criteria for Fulton County School District

Primary Criteria:

Geographic proximity—Distance traveled using available routes of transportation.

Capacity—Number of students who can be accommodated at the school, taking into account the number of classrooms and resource rooms needed for art, music, laboratories, foreign language, English to Speakers of Other Languages (ESOL), special education, and Talented and Gifted (TAG) programs.

Projected enrollment—Number of students assigned to a school taking into account the future projected enrollment.

Secondary Criteria:

When primary criteria provide for more than one option, the options should be evaluated on the basis of:

Traffic patterns—Factors impacting accessibility of the school from all portions of the attendance zone, including travel time, traffic flow in the area, safe operation of school buses, and other safety considerations.

Previous rezoning—School system seeks to avoid rezoning neighborhoods more than once during a three-year period if facility sizes and geographic distribution of student populations allow.

Special programs—Special programs are those serving children with special needs that require use of additional space over and above a regular classroom. Where possible, the school system avoids setting attendance zones that would place a disproportionate number of special programs at a school.

School feeder alignment—Where possible, consideration should be given to the alignment of elementary, middle, and high school attendance boundaries. (Fulton County Public Schools, 2001)

Third, once criteria have been developed and tentatively applied, school district leaders need to solicit input from all affected parties, especially parents. It is important that people be given several channels through which to express concerns. Some individuals may feel uncomfortable voicing their opinions in a large public forum.

One final suggestion concerns the actual decisions on re-districting and school consolidation. School district leaders should be sensitive to non-economic factors as well as cost-savings. Especially in cases involving school closing, the very existence of a small community can be threatened. Community members may be willing to support alternative cost-saving measures in order to preserve their local school.

Resegregation

In the wake of the *Brown* decision in 1954, America as a society made a commitment to integration. The principle of separate but equal, established in 1896 by the Supreme Court in *Plessy v. Ferguson*, was rejected. Separate schools for blacks and whites were judged to be inherently unequal. A half century after the *Brown* decision, however, black students were more segregated than they had been since the late 1960s (Frankenberg, 2007, p. 9). The problem of segregation was even greater for Latino students (Orfield & Lee, 2006).

Various reasons are offered to explain this reversal of progress. White flight has left many communities with a predominantly minority population base. Elsewhere, whites have remained, but opted to enroll their children in private and parochial schools. Some believe discriminatory housing practices have helped to preserve racially isolated neighborhoods. When Reardon and Yun (2005, p. 67) investigated residential segregation in the South, however, they discovered that residential segregation has been declining as school segregation has been increasing.

A relatively recent argument for the jump in racially isolated schools involves the educational accountability movement. Wells and Holme (2003, p. 187) contend that the increase in high-stakes testing along with public access to test results and school rankings has provided the impetus for relatively well-to-do families to abandon low-ranked schools. Since socioeconomic status is highly correlated with race, the result was a reduction in white students in the lower-performing schools they studied.

School district leaders, for their part, have tried in many cases to prevent reversion to segregated schools. Initially their efforts often were prompted as much by the threat of legal action and court orders as they were by a genuine commitment to integration. More recently, though, as the courts have backed away from taking action to promote integration, school district leaders have taken the initiative. It is useful to review some of the measures that have been and are being taken to realize the intent of the *Brown* decision.

Court-ordered busing was one of the first strategies used to desegregate public schools, but as the years have gone by and white flight has increased, busing has lost some of its appeal. Minority parents question the value of having their children endure long bus rides just so they can attend another racially isolated school (Peterson, 1998). Some school systems have chosen to develop magnet schools as a way to promote integration. Students, of course, still must be bused to magnet schools, but they typically are drawn from all over the community, not just one neighborhood. By offering a distinctive curriculum, such as one focused on science and technology or the arts, magnet schools are designed to attract a diverse student body and lure back students who previously withdrew from public schools. By 2002, 3,100 magnet schools existed in the United States (Rossell, 2005). Most were located in large school systems.

Rossell (2005) reports that the most popular type of magnet school structure is one in which an entire school is dedicated to the magnet program. These magnets are less common, however, than program-within-a-school magnets, where the magnet program shares space with a regular public school. The latter type of magnet may experience some difficulties when the make-up of the magnet program differs greatly from the make-up of the regular school. Rossell believes that the spread of magnet programs in recent years has more to do with interest in school choice than with a commitment to desegregation.

The increase in opportunities for public school parents to choose their children's schools presents school district leaders with additional challenges related to resegregation. Nowhere have these challenges been any greater than San Francisco. In 1994 Chinese American parents sued San Francisco Unified School District on the grounds that their children were being kept out of their preferred schools simply because of their ethnicity. In the court ruling handed down in 1999, the school district was forbidden from using race and ethnicity to make school assignments. Parents were allowed to submit a wish list of up to seven schools. The result has been differential preferences based on parents' race or ethnicity and the subsequent resegregation of San Francisco schools (Fulbright & Knight, 2006).

Given the choice, many relatively well-off parents desire neighborhood schools for their children. While neighborhood schools may not necessarily promote the integration of a particular school, this policy can have the effect of keeping some parents from leaving a school system. Cities like Richmond, Virginia, where large numbers of white parents fled following court-ordered busing, have been able to retain a small percentage of white families by embracing neighborhood schools. Neighborhood schools may not only benefit white parents, however. For the 2007–2008 school year, eight of nine neighborhood schools in Richmond made adequate yearly progress (*Church Hill People's News*, 2007). All of these schools were predominantly or entirely African American. School district leaders in Richmond also have tried to cluster white students in the same elementary class when the number of white students at a particular grade level was very small. While this policy appealed to white parents, it was rejected by federal authorities.

When the Supreme Court struck down the desegregation plan adopted by the Jefferson County, Kentucky, school system, school district leaders had to search for other ways to combat resegregation. No longer permitted to use a student's race to make school assignment and transfer decisions, district officials explored pairing lower-income and higher-income regions of Jefferson County, including Louisville, in order to form attendance areas that included a diverse mix of students (Gewertz, 2007).

Nowhere has the option of socioeconomic integration gained a greater foothold than Wake County, North Carolina, a school system of 134,000 students that includes the city of Raleigh. Figure 2.1 contains the student assignment policy adopted by the school board on January 10, 2000. The policy permits district officials to consider a variety of factors in making student assignments. These factors include instructional program, facility utilization, diversity in student achievement, diversity in socioeconomic status, the percentage of students who will remain at the same school (stability), and proximity of home to school. The last criterion is based on a maximum travel time to and from school that is established by the school board.

The goal of school district leaders in Wake County was to keep the proportion of students who are eligible for free and reduced-price meals to no more than 40 percent in each school. Given the correlation between socioeconomic status and race/ethnicity, the effect of this policy has been to ensure diversity throughout the school system. That is until recently. In 2000 when the student assignment policy was adopted, 20 percent of the district qualified as low-income. An influx of Hispanic immigrants, however, has pushed that number to 27 percent (Maxwell, 2007). School district leaders admit that it is harder to keep all schools from exceeding the 40 percent poverty maximum. The benefits of the student assignment policy, at least during its initial years, were manifested in the achievement of students from low-income families. The income-achievement gap narrowed more for Wake County students than for the state of North Carolina in general (Flinspach & Banks, 2005, p. 273).

The Wake County Public School System believes that maintaining diverse student populations in each school is critical to ensuring academic success for all students, and this belief is supported by research. The school system also must consider such factors as cost effective use of facilities.

Each student enrolled in the Wake County Public School System shall be assigned to the school of his or her grade level serving the attendance area in which that student's parents or count-appointed guardian lives. Exceptions will be made as necessary to limit enrollment of a school due to overcrowding or for special programmatic programs. Each student will have the option of applying for admission to one of the magnet educational programs or year-round programs, which will be offered in designated schools.

All of the following factors, not in priority order, will be used in the development of the annual student assignment plan:

A. Instructional program; e.g., magnet programs, special education, ESL, etc.
B. Adherence to K–5, 6–8, 9–12 grade organization.
C. Facility utilization, including crowding (projected enrollment should be between 85 percent and 115 percent of approved campus capacity). New schools may operate with less than 85 percent of capacity enrolled if some grade levels will not be assigned during the first year or if significant growth is anticipated in the following year.
D. Diversity in student achievement (percentage of students scoring below grade level should be no higher than 25 percent, averaged across a two-year period). Schools with more than 25 percent of students below grade level will receive an instructional review to ascertain the reasons for the low achievement; improvement trends will be considered in deciding whether to address this issue in development of the assignment plan.
E. Diversity in socioeconomic status (percentage of students eligible for free or reduced price lunch will be no higher than 40 percent). Schools with more than 40 percent of students eligible for free or reduced price lunch will receive an instructional review; improvement trends will be considered in deciding whether to address this issue in development of the assignment plan.
F. Stability (the percentage of students who will remain at the same school).
G. Proximity (no student will travel more than the maximum time established by board policy).

Beginning in the fall 2000, the board will review and approve the factors to be considered in developing the student assignment plan and will approve the list of factors and ways to measure those factors by their first meeting in October each year.

Revised: January 10, 2000

Figure 2.1 Wake County Policy 62000, Student Assignment. Source: Wake County Public School System Board Policy.

If many schools and school systems are resegregating, it is not for want of effort on the part of school district leaders. To date, no strategy for preventing or reducing resegregation has proven to be uniformly effective or without controversy. Some measures, such as neighborhood schools and choice-based programs, can appear to be concessions to white parents. Other initiatives risk rejection by courts that are increasingly reluctant to engage in "social engineering." It may be that the best strategy in the long run for school district leaders committed to integrated schools is to focus on providing the highest quality instructional program for *all* students. This challenge will be taken up in Chapter 6.

When white parents fled desegregated schools, they frequently headed for homogeneous suburban communities. With their children comfortably enrolled in predominantly white schools, they resisted attempts by urban school systems to bus children from the inner city to high-performing schools in the suburbs. Today, however, the demography of the suburbs is rapidly changing, and with it, the role of suburban schools. It is worth noting, in fact, that when President Clinton addressed his commission on race relations in the fall of 1997, he chose a suburban community, not an urban area, as a good place to investigate how people from diverse cultures and backgrounds live, work, and go to school together (Lipton & Benning, 1997).

The suburban community spotlighted by President Clinton was Fairfax County, Virginia. One of the wealthiest counties in the United States, Fairfax was rapidly becoming one of the most diverse. No individuals were more acutely aware of this change than the leaders of Fairfax County Public Schools (FCPS). Fairfax already had a well-established African American population that constituted approximately 10 percent of the county's residents. Many of the black students in Fairfax schools came from relatively well-to-do families, reflecting the fact that the suburbs surrounding Washington, D.C. led the nation in African American prosperity.

In the 1990s, Fairfax welcomed 112,841 immigrants (Duke, 2005, p. 70). By 2000, over one in four of the county's one million residents were foreign born. Hispanics accounted for 31 percent of this number, but the largest percentage of newcomers came from Asia. A language other than English was spoken in three out of every ten Fairfax homes. In 2001, the most frequently spoken foreign languages by students in FCPS included Spanish (9,825), Korean (1,713), Urdu (1,004), Vietnamese (986), Arabic (771), Farsi (646), Chinese (460), Punjabi (220), Hindi (167), and Somali (167) (Duke, 2005, p. 71).

As if accommodating the needs of non-English-speaking students was not challenging enough, FCPS also hosted a growing number of economically disadvantaged students. Earlier it was noted that the number of school-age children whose household incomes fell below the federal poverty line in the 1990s rose 134 percent, from 5,099 to 11,955, even as the median annual household income for Fairfax County approached $100,000. That number has steadily increased. By 2008, over 34,000 Fairfax students, out of a total enrollment of 168,384, qualified for free or reduced-price meals. This number included a growing number of homeless students.

Poverty often is accompanied by mobility, as families are forced to vacate homes and apartments and move to less expensive living quarters. Student mobility represents the change in student membership over the course of the school year. The mobility rate for FCPS in 2006–2007 topped 15 percent, and some schools' rate exceeded 30 percent (Student Mobility, 2006–2007, 2008).

While Fairfax County's changing demography may represent an extreme example of suburbs becoming more like urban areas, it is clearly the case that the make-up of America's suburbs is changing. In 1999 large cities and their suburbs had nearly equal numbers of poor residents, but by 2005 the suburban poor outnumbered their city counterparts by more than a million (Berube & Kneebone, 2006, p. 1). Once synonymous with homogeneity, suburbs have become symbols of American diversity. While the white population of big-city suburbs rose by 7 percent between 2000 and 2006, the same period saw the suburban Asian population climb by 16 percent, the black population by 24 percent, and the Hispanic population by 60 percent (An age of transformation, 2008). Unlike their predecessors, today's immigrants are opting to bypass cities and move directly to the suburbs. With increasing suburban diversity and poverty have come a host of new challenges for school systems and their leaders.

The new suburbanites bring with them the academic issues associated with poverty and English language learners. Cultural differences among newcomers and between newcomers and long-time residents sometimes result in social tension and disruptive incidents. To cope with feelings of isolation and alienation, young newcomers may choose to join gangs and engage in criminal activities. Suburban schools no longer are sanctuaries from the racial problems and violence thought to characterize only inner-city schools. Less sedentary than long-time suburban residents, the newcomers are more likely to move around, creating disruptions in their children's education. With growing diversity also comes the prospect of differential expectations and potentially discriminatory school practices such as tracking. Advocates for newcomers have learned to be on the lookout for inequities in course-taking and in student discipline. Newcomers often are suspended and expelled from school at much higher rates than other students.

School district leaders must do all they can to ensure that suburban newcomers enjoy the same educational benefits as long-time residents. A crucial step in this process involves establishing procedures for the early assessment of academic needs. Many newcomers arrive on the doorsteps of suburban schools with deficiencies in language and other content areas of the curriculum. Early detection of these deficiencies increases the likelihood that newcomers can catch up to their peers. The next section focuses on the challenges associated with English language learners (ELLs).

Not all of the needs of newcomers are purely academic. It is not uncommon for new residents to require the assistance of social service agencies and health clinics. To reduce the attraction of gang membership, young newcomers benefit from positive role models and teachers with backgrounds similar to their own. When Fairfax's immigrant population began to swell, the school board approved the creation of the position of language-access coordinator (Duke, 2005, p. 71). This individual is responsible for communicating to non-English-speakers about what the school system has to offer. Some large school systems operate intake centers for newcomers. Before students are assigned to schools, they spend time at an intake center receiving relevant information in their native language and having their academic needs assessed.

Though clearly a step in the right direction, intake centers need to be closely monitored by school district leaders to ensure that they function effectively. When the Council of the Great City Schools conducted an assessment of Seattle's efforts to address the needs of its large ELL population, the visiting team of experts raised questions about the urban district's Bilingual Orientation Centers (Raising the Achievement of English Language Learners in the Seattle Public Schools, 2008, pp. 45–46). Confusion existed, for example, regarding the central purpose of the centers. While some believed the centers were designed for social acculturation and assistance with students' emotional development, others thought that more of an academic focus was needed. In the centers' classrooms, little effort was made to differentiate students by language proficiency. Over-age English language learners at the secondary level had no clear pathway to graduation. One of the greatest concerns identified by the visiting team involved the absence of clear exit criteria governing when ELLs were ready to leave the Bilingual Orientation Centers and enter a regular school or how their appropriate grade-level would be determined.

As suburban school systems become more diverse, school district leaders must ensure that newcomers are subject to the same high expectations as other students. Tracking can undermine these efforts by concentrating large numbers of newcomers in less rigorous courses. Faced with growing diversity, the Rockville Centre School District in New York, for example, eliminated the lowest high school track, a move that made a demonstrable difference in student achievement and school culture (Heubert & Hauser, 1999). Other measures include opening enrollment in Advanced Placement classes, sensitizing guidance counselors to the value of assigning newcomers to challenging courses, and providing teachers with staff development that addresses differentiated instruction.

The requirement under the No Child Left Behind Act to disaggregate student achievement data by student sub-group means that there is no longer any excuse for lack of awareness of newcomers' performance. Where data indicate problems, timely and targeted interventions must be provided. School district leaders should provide resources to principals so that they can initiate these interventions and then hold them accountable for doing so. It also is important for district leaders to monitor disciplinary referrals, suspensions, and expulsions to make certain that newcomers are not accounting for a disproportionately large number of disciplinary actions.

What's Best for English Language Learners

As the number of English language learners attending public schools grows, school district leaders are faced with the challenge of determining how best to instruct them. The challenge is all the greater when recent immigrants are illiterate in their native language. Despite the efforts of educators to accommodate the needs of newcomers, the achievement gap nationally in reading between fourth-grade English learners and non-English learners was 35 points in 2005 (Gersten et al., 2007, p. 4).

Many factors contribute to the difficulties of teaching English language learners. First, there is a lack of qualified teachers. A 2008 report from California's Commission on Teacher Credentialing, for example, found more than 11,000 out-of-field instructors of English language learners from 2003 to 2007 (Out-of-Field Teaching, 2008). In California schools that are predominantly minority and ELL, roughly one of every four teachers lacks the appropriate credential (Verdugo & Flores, 2007, p. 174).

A second issue concerns the requirements for testing English language learners under the No Child Left Behind Act. Schools initially are permitted to make "reasonable accommodations," such as testing ELL students in their native language, but only for a limited period of time. The law's intent is clearly to get to a point as quickly as possible when ELLs can be tested in English. Many educators feel that this pressure ensures low performance.

Consensus regarding the best way to instruct ELLs is lacking, posing a third concern for school district leaders. At least four competing instructional models are available. *Immersion* calls for ELLs to learn exclusively in English. Teachers use relatively simple language to instruct students in various curriculum subjects. *Transitional bilingual education* calls for students to receive some instruction in their native language at the same time that they are getting concentrated English-language instruction. *Developmental bilingual education* focuses on building students' proficiency in their native language while they are learning English as a second language. A fourth option, *two-way immersion*, places English language learners and English speakers together in the same classes. In this integrated learning environment, English speakers learn the native language of the non-English speakers while the latter learn English.

Advocates abound for each approach to instruction. The decision about which approach to adopt has become so highly politicized, in fact, that it is often taken out of the hands of educators. School boards and state and federal officials frequently are compelled to get involved. Arizona, for example, adopted regulations requiring all English language learners to be taught specific English skills in classrooms separate from other students for four hours a day (Zehr, 2008). Experts have noted that there is no rigorous research support for this requirement (Ibid.).

Given the issues surrounding English language instruction for newcomers, what can school district leaders do? The first step is to become familiar with the growing body of research on instruction for ELLs. Controversies notwithstanding, research supports some practices more than others. School district leaders should advocate for these preferred practices.

Of the four general approaches noted above, two-way immersion, also known as dual language education, seems to show the greatest promise. Collier and Thomas (2004) surveyed research and found that two-way immersion enables ELLs who begin in early elementary school to reach grade-level achievement in English by fifth or sixth grade. The presence of native-English-speaking peers in the same classroom clearly enhances instruction and expedites English language acquisition for ELLs. Collier and Thomas stress the importance of maintaining at least a 70:30 balance of English language learners to native-English-speakers.

When the federal Institute for Education Sciences commissioned a guide for effective instruction for ELLs, the authors offered four recommendations for which they found strong research support (Gersten et al., 2007, p. 6):

1. Conduct formative assessments with English learners using English language measures of phonological processing, letter knowledge,

and word and text reading. Use these data to identify English learners who require additional instructional support and to monitor their reading progress over time.

2. Provide focused, intensive small-group interventions for English learners determined to be at risk for reading problems. Although the amount of time in small-group instruction and the intensity of this instruction should reflect the degree of risk, determined by reading assessment data and other indicators, the interventions should include the five core reading elements (phonological awareness, phonics, reading fluency, vocabulary, and comprehension). Explicit, direct instruction should be the primary means of instructional delivery.

3. Provide high-quality vocabulary instruction throughout the day. Teach essential content words in depth. In addition, use instructional time to address the meanings of common words, phrases, and expressions not yet learned.

4. Ensure that teachers of English learners devote approximately 90 minutes a week to instructional activities in which pairs of students at different ability levels or different English language proficiencies work together on academic tasks in a structured fashion. These activities should practice and extend material already taught.

Of the four recommendations, the first may be the most critical. School district leaders must ensure that newcomers' language skills are assessed as soon as possible. Subsequent intervention and instruction depends on timely and accurate assessment. It also is important for ELLs to receive instruction in academic as well as conversational English. The ability of ELLs to progress in school and eventually graduate is contingent on becoming familiar with the vocabulary used in academic subjects.

The commissioned report from the Institute for Education Sciences acknowledged that the research base for elementary education of ELLs is much stronger than that for secondary education (Gersten et al., 2007, p. 5). Secondary schools pose special challenges for ELLs. Ruiz-de-Velasco and Fix (2000, p. 4) noted, for example, that "the departmentalization of secondary schools…effectively barred language and content teachers from collaborating to improve immigrant student outcomes." Secondary school schedules that divide the day into 40–50 minute segments also inhibit effective instruction for ELLs, who benefit from sustained and systematic instruction (Ruiz-de-Velasco & Fix , 2000).

Problems associated with educating older ELL students help explain why the dropout rate for Hispanic students is higher than other groups. In a unique study, Calaff (2008) spent a year shadowing nine Hispanic high school students who were participating in a college preparation program with a good track record. Instead of encountering the tracking and discrimination that discourages many ELL students in high school, these nine students were exposed to a rigorous academic curriculum. They were treated with care, expected to meet the same standards as other students, exposed to the latest instructional technologies, and supported by teachers and counselors. School staff embraced cultural and linguistic diversity. These "keys" to effective ELL instruction in high school are more likely to be in place when school district leaders *expect* them to be in place.

Sound advice for school district leaders committed to improving the educational opportunities for ELLs can be found in the previously mentioned report to the Seattle Public Schools (Raising the Achievement of English Language Learners in the Seattle Public Schools, 2008). The visiting team began by recommending that the superintendent (1) formulate a clear vision for the district's ELL instructional program, (2) see that the vision is incorporated into the district's strategic plan, and (3) provide the school board with regular reports on the progress of ELL reforms. When the education of ELLs is not treated as a high district priority, school-based personnel are more likely to focus on other concerns. The result can be confusion, inadequate support, and lack of direction.

The Seattle report goes on to recommend that the school district accountability office establish explicit districtwide academic achievement targets for ELLs as well as other subgroups. To ensure that these targets are taken seriously, the evaluation of principals and instructional personnel should be tied to achievement gains and the bilingual education program should be subject to a quality review. The results of this review should be shared with the community.

As for the actual instructional program for ELLs, the report advocated two broad components: (1) an enhanced "sheltered English-plus" program characterized by a strong native language support structure and (2) a dual language proficiency program. The authors of the report recommended that the school system decrease its reliance on its traditional English as a second language (ESL) pull-out instructional program. The "sheltered English-plus" program requires that ELL students remain in mainstream classes with English-speaking peers and receive in-class support from ESL teachers.

Educational opportunities for English language learners depend on school district leaders addressing their needs in a comprehensive and well-coordinated way. Given the increasing diversity of American society, school systems no longer can afford to treat programs for ELLs as add-ons and after-thoughts.

EXECUTIVE CONCLUSION

Contemporary school districts are constantly in flux. Enrollments grow and shrink. The make-up of the student body changes. Immigration brings large numbers of English language learners. Long-time residents move to new neighborhoods. Each demographic shift presents school district leaders with new challenges. The more leaders are able to anticipate these changes, the better they will be able to confront the challenges in constructive ways. Parents count on school districts to provide the best education possible for their children, regardless of who their children are or where they come from.

Demography and politics go hand in hand. Community residents often organize based on their race, ethnicity, socioeconomic status, or other distinguishing feature. Each group may pressure school district leaders to address their special interests. Pressures can become especially great when school systems face the prospect of school redistricting and con-solidation. Economic concerns have to be balanced against community support and good educational practice. School district leaders must make sure that decisions prompted by demographic changes are based on clearly articulated criteria and determined as transparently as possible.

One of the most difficult demographic changes confronting school district leaders involves racial and ethnic resegregation. American society presumably is committed to integration. The educational disadvantages of segregation have been acknowledged for decades and recognized by the courts and educators. School systems have implemented various initiatives aimed at preventing and reducing resegregation. These efforts include busing, magnet schools, and pupil assignment based on socioeconomic status. Each is credited with a limited degree of success, but the most effec-tive antidote to resegregation probably is a district focus on maintaining as academically rigorous an instructional program as possible.

Leaders of contemporary suburban school districts are less likely to face resegregation than growing diversity. American's suburbs no longer are exclusive havens for the white middle class. Suburban schools are enrolling increasing numbers of racial and ethnic minorities as well as students who qualify for free and reduced-price meals. To serve these newcomers, school district leaders must re-think how they plan, program, and allocate resources. Partnerships must be forged with community agencies and service providers. School data must be closely monitored to make certain that newcomers are not left behind or subjected to dis-criminatory practices. High expectations for all students should be every school district leader's mantra.

These provisions are especially applicable to English language learners. No longer can the education of ELLs be treated as a relatively low priority.

The future of American society in no small measure depends on the public schools' ability to provide ELLs with a high quality education. This means that school district leaders must understand which approaches to ELL instruction are most likely to be effective. Strategic plans should include targets and benchmarks for the academic achievement of English language learners. School district leaders have to mobilize resources to support hiring teachers qualified to teach ELLs and provide staff development for other teachers on how to address the needs of ELLs.

REFERENCES

An age of transformation. (September 15, 2008). *Economist.* Accessed from: www.economist.com/displaystory.cfm?story_id=11449846

Berube, A., & Kneebone, E. (2006). *Two Steps Back: City and Suburban Poverty Trends 1999–2005.* Washington, D.C.: The Brookings Institution.

Calaff, K.P. (2008). Supportive schooling: practices that support culturally and linguistically diverse students' preparation for college. *NASSP Bulletin,* 92(2), 95–110.

Chandler, M.A. (April 1, 2008). Parents sue to halt school boundary changes. *The Washington Post,* B-2.

Church Hill People's News. (August 23, 2007).

Collier, V.P., & Thomas, W.P. (2004). The astounding effectiveness of dual language education for all. *NABE Journal of Research and Practice,* 2(1), 1–20.

Duke, D.L. (2005). *Education Empire: the Evolution of an Excellent Suburban School System.* Albany: State University of New York Press.

Duke, D.L., & Trautvetter, S. (2001). *Reducing the Negative Effects of Large Schools.* Washington, D.C., National Clearinghouse for Educational Facilities.

Duncombe, W., & Yinger, J. (2007). Does school district consolidation cut costs? *Education Finance and Policy,* 2(8), 341–375.

Flinspach, S.L., & Banks, K.E. (2005). Moving beyond race. In J.C. Boger & G. Orfield (eds.), *School Resegregation.* Chapel Hill: University of North Carolina Press, 261–280.

Fowler, F.C. (2004). *Policy Studies for Educational Leaders,* Second edition. Columbus, OH: Pearson.

Fowler, W.J., & Walberg, H.J. (1991). School size, characteristics, and outcomes. *Educational Evaluation and Policy Analysis,* 13(2), 189–202.

Frankenberg, E. (2007). School integration — the time is now. In E. Frankenberg & G. Orfield (eds.), *Lessons in Integration.* Charlottesville: University of Virginia Press, 7–27.

Fulbright, L., & Knight, H. (May 24, 2006). With more choice has come resegregation. *San Francisco Chronicle,* A-1.

Fulton County Public Schools, Redistricting Policy. (2001). Accessed from: www.fultonschools.org/redistricting/process_NFSpring08.htm

Garofano, A., Sable, J., & Hoffman, L. (2008). *Characteristics of the 100 Largest Public Elementary and Secondary School Districts in the United States: 2005–06.* Washington, D.C.: U.S. Department of Education, National Center for Education Statistics.

Gersten, R., Baker, S.K., Shanahan, T., Linan-Thompson, S., Collins, P., & Scarcella, R. (2007). *Effective Literacy and English Language Instruction for English Learners in the Elementary Grades.* Washington, D.C.: U.S. Department of Education, Institute for Education Sciences.

Gewertz, C. (November 14, 2007). Urban leaders assess methods for integrating schools. *Education Week,* p. 9.

Heubert, J.P., & Hauser, R.M. (1999). *High Stakes: Testing for Tracking, Promotion, and Graduation*. Washington, D.C.: National Academy Press.

Largest 100 districts. (May 7, 2008). *Education Week*, p. 5.

Lee, V.E. & Smith, J.B. (1997). High school size: which works best and for whom? *Educational Evaluation and Policy Analysis*, 19(3), 205–227.

Lipton, E., & Benning, V. (October 2, 1997). With Fairfax's celebrated ethnic mix, rewards and problems. *The Washington Post*, D-1, D-5.

Maxwell, L.A. (October 10, 2007). Wake County, N.C., may raise cap on poor students. *Education Week*, p. 8.

Orfield, G., & Lee, C. (2006). *Racial Transformation and the Changing Nature of Segregation*. Cambridge, MA: The Civil Rights Project at Harvard University.

Out-of-field teaching. (September 3, 2008). *Education Week*, p. 5.

Peterson, B. (1998). Neighborhood schools, busing, and the struggle for equality. *Rethinking Schools*, 12(3), 1–8.

Raising the achievement of English language learners in the Seattle Public Schools. (2008). Washington, D.C.: Council of the Great City Schools.

Reardon, S.F., & Yun, J.T. (2005). Integrating neighborhoods, segregating schools. In J.C. Boger & G. Orfield (eds.), *School Resegregation*. Chapel Hill: University of North Carolina Press, 51–69.

Rossell, C. (2005). Whatever happened to magnet schools? *Education Week*, 4(2), 44–49.

Ruiz-de-Velasco, J., & Fix, M. (2000). *Overlooked & Underserved: Immigrant Students in U.S. Secondary Schools*. Washington, D.C.: The Urban Institute.

Schulte, B. (September 27, 2008). Student privacy spotlighted in Va. *The Washington Post*, pp. B-1, B-5.

School consolidation. (1985). ERIC Digest Number 13, ED 282346.

Student mobility, 2006–2007. (2008). Fairfax, VA: Fairfax County Public Schools.

Turque, B. (September 20, 2008), D.C. school rolls decline, preliminary tally shows. *The Washington Post*, B-1.

U.S. Census Bureau News. (May 17, 2007). Washington, D.C.: U.S. Department of Commerce.

Verdugo, R.R., & Flores, B. (2007). English-language learners: key issues. *Education and Urban Society*, 39(2), 167–193.

Wake County Policy 6200, Student Achievement. (January 10, 2000). Raleigh, NC: Wake County Public Schools.

Wasley, P.A., Fine, M., Gladden, M., Holland, N.E., King, S.P., Mosak, E., & Powell, L.C. (2000). *Small schools: great strides*. New York: Bank Street College of Education.

Wells, A.S., & Holme, J.J. (2005). No accountability for diversity. In J.C. Boger & G. Orfield (eds.). *School Resegregation*. Chapel Hill: University of North Carolina Press, 187–211.

Zehr, M.A. (September 3, 2008). Arizona still grappling with balance on mandated ELL instruction. *Education Week*, p. 14.

3

THE CHALLENGES OF SCHOOL DISTRICT
GOVERNANCE

SCHOOL DISTRICT POLITICS, CHICAGO-STYLE

Not one to mince words, U.S. Secretary of Education William Bennett came to Chicago in 1988 and pronounced the city's schools the worst in the nation. Bennett, of course, was not saying anything that many Chicagoans did not know already. The previous year a 19-day teachers' strike delayed the opening of school. More than a thousand citizens marched on city hall to demand that Mayor Harold Washington intervene to settle the strike.

Intervention did not stop at the Mayor's office, however. Angry citizens and business groups brought the fight to the Illinois legislature, which passed a landmark bill in 1988. The bill created elected local school councils (LSCs) at every Chicago public school. Each LSC was to consist of 11 teachers, parents, and other community members, but parents and community members had to constitute a majority. The LSC was granted the authority to (1) hire and fire principals, (2) control academic programs through approval of mandated annual School Improvement Plans, (3) oversee the school's share of state Title 1 funds, and (4) contract for support services.

The legislation instituted several other reforms related to governance. Each school was required to have a Professional Personnel Advisory Committee (PPAC), composed of teachers, to advise the principal and LSC on instructional and professional issues. At the district level, the school board, which traditionally had been appointed by the major and

56

was highly partisan politically, was stripped of much of its authority. Control over school finances shifted to the newly formed School Finance Administration, which was run by business leaders instead of educators. The size and power of the central office of Chicago Public Schools was substantially curtailed.

Just as Chicagoans were adjusting to these dramatic changes, a second wave of governance reforms washed over the school system. In 1995 legislation was passed that eliminated the central school board along with the position of superintendent. The management of the school system was placed in the hands of the Reform Board of Trustees, which was appointed by the mayor. In effect, Chicago Public Schools was governed by city hall. The Board of Trustees was led by a Chief Executive Officer (CEO), who also was a mayoral appointee. The CEO was given the authority to lay off and reassign principals in low-performing schools, a move that clearly undercut the power of the LSCs. The legislation also encouraged the privatization of school support services and reduced the bargaining power of the teachers union. Teachers lost control over academic-related decisions, including student retention and promotion decisions. A moratorium on teachers' right to strike also was imposed.

These dramatic changes resulted from several concerns. The school system needed to win back the confidence of middle class parents who had abandoned Chicago schools. Student achievement decline had to be arrested and provisions put in place for holding educators accountable for educational outcomes. Finally, responsibility for the schools needed to be balanced. The LSCs did not always demonstrate a capacity for wise school governance. The 1995 legislation ensured that the mayor would assume a significant measure of responsibility for school performance.

※※※※※

Chicago's experience at the end of the 20th century illustrates many of the challenges associated with governing contemporary school systems. Two such challenges involve the expanding role of state and local government in the operation of schools. These changes have been accompanied, not surprisingly, by the increased politicization of public education. School district leaders now confront a gauntlet of special interest groups with varying agendas for the schools. The impact of such tectonic shifts has been to erode much of the traditional authority of school boards, teachers, superintendents, and unions. When changes of the kind undertaken in Chicago are coupled with the federal government's expanded role in the wake of the No Child Left Behind Act, school district leaders are left wondering how much of the education process remains under their control.

THE RHETORIC AND REALITY OF SCHOOL
DISTRICT GOVERNANCE

The landscape of school district governance is littered with illusions, half-truths, and nostalgia. To gain a clearer view of the challenges associated with school governance, school district leaders first must be able to distinguish fact from fiction. Fiction often takes the form of narratives, and several of the more popular narratives related to school governance are examined in this section.

The "narrative of the closed door" holds that teachers, not school boards, superintendents, and principals, really are in control of public education. Once the classroom door is closed, teachers are free to do whatever they please. Characterized as "street-level bureaucrats," teachers in this narrative "have the power to unmake or remake policy faster than policy can influence organizational priorities and practices" (Malen, 2006, p. 97).

While many observers acknowledge that teachers, if they so choose, can ignore policies and administrative directives, it is doubtful in today's public schools that they can do so for long. Teaching practice is under greater scrutiny than at any time in recent memory. Principals who fail to ensure a measure of instructional uniformity may find themselves facing removal. The image of the autonomous professional educator trusted by the community to make the correct judgment for every child in his or her charge has given way in many school systems to a tightly coupled accountability system marked by frequent monitoring and performance evaluation. Whether such a change constitutes a step forward or backward, of course, is an empirical question. It should be noted, though, that teachers are not the only professionals facing the demands of greater accountability.

Another narrative related to school governance involves the notion that public education is a non-partisan concern. Decision making regarding the operation of public schools, in other words, is supposed to be "above" politics. Considerable nostalgia surrounds this narrative. Those whose memories are short or who read little history conjure up images of a bygone time when civic-minded school boards set aside special interests and considered only what was best for the children of the community. To this day in many localities, school board members are not permitted to run on the ticket of a political party.

Students of school district governance, of course, reject the notion that politics stops at the schoolhouse door. Examples abound of school board members who cut deals in order to secure benefits for their constituents. Public education is big business, accounting for billions of dollars annually. Whenever such large sums of money are involved, the prospects for politics are great. Education also entails the transmission of values, another impetus for politics. Every time a social issue arises, school district leaders face pressures to address the issue in the curriculum. Considerable contentiousness often swirls around how best to address social issues.

Public education is one of the cornerstones of a democratic society. Presumably politics in a democratic society is not a negative phenomenon. Politics represents the process by which the voices of the people are heard. Under such circumstances, it seems odd that anyone committed to democracy would expect school governance to be anything but political. Perhaps critics of the politicization of school district governance differentiate between "good" politics and "bad" politics. If so, it would be interesting to examine what they regard as "bad" politics. Could it be that "bad" politics is associated with outcomes that they oppose?

A third narrative concerns the local control of public education. The story traces its origins to the birth of the common school in the nineteenth century. Local villages and towns, not state legislatures or the federal government, took the initiative to establish publicly funded schools. People reasoned that the educational needs of children were best determined and addressed by those who paid the bills, namely local taxpayers.

Over time, of course, an increasing portion of the bills was paid by non-local funds. States became more active players in overseeing the operation of local schools. With the passage of the Elementary and Secondary Education Act in 1965, the federal government also began to play a role, especially with regard to issues of educational equity. Parents and educators expressed resentment over threats to local control, but they willingly accepted the funds that flowed from Washington, D.C. and statehouses. By the last decades of the 20th century, local control, which once had been regarded as the preferred route to an educated citizenry, was increasingly seen as an obstacle.

This chapter addresses some of the challenges associated with the governance of contemporary school systems, Every school district leader probably has had or will have occasion to ask at least one of the following four questions.

The Challenges of School District Governance

1. Can school district governance be both democratic and effective?

2. Given greater involvement in local education by states and the federal government, what do school district leaders actually control?

3. How are big city mayors reshaping school district governance?

4. Is it better to centralize or decentralize district decision making?

THE BURDEN OF DEMOCRACY

At a particularly tense point in the movie, *Crimson Tide*, Gene Hackman, who plays the commander of a submarine loaded with nuclear weapons and facing a possible attack by a renegade Russian admiral, confronts Denzel Washington, the second in command. Washington is concerned that Hackman is overstepping his authority by preparing a preemptive strike without proper authorization. Hackman responds that the Navy's duty is to protect democracy, not practice it. Given the challenges associated with governing school districts democratically, some school district leaders might agree with Hackman's point. Governing school districts democratically requires a tolerance for amateurs, the patience to hear from all stakeholders, and the courage to resist pressure from special interest groups.

In 1990 two political science scholars published a controversial analysis of the problems with public schooling in the United States. *Politics, Markets, and America's Schools* (Chubb & Moe, 1990) concluded that U.S. students were falling behind their peers in other countries because of how their school systems were governed and managed. The authors stated their belief that "the existing institutions of democratic control are simply inconsistent with the autonomous operation and effective organization of schools" (p. 183). Chubb and Moe reasoned that the most effective public schools operate relatively free of school board politics and heavy bureaucratic control. As they put it, "the direct influence of boards is stronger over schools that are ineffectively organized than it is over schools that are effectively organized" (p. 156). Their solution was to emulate the private sector and stimulate the development of education markets.

School district leaders did not escape Chubb and Moe's indictment. Too much central office bureaucratization, according to their analysis of effective and ineffective schools, constrained principals and prevented them from exercising the kind of on-site leadership associated with high performance. Chubb and Moe were especially critical of district bureaucrats who interfered with principals' efforts to hire staff and determine curriculum.

Whether or not school district leaders should decentralize decision making will be taken up later in this chapter. As for the role of school boards, a popular complaint has been that many, if not most, board members are amateurs when it comes to the professional practice of education. Is the practice of medicine in hospitals turned over to non-physicians? Hospital boards presumably focus on the business side of operations, leaving decisions regarding medical care to the experts. While many school board members clearly appreciate this distinction, others engage in what is frequently referred to as "micromanagement." One of the most daunting challenges for superintendents is constraining the tendency of board members to assume responsibilities better left to educators.

The primary duties of school boards are to set district policy, approve the budget, and hire and evaluate the superintendent. In undertaking these duties, school board members, whether elected or appointed, are expected to see that the public's interests in public education are properly represented. Herein, however, lies another challenge. Who constitutes the "public?" To what extent do board members represent the make-up of the population? Are special interest groups part of the public? What should school board members do when the majority of their constituents do not have children in the public schools? Do board members have a special obligation to serve the needs of parents and young people?

When Kowalski (2006, pp. 132–133) reviewed data on the make-up of school boards, he found that they are gradually becoming more representative of the population in general. Once made up largely of white males, boards now include many women. In 2001, slightly more than 40 percent of school board members were women. In the same year, though, only 14 percent of board members were reported to be non-white.

At various times in their history, school boards have been accused of catering to the interests of power elites, teacher unions, and other special interest groups (Petersen & Fusarelli, 2008, p. 119). In one of the few systematic studies of contemporary school board politics, Hess and Leal (2005, p. 24) found that board members did not feel that special interest groups wielded much influence over school board decisions and elections. That said, they noted that teacher unions generally were perceived to be the leading special interest group in local board politics, especially in large urban districts. Hess and Leal also found, not surprisingly, that the influence of race-based special interest groups increased with the size of the African American and (to a lesser extent) Hispanic population. Still, when superintendents were polled in 2002 regarding the political proclivities of their school boards, only 19 percent indicated that their boards were aligned with a distinct community faction (Hess, 2002).

The interests of a community's young people can be served best when school board members are able to set aside their differences, avoid partisan politics, and commit to a common mission and vision for the school system. When consultants are commissioned to advise struggling school districts on how to improve, they often begin at the top by insisting that board members reach consensus regarding district priorities and then convey these priorities to the superintendent. Such was the advice given to the Richmond, Virginia, school system, by a visiting team from the Council of the Great City Schools. Invited to assess the struggling school system, the team examined all aspects of district operations and issued a lengthy report on how to raise student achievement. The report opened with the observation that "the Richmond school district has had trouble hitting its mark over the years because so many people in the system are aiming in different directions" (*Charting a New Course...*, 2003, p. 11). The report recommended that the school board, which had been characterized by contentiousness and frequent split votes, coalesce around a "shared vision for where they want the district to go and what they want the schools to look like" (p. 12).

As a result of the Council of the Great City School's report, the Richmond School Board reached consensus on a set of priorities that focused squarely on improving student literacy and ensuring school safety. Board members set measurable goals for academic improvement and timelines for the attainment of goals. The school board then charged the superintendent, Deborah Jewell-Sherman, with establishing school-by-school academic targets and taking the steps necessary to enable school personnel to reach these targets. And the rest, as they say, is history. Within three years, Richmond more than doubled the number of schools that were fully accredited. So successful were Richmond's efforts to raise student achievement that educators from high-performing Fairfax County Public Schools visited Richmond to learn how the school system was managing to close the achievement gap between African American and white students.

Many of the recommendations in the Council of the Great City Schools report to Richmond were supported by an earlier study funded by the Council and conducted by MDRC researchers (Snipes, Doolittle, & Herlihy, 2002). The study compared various aspects of four urban school systems that had achieved dramatic success in raising student achievement with four less successful school systems. Of particular relevance to the present discussion, the four successful districts were characterized by the following features:

- The school board focused on policy and left management to the central office.
- The school board's top priority was raising student achievement.
- The school board was quick to create a vision for the district.
- The school board sought a superintendent who embraced its vision.
- The school board insisted that the superintendent be held accountable for goals.
- Once hired, the superintendent worked with the school board to refine the board's initial vision.
- The school board and the superintendent developed a stable and lengthy relationship. (Snipes et al., 2002, p. 63)

As for the less successful comparison districts, they differed on virtually every aspect listed above. These school boards were easily distracted from issues related to student achievement. They were slow to define a vision for the district and unable to agree on goals to which to hold the superintendent accountable. Instead of alignment between the school board and the superintendent, each entity appeared to move in a different direction. This fact undoubtedly helped to explain the high turnover rate for superintendents in the comparison districts.

Delagardelle (2008, pp. 211–212) reported on an extensive series of studies of the relationship between school board actions and student achievement. Five primary roles of school boards were found to be associated with achievement gains: (1) setting clear expectations for outcomes, (2) holding themselves and district staff accountable for achieving the expectations, (3) ensuring that the conditions for success were present in the school district, (4) building the collective will of the district staff and the community to improve student learning, and (5) engaging in continuing board development and learning. Delagardelle (2008, p. 221) concluded with the following observation, "How board-superintendent teams understand and carry out their roles can make the difference between dysfunctional leadership teams incapable of leading change and highly effective leadership teams that build district wide capacity to ensure every student succeeds."

Returning to the focal question for this section, there is no reason to believe that democratically chosen school boards and educational effectiveness are necessarily incompatible. Plenty of examples of successful school systems led by elected school boards can be found. Two keys to effectiveness are aligned leadership between school boards and superintendents and continuity of leadership. It is obviously more difficult for aligned leadership to develop when school board members and superintendents only remain in office for brief periods of time.

THE LIMITS OF LOCAL CONTROL

There are few traditions more cherished by Americans than local control, especially when it comes to the operation of public schools. If the opinions of many contemporary school district leaders are any indication, however, an observer might wonder what aspects of schooling still remain under the control of school boards and school district administrators. It would seem that much of a school district leader's time is spent ensuring that district personnel comply with rules, regulations, guidelines, and laws that derive from non-local sources.

Beginning with the *Brown* decision in 1954, the courts began to play a major role in determining who had to be served by the public schools and how they had to be served. Then the federal government, starting with the Elementary and Secondary Education Act of 1965, became an active player in the world of public education. During the Reagan presidency, the federal role diminished somewhat with the shift from categorical to block grants to states. States found themselves exercising greater discretion over the allocation of federal education funds. While much of this discretionary authority has continued, the passage of the No Child Left Behind Act in 2002 provided a dramatic reminder that Washington had no intention of leaving public education exclusively to states and localities.

It might be instructive to survey some of the aspects of schooling where local school district leaders do not exercise unfettered authority. School districts, for instance, have little control over who they must serve. Court decisions and federal laws have determined that schools are obligated to educate, among others, students with special needs, homeless students, non-English speakers, and undocumented minors from other counties. Most states set performance standards that schools and districts must meet in order to maintain accreditation and meet the requirements of adequate yearly progress under the No Child Left Behind Act. These standards also specify the course and credit requirements needed to earn a diploma and the number of hours of instruction required to earn a credit.

When it comes to what must be taught in local schools, states exercise considerable influence. By designating the courses required to earn a diploma, establishing curriculum guidelines, and developing standard-ized tests aligned to state curriculum guidelines, states determine to a considerable degree what content will be covered in local schools and classrooms. Some states even approve the textbooks that can be used in public schools.

While most states leave matters related to the delivery of instruction to local educators, they do exercise some control over the conditions under which instruction is to take place. Some states, for example, have adopted policies regarding maximum class size, especially for the early grades. Other policies govern the length of the school year and various aspects of school discipline and safety. The No Child Left Behind Act requires that schools employ "highly qualified" teachers, but the defini-tion of what constitutes "highly qualified" is left up to the states. Many states also have policies regarding staffing ratios for school administrators, guidance counselors, and other professional personnel.

A relatively recent development in state control concerns low-perform-ing schools. Prompted in part by the sanctions specified for chronically low-performing schools under the No Child Left Behind Act, states offer various types of assistance to struggling schools and school systems. Help ranges from visiting teams of educators to trained turnaround specialists.

When school districts fail to make required improvements, 24 states have provisions for taking over school district operations. By 2001, school district takeovers had occurred in 18 states and the District of Columbia (Wong & Shen, 2001). Takeovers initially were prompted by concerns regarding finances and mismanagement, but low student achievement increasingly has been cited as a justification for state intervention. States also may permit the creation of charter schools, thereby introducing the element of competition to spur better performance.

The seeming erosion of local control of public education is closely associated with finance. School districts depend to varying degrees on local, state, and federal funds. Non-local funds typically have strings attached. Concerns over too much federal control under the No Child Left Behind Act, in fact, have led some states to consider rejecting Title 1 assistance from Washington. It also should be noted that school district leaders frequently complain about under-funded and unfunded mandates when the federal government and state governments promulgate requirements for local schools without allocating adequate funds to address the new requirements.

The educational aims of local school district leaders do not always coincide with the aims of state and national leaders. The latter often are motivated by the understandable desire to reduce variations across schools and school systems. The intent is to promote greater educational equity. Local school district leaders, on the other hand, frequently focus on educational excellence. Their intent is to distinguish the education available in their schools from the education offered in neighboring school districts. Developing distinctive programs can boost real estate values and attract business. From the perspective of many school district leaders, the increased role of state and federal authorities in local education serves to inhibit innovation and limit competition between school districts.

Since state and federal efforts to influence local education are unlikely to diminish, the challenge for school district leaders is to respond to external mandates designed to promote equity while simultaneously engaging local educators and community members in the quest for educational excellence. Ultimately, it is the continuous pursuit of educational excellence more than its achievement that may matter the most. Actually attaining excellence can lead to undesirable consequences, including over-confidence and complacency.

THE RISE OF BIG CITY MAYORS

Local control of education, in one sense, is not eroding. In some of the nation's largest and most troubled school systems, popularly elected mayors have begun to play a prominent role in local public education.

The rise of mayoral control constitutes another governance challenge for school district leaders.

The mini-case that opened this chapter described how Chicago's mayor assumed leadership over a foundering school system. The mayor created a separate authority to oversee school system finances, disbanded the school board and formed his own governing body, and appointed a chief executive officer to handle the day-to-day operations of the school district.

Since the advent of mayoral control in Chicago in 1995, a number of American cities with low-performing school systems have experienced efforts by mayors to increase their influence over local education. The cities include Cleveland, Detroit, Los Angeles, New York, Richmond, and Washington, D.C. Some of these efforts by mayors to turn around entire school systems have been more successful than others. Expanded mayoral influence, of course, may be viewed in various ways, depending on one's perspective. While some consider such initiatives to be "power grabs" by politicians who lack the expertise to govern public education, others regard mayoral moves as preferable alternatives to state takeovers of local school systems.

Mayors can expand their influence in a variety of ways. Wong and Shen (2008, pp. 347–351), for example, identify five different forms of mayoral influence over school governance. The least intrusive form of mayoral influence is the mayoral-led "blue ribbon panel." The traditional governance system remains in tact, while the panel studies the city's schools and produces a report intended to impact district operations. The next option involves the creation of a standing office under the mayor's supervision to monitor the city's schools and advise the mayor on education issues. The third alternative finds the mayor endorsing a slate of candidates for the school board. By backing candidates who support their positions, mayors hope to exercise more direct influence over school systems.

The last two options represent the highest levels of mayoral influence. Mayors in New York and Oakland (CA) gained the authority to appoint some members of the school board. In the cases of Boston and Chicago, the entire school board is appointed by the mayor.

Opinions vary concerning the impact of mayoral control, especially with regard to student achievement. Bryant (2007, p. 26) is critical of mayoral efforts to lead school systems:

> Mayoral control is a simple and wrong solution to the complex challenge of raising student achievement. Although research demonstrates that in a few cities mayoral takeover has reined in administrative costs and oversight, research also indicates that overall student achievement does not increase under mayoral control.

Wong and Shen (2008, pp. 333–335), in by far the most sophisticated statistical analysis of the impact of mayoral influence on student achievement, offer a more nuanced view. When the mayor has the power to appoint a majority of the school board, there is a positive impact on elementary reading achievement. When the mayor has the power to appoint all school board members, however, elementary reading achievement actually declines. Wong and Shen recommend that mayoral control be balanced by a nominating committee charged with developing a slate of school board candidates. They caution against unfettered mayoral control of public schools.

Bryant (2007, p. 26) prefers a governance model in which school boards and mayors form partnerships. She cites the example of San Francisco, where Mayor Gavin Newsom and the school board forged an alliance that has proven productive in advancing the interests of San Francisco youth.

Richmond's experience with a mayor who wanted expanded power over the schools constitutes an example of how not to proceed. Despite the school district's impressive gains under Superintendent Deborah Jewell-Sherman, newly elected Mayor Doug Wilder sought to assume direct control of the school system. When he failed to get support from the Richmond City Council, he tried to act on his own. At one point, he even attempted to move the superintendent and school board out of their offices in City Hall without their knowledge or permission. Ultimately, Wilder lost so much credibility with local voters that he was compelled not to run for re-election. Regrettably, however, Deborah Jewell-Sherman also decided to leave. The highly acclaimed leader had had enough of the mayor's persistent meddling in school district affairs.

Sometimes urban school district leaders may need to get directly involved in local politics in order to ensure good working relations with local authorities. *The Little School System That Could* (Duke, 2008) recounts the story of Superintendent Tom DeBolt and his efforts to transform the Manassas Park school system in northern Virginia. When he was unable to enlist the active support of the Manassas Park City Council for badly needed capital improvements, DeBolt became personally involved in the local Republican Party. Joining him was School Board Chairman Frank Jones. Together they managed to see that education-friendly candidates ran for the city council. Eventually, by working closely with the new city council, DeBolt and Jones managed to gain approval for a capital improvement program, significant increases in teacher salaries, and a revenue-sharing agreement that guaranteed the school system 57 percent of local revenues. These developments provided the impetus for the transformation of the perennially low-performing school system.

There is no question that finding ways to work with mayors and city councils represents a major challenge for urban school district leaders, but it is a challenge that cannot be avoided if school districts are to continue to be guided by professional educators.

Efforts by mayors to increase control over school systems constitute one form of organizational centralization. Opinions vary on the desirability of centralization. In the next section, the costs and benefits of school district centralization will be examined.

TO CENTRALIZE OR NOT TO CENTRALIZE

Prescriptions for how best to govern school districts include calls for both greater centralization and greater decentralization of decision making. An analysis of each option reveals costs and benefits. Determining whether particular conditions are better served by centralized or decentralized decision making is one of the most important challenges facing school district leaders.

The history of American education is punctuated by periods when the value of greater decentralization has been stressed. Sometimes the focus on decentralization was prompted by controversy. Such was the case in New York City when racial tensions erupted in the late 1960s (Rogers, 1969). Minority parents grew concerned that the predominantly white power structures of the city's school system and teachers union were not responsive to the needs of their children. As a result, the enormous school system was sub-divided into community districts, each with its own school board and superintendent.

Rapid growth in enrollments also can lead to school district decentralization. In the wake of Baby Boomer growth in the 1960s, Fairfax County Public Schools sub-divided into four divisions, each headed by an "area superintendent." Unlike New York City, however, the divisions did not have their own school boards. According to a high-ranking Fairfax administrator, decentralization "enabled supervisory personnel to maintain close and effective contact with school-based personnel despite rapid growth" (Duke, 2005, p. 36).

Decentralization efforts do not always focus on breaking up large school systems into more responsive and manageable units. Sometimes decentralization targets individual schools, the intention being to improve performance and encourage innovation. Variously referred to as site-based management, school-based management, shared decision making, and school restructuring, initiatives aimed at devolving greater authority on local schools have been traced back to the mid-1960s (Cuban, 2004, p. 110). The movement got a boost following the publication of *A Nation at*

Risk in 1983. School reformers intent on raising the overall level of student achievement drew inspiration from corporations that were reaping productivity benefits by shifting decision-making responsibility downward. The press for decentralization grew so great by 1990 that Kentucky's legislature mandated school-based management in its omnibus Kentucky Education Reform Act (KERA). KERA required every school in the state to create a school council consisting of three teacher representatives, two parent representatives, and the principal. Each council was authorized to make policy decisions regarding school budget (including staff salaries), professional development, curriculum, instructional practices, textbooks, allocation of positions, daily school schedule, assignment of students to programs and classes, and extracurricular programs (*The Progress of Education...*, 2001).

As indicated at the beginning of the chapter, Chicago also implemented school councils at about the same time as KERA was passed. Concern over how these councils were functioning, however, eventually led to a reduction in their authority. Still, the principle of greater community participation in school decision making remained intact in Chicago.

Some school systems have preferred to increase the authority of principals and teachers, but not necessarily parents and community members. In New York City, Mayor Bloomberg decided that his efforts to re-centralize the giant system were not working well. Besides scrapping the ten "regions" that had been set up to replace the community districts and reinstituting the 32 community districts, Bloomberg backed a plan in 2007 to give principals "more power over hiring and firing staff, controlling educational programming, and managing their schools' budgets" (Gewertz, 2007). Many school district leaders have instituted similar provisions that give principals extraordinary powers to turn around low-performing schools.

In other school systems, interestingly, such powers have been reserved as rewards for principals in high-performing schools (Jacobson, 2008). In Richmond, for example, Deborah Jewell-Sherman maintained direct control over principals in low-performing schools, deciding, among other things, what reading programs they had to use and what kinds of staff development their teachers received. As schools improved, principals were accorded greater discretion over decision making. As Yvonne Brandon, Jewell-Sherman's deputy superintendent, argued, "It's easier to loosen up than tighten up."

Perhaps the most extreme form of decentralization involves the semi-privatization of individual public schools. One way to accomplish this process is through the conversion of public schools to charter schools. New Orleans and the District of Columbia have extensive charter school programs. Regulations governing charter schools vary from state to state. In Arizona, for example, charters are granted by the state. Virginia, on the other hand, gives authority to local school boards to approve charter schools. Charter schools operate semi-autonomously, free to determine such matters as what to teach, how to allocate resources, and the length of the school day and school year. Charter schools typically are not constrained by union contracts with school districts. Most charter schools, however, are subject to some state and local restrictions. Usually charter schools, for example, are not allowed to deny access to any group of students.

Another form of semi-privatization involves contractual arrangements between school districts and private management firms. Such initiatives typically are prompted by sustained low performance and fiscal mismanagement. In 2002, for instance, the state of Pennsylvania took over the troubled Philadelphia school system. The city's nine-member school board was replaced with an appointed School Reform Commission (SRC) composed of three members appointed by the governor and two members appointed by the mayor. The SRC adopted a "diverse provider" model that called for management of 45 of the district's lowest performing elementary and middle schools by seven for-profit and nonprofit organizations. It is worth noting that an evaluation of the privately managed schools undertaken four years after the experiment began found no statistically significant differences in reading or mathematics achievement between the 45 schools and other Philadelphia elementary and middle schools (Gill, Zimmer, Christman, & Blanc, 2007).

School district leaders must weigh the costs and benefits of decentralization. The benefits of decentralization have been widely reported (Chubb & Moe, 1990; Ouchi, 2003; Somech, 2002). Decentralization has been linked to greater teacher job satisfaction, higher quality decision making, teacher professionalization, and improved student achievement. Since there are so many forms that decentralization can take, it is impossible, though, to generalize across all of them. A review of research on school-based management commissioned by the Education Commission of the States (*The Progress of Education...*, 2001) reported that this form of decentralization led to higher levels of reform in curriculum and instruction and greater teacher morale. Ouchi (2003) drew on the experience of three large school systems to advocate for greater discretionary authority for principals. Enabling principals to control their budgets and function as "entrepreneurs" was the key, according to Ouchi, to higher performance. Chubb and Moe's (199) claim that central office bureaucracies and school board politics inhibit schools from taking effective action to raise student achievement already has been noted.

The case for decentralization is not conclusive, however. Ryan (2001) questioned whether large school districts that purport a commitment to decentralization actually implement measures to increase school-based control. Drawing on Cleveland's experience, he noted the potential contradictions in any *centrally mandated* effort to increase school-based decision making. As he put it, "Grassroots authority is difficult to maintain if social policy is conceptualized in terms of centrally planned blueprints" (p. 38). Ultimately, the reform process in Cleveland revealed serious doubts by central office leaders that local schools and parent groups were capable of making the kinds of decisions needed to raise student achievement.

An investigation of some of the most impressive school district turnarounds in recent years finds a relatively high degree of centralization. In Duval County, Florida, and Boston, Massachusetts, for instance, new superintendents refused to leave improvement efforts up to school-based personnel. Drawing on the expertise of central office administrators and outside consultants, John Fryer and Tom Payzant saw to it that a district-wide approach to school reform was generated (Reville, 2007; Supovitz, 2006). A more in-depth discussion of these efforts appears in Chapter 6. A similar strategy was undertaken in Norfolk and Richmond, Virginia. In both cases, a centrally dictated program of curriculum alignment coupled with a common instructional model for all schools enabled the two troubled school systems to make remarkable gains in student achievement in a relatively short time.

In school systems characterized by substantial variations in success across schools, centralized decision making and governance may be the only way to ensure some degree of overall equity. Allowing each school to pursue its own reform agenda can give rise to large gaps in performance, especially when some schools are blessed with better leadership and stronger faculties than others. Centralization also may be the preferred strategy during periods of turbulence and retrenchment. Leaving decisions about budgets and program priorities up to individual schools when conditions are characterized by uncertainty and diminished resources can lead to an escalation of tensions and infighting (Brouillette, 1996, p. 193; Duke, 1984). Rather than watch school personnel struggle over how and where to cut back, school district leaders may be advised to assume responsibility for guiding schools through the treacherous waters of financial crisis.

Since both centralized and decentralized decision making involve benefits and costs, school district leaders may wish to seek some balance between the two strategies. Marsh (2002, p. 36), in fact, concludes after reviewing the literature on education reform that districts' success "in enacting school-level improvement often hinges on a delicate balance between centralized and decentralized control." School-based personnel need to know that their perspectives and suggestions are valued. At the same time, school district leaders have an obligation to ensure some degree of uniformity across all schools.

EXECUTIVE CONCLUSION

Few areas of school district operations generate as much opinion and controversy as governance. Much of this tension is the result of trying to exercise professional responsibilities within the context of a democratic governance structure. All stakeholders expect to have their voices heard in a democracy, and that includes educational leaders and teachers. Should the voices of some stakeholders be accorded greater importance than others? Who should decide which stakeholder views to heed? Questions such as these keep school district leaders awake at night.

Some observers believe that many of the problems of public education derive from a system of school district governance that places too much control in the hands of non-educators. Others insist that school boards are an important expression of democratic principles and that they can function effectively as long as board members refrain from "micromanaging" the daily operations of schools and districts. One of the challenges facing superintendents is learning how to work with school boards to minimize meddling, partisanship, and political conflict. The interests of students are best served when school boards and central office personnel do not work at cross-purposes, but instead forge productive partnerships.

Another challenge for school district leaders involves determining what aspects of public education they actually can control. As state legislatures, federal authorities, and the courts have played an increasingly influential role in shaping public education, local control of schools has steadily eroded. School district leaders often feel like managers whose primary responsibilities involve ensuring compliance with laws and regulations. Still, examples abound of school district leaders who find ways to exceed expectations and undertake bold new initiatives that set their school systems apart from the mainstream.

Over the past few decades, school district leaders in some large urban systems have had to contend with mayors as well as state legislatures, federal authorities, and the courts. Prompted by concerns over mismanagement and low performance, big city mayors have become increasingly active in local school matters. Sometimes their efforts are limited to relatively benign forms of influence. In other cases, mayors actually have taken over control of school systems. The results of mayoral intervention are mixed, but one thing is clear. There is much to gain by school district leaders and mayors working closely together to mobilize public support and generate resources for schools.

Governance issues frequently arise in the context of debates over the costs and benefits of decentralization. Sharing decision making with principals, teachers, and community members has the potential to enhance staff morale, improve the quality of many decisions, and even raise student achievement. Decentralization, however, also can lead to petty squabbling and inequities across schools. Decentralization may not be well-suited to situations in which budgets are being reduced and where a large number of schools are chronically low-performing. When school systems are not unusually stressed, though, a balance of centralized and decentralized decision making may constitute the best strategy.

REFERENCES

Brouillette, L. (1996). *A Geology of School Reform*. Albany: State University of New York Press.

Bryant, A.L. (December 12, 2007). Should the mayor be in charge? *Education Week*, p. 26.

Charting a New Course for the Richmond Public Schools. (2003). Washington, D.C.: The Council of the Great City Schools.

Chubb, J.E., & Moe, T.M. (1990) *Politics, Markets, and America's Schools*. Washington, D.C.: Brookings.

Cuban, L. (2004). A solution that lost its problem: centralized policymaking and classroom gains. In N. Epstein (ed.), *Who's in Charge Here?* Washington, D.C.: Brookings Institution Press, 104–130.

Delagardelle, M.L. (2008). The Lighthouse Inquiry: examining the role of school board leadership in the improvement of student achievement. In T.L. Alsbury (ed.), *The Future of School Board Governance*. Lanham, MD: Rowman & Littlefield, 191–223.

Duke, D.L. (2008). *The Little School System That Could: The Transformation of a City School District*. Albany: State University of New York Press.

Duke, D.L. (2005). *Education Empire: The Evolution of an Excellent Suburban School System*. Albany: State University of New York Press.

Duke, D.L. (1984). *Decision Making in an Era of Fiscal Instability*. Bloomington, IN: Phi Delta Kappan.

Gewertz, C. (January 24, 2007). NYC to scrap regions, give principals more authority. *Education Week*, 7.

Gill, B., Zimmer, R., Christman, J., & Blanc, S. (2007). *State takeover, School Restructuring, Private Management, and Student Achievement in Philadelphia*. Santa Monica, CA: RAND.

Hess, F.M. (2002). *School boards at the dawn of the 21st century: conditions and challenges of district governance*. Washington, D.C.: National School Boards Association.

Hess, F.M., & Leal, D.L. (2005). School house politics: expenditures, interests, and competition in school board elections. In W.G. Howell (ed.), *Besieged: School Boards and the Future of Education Politics*. Washington, D.C.: Brookings Institution Press, 228-253.

Jacobson, L. (March 5, 2008). States eye looser rein on districts. *Education Week*, 1, 18.

Kowalski, T.J. (2006). *The School Superintendent*, second edition. Thousand Oaks, CA: Sage.

Malen, B. (2006). Revisiting policy implementation as a political phenomenon. In M.I. Honig (ed.), *New Directions in Education Policy Implementation*. Albany: State University of New York Press, 83–104.

Marsh, J.A. (2002). How districts relate to states, schools, and communities: a review of emerging literature. In A.M. Hightower, M.S. Knapp, J.A. Marsh, & M.W. McLaughlin (eds.), *School Districts and Instructional Renewal*. New York: Teachers College Press, 25–40.

Ouchi, W.G. (2003). *Making Schools Work*. New York: Simon & Schuster.

Petersen, G.J., & Fusarelli, L.D. (2008). Systemic leadership amidst turbulence: superintendent-school board relations under pressure. In T.L. Alsbury (ed.), *The Future of School Board Governance*. Lanham, MD: Rowman & Littlefield, 115–134.

The Progress of Education Reform 1999–2001: School-based Management. (2001). Denver, CO: Education Commission of the States.

Reville, S.P. (ed.). (2007). *A Decade of Urban School Reform*. Cambridge, MA: Harvard Education Press.

Rogers, D. (1969). *110 Livingston Street*. New York: Vintage.

Ryan, P.J. (2001). Can't let go. *Education Next*, 1(4), 36–41.

Snipes, J., Doolittle, F., & Herlihy, C. (2002). *Foundations for Success: Case Studies of How Urban School Systems Improve Student Achievement*. Washington, D.C.: The Council of the Great City Schools.

Somech, A. (2002). Explicating the complexity of participative management: an investigation of multiple dimensions. *Educational Administration Quarterly*, 38(3), 341–371.

Supovitz, J.A. (2006). *The Case for District-based Reform*. Cambridge, MA: Harvard Education Press.

Wong, K.K., & Shen, F.X. (2008). Education mayors and big-city school boards: new directions, new evidence. In T.L. Alsbury (ed.), *The Future of School Board Governance*. Lanham, MD: Rowman & Littlefield, 319–356.

Wong, K.K., & Shen, F.X. (2001). Does school district takeover work? Assessing the effectiveness of city and state takeover as a school reform strategy. Paper presented at the 97th annual meeting of the American Political Science Association, San Francisco.

2
Operational Challenges

4

THE CHALLENGES OF SCHOOL DISTRICT
ORGANIZATION

RESTRUCTURING FOR INSTRUCTIONAL REFORM[1]

Faced with growing diversity and declining student achievement, San Diego City Schools (SDCS), California's second largest school district with 138,000 students, was in desperate need of leadership at the close of the 20th century. The school hired Alan Bersin, a former U.S. District Attorney, to be superintendent. Bersin, in turn, recruited Anthony Alvarado, superintendent of New York City's Community School District #2, to serve in the newly created role of Chancellor of Instruction. Alvarado was charged with spearheading a sweeping restructuring initiative aimed at improving the quality of instruction and boosting literacy in San Diego schools and thereby raising student achievement.

Bersin and Alvarado understood that the school district had an important role to play in directing and supporting instructional improvement in the schools. They also realized that this role could not be played unless and until significant changes occurred in the organization of the school district and its central office. The organizational structure in place when Bersin arrived involved seven divisions reporting directly to the superintendent. They included (1) Planning, Assessment, Accountability, and Development, (2) Internal Auditing, (3) Finance, (4) Administrative Services, (5) Educational and School Services, (6) Communications and Community Relations, and (7) Legal Counsel. Only two of these divisions dealt directly with teaching and learning. In addition, five area superintendents, each supervising several cluster leaders who were responsible for high schools and their feeder systems, reported to the Deputy Superintendent for Educational and School Services. So, too, did 14 academic and co-curricular programs ranging from gifted and talented education and libraries to alternative education and athletics.

To send a clear message that instructional matters were of the utmost importance, Bersin reorganized the central office into three divisions: the Institute for Learning, Administrative and Operational Support, and the Center for Collaborative Activities.

Headed by Alvarado, the Institute for Learning consolidated in one division responsibilities for curriculum, teaching strategies, and the professional development of teachers and principals. The five area superintendents were replaced by seven "instructional leaders" who reported directly to Alvarado. Each instructional leader was responsible for monitoring and guiding a "learning community" of roughly 25 San Diego principals. It was in their learning community that principals received most of their professional development and training in high-quality instructional practices.

The Administrative and Operational Support division included offices for business services, human resources, finance, and educational services (materials, library services). The Center for Collaborative Activities, a much smaller division than the other two, was designed to promote collaboration between departments and programs as well as between SDCS and the community.

Bersin's restructuring initiative aimed to bring coherence to the proliferation of special programs that had been implemented over the years to address various instructional issues. Often a new program was created when the school district received a grant or responded to a new government initiative. As the number of programs expanded, so too did organizational complexity and the potential for coordination problems. Bersin saw to it that the management of special programs was consolidated and centralized under Alvarado, thereby cutting overhead expenses and ensuring that all programs supported the same priorities. Bersin insisted that budget and operations managers work closely with Alvarado's division to direct funds to district instructional priorities.

Another key element of Bersin's restructuring plan involved downsizing the central office in order to free up more resources for the schools. Every central office employee was asked to specify how what they did supported teaching and learning. Those whose answers revealed a tenuous link to district priorities lost their jobs. By eliminating over 100 central office positions, Bersin was able to increase staffing in San Diego's low-performing schools.

✳✳✳✳✳

School district leaders typically do not have the luxury of being able to design their school systems from scratch. They inherit organizational structures that have been expanded, modified, reduced, and otherwise adjusted over the years as circumstances dictated. The organizational structure that was adopted a decade earlier to cope with a substantial growth in enrollment may not be well suited to the subsequent reality of declining enrollment. Determining when it is necessary to restructure and how that restructuring should be achieved pose significant challenges for school district leaders. Let us consider some of the reasons why restructuring may be called for.

WHY DO SCHOOL DISTRICTS RESTRUCTURE?

The organizational structure of a school district is most readily understood by looking at an organization chart. An organization chart typically is a graphic representation of an organization's formal hierarchical system of authority and control. It provides a picture of the intended distribution of responsibilities and reporting relationships. Looking at an organization chart should provide the viewer with a clear idea of the units into which the organization is divided and how they are related to each other.

The idea of reorganizing or restructuring is based on several assumptions, the first of which is that the structure of an organization is related in some way to how organization members perform their duties. If there was no link between structure and behavior, there would be little reason, beyond purely symbolic gestures, to invest much time or energy in restructuring.

Bolman and Deal (1997, p. 40) note additional assumptions that support a structural perspective on organizations. Organizations, they observe, exist to achieve established goals and objectives. The structure of an organization presumably makes it possible for these goals and objectives to be achieved. The organization's structure enables employees to undertake a variety of specialized functions that together contribute to a finished product or service. It is further assumed that without structure employees might duplicate functions, work at cross-purposes with other employees, disregard organizational priorities in favor of self-interest, or otherwise fail to help achieve goals and objectives as efficiently and effectively as possible. When an organization is not functioning as efficiently and effectively as possible, Bolman and Deal point out that restructuring is one strategy for correcting the situation.

When Alan Bersin became superintendent of San Diego City Schools, the school district was considered by many people in the community to be failing in its mission to provide a quality education for many of its students. As a new leader, Bersin could have chosen a variety of "first steps" to improve performance. He might have elected, for example, to seek additional resources or remove principals in low-performing schools. Instead, he decided to restructure district operations, as indicated in the opening vignette.

It is not unusual, of course, for new superintendents to commence their tenure by announcing some form of reorganization. Often, however, reorganization turns out to be mostly a symbolic gesture, a signal that leadership has changed. Cynical observers frequently refer dirisively to such reorganization as "re-arranging the deck chairs on the *Titanic*." Titles are changed, a few people are moved around, the name of a division is modified, but by and large little of substance changes.

Bersin's restructuring plan was anything but a symbolic gesture. He wanted to "jolt" the system, and jolt it he did. He believed that effective instruction and literacy had to be the foci of attention if student achievement was to improve, but before schools could devote time and energy to literacy, the capacity of the central office to support teaching and learning needed to be increased. Capacity-building required program consolidation, resource re-allocation, and a new arrangement for monitoring and developing school principals. Creating the role of Chancellor of Instruction and hiring a leader with a proven track record for instructional improvement freed Bersin to focus on the political and financial aspects of restructuring.

The ultimate purpose of restructuring in San Diego was to raise student achievement. Such an impetus is not uncommon among restructuring school districts. In a large study of Title I schools, nearly a quarter of the schools identified for improvement under the No Child Left Behind Act reorganized district office staff in order to focus more effectively and efficiently on instructional improvement and higher student achievement (LeFloch et al., 2007, p. 178). The secondary purpose of San Diego's restructuring was to improve operational efficiency. School district central offices are frequent targets of criticism concerning efficiency. Cost-conscious citizens question whether district offices are overstaffed and express a desire to see funds transferred from central administration to schools and classrooms.

That such concerns may be valid can be seen in the case of the Richmond Public Schools at the beginning of the 21st century. Virginia governor Mark Warner initiated a state efficiency review process in 2004 and targeted Richmond for one of the first reviews (*School Efficiency Review...*,

2004). Part of the review process involved comparing administrative staff-ing expenditures in Richmond with spending in nine similar urban school divisions in Virginia. Excluding Richmond, the average administrative expenses per pupil for the nine peer divisions was $196.61. Richmond, however, spent $345.18 per pupil for administration. Over one-third of the money spent annually by Richmond for administration went to fis-cal services. The review questioned why such a large sum was needed to cover the management of division finances.

The message of Richmond's efficiency review was hard to ignore. Since student achievement in Richmond was lower than practically every other school division in the state, Richmond was paying a lot for administra-tion and getting relatively little in return. Such findings often serve as the impetus for restructuring.

Other impetuses include enrollment growth and decline. During the Baby Boom in the 1950s and 60s, Fairfax County Public Schools, for example, grew from just under 15,000 students to over 130,000 students. The number of schools mushroomed from 48 to 168. Having all of these schools report to three directors (one each for elementary, intermediate, and secondary), who in turn reported to the assistant superintendent for instruction, became cumbersome. Complaints were heard from school principals that it took too long to get approval for school-based initiatives. Following a consultant's report, Fairfax restructured in the late 1960s. The school system was divided into four "areas," each with its own area super-intendent and support staff. This arrangement presumably enabled central office service providers to be more responsive to school-based needs.

The area-office system remained in effect in Fairfax until the late 1990s. At that point a new superintendent concluded that the "areas" covered too many schools to permit the effective delivery of services. An additional concern involved the growing independence of area su-perintendents, each of whom oversaw more schools than existed in most school systems (Duke, 2005, p. 143). Given the state's push for greater accountability, Fairfax could not afford great variations across sections of the school system. Dan Domenech's answer was to restructure Fairfax into eight clusters, each consisting of three high schools and the middle and elementary schools that fed into them. Instead of a large area office staffed with dozens of professionals, cluster offices consisted of a cluster director, a coordinator, and an administrative assistant. Each cluster direc-tor was responsible for monitoring the effectiveness of 20 to 30 schools, evaluating principals, and responding to parent concerns that could not be resolved at the school level.

School districts like Fairfax restructure to cope with enrollment growth and concerns regarding central office responsiveness to the needs of local schools. Logic seems to dictate that central office expansion during periods of growth would be balanced by central office contraction during periods of enrollment decline. While the number of central office personnel often shrinks when enrollment drops, the configuration of organizational units is less likely to change significantly.

One reason why Fairfax switched from areas to clusters concerned the fact that area superintendents had become semi-autonomous over the years. School board members complained that the area system hindered their efforts to respond to the concerns of constituents. Politics, in other words, served as an additional impetus to restructuring. Politics also was involved when Fairfax added the Office of Minority Student Achievement (OMSA) to its central office in the 1980s. Pressure from the African American community regarding the achievement gap between black and white students had been building for years in the huge school system. The school board eventually was compelled to create the Office of Minority Student Achievement as a good faith gesture. The OMSA was charged with monitoring the progress of African American and other minority students, keeping school board members informed, and recommending measures to close the achievement gap.

The example of Fairfax's Office of Minority Student Achievement illustrates the fact that structural change sometimes is limited to the addition of a new unit. It is not uncommon for units to be added as a result of new federal, state, and school board mandates. Following passage of the Elementary and Secondary Education Act in 1965, for instance, many school districts created an office to handle Title 1 programs and funds. Another major impetus for the addition of new central office units was Public Law 94-142, the Individuals with Disabilities Education Act. Passed originally in 1975 and re-authorized periodically afterwards, the IDEA involves so many regulations, funding provisions, and monitoring requirements that school districts have been forced to create separate offices and sometimes entire divisions devoted exclusively to special education.

Once an organizational unit comes into existence, it is subject to possible reorganization. Reorganization frequently entails adding new positions and redefining the responsibilities associated with existing positions. In the early 21st century, for example, the Special Education Department of the Norfolk, Virginia, school system added two senior coordinators to its six existing senior coordinators. This move enabled the department director to make across-the-board changes in assignments. One coordinator for secondary special education replaced the two coordinators for middle schools and high schools. The position that was freed up by this consolidation was assigned to an individual to coordinate monitoring and compliance activities. One of the new coordinator positions was devoted to early childhood special education services, an area that had grown rapidly. The other new coordinator oversaw a variety of support services, including speech therapy, occupational therapy, physical therapy, adaptive physical education, vision and hearing impaired programs, and homebound instruction. These additions and changes enabled the remaining four senior coordinators to focus exclusively on instructional support in the schools.

Besides new mandates, political pressure, a desire for greater responsiveness, enrollment changes, and pressure for improved effectiveness and efficiency, imitation sometimes serves as a reason for restructuring. The theory of institutional isomorphism (DiMaggio & Powell, 1983) holds that various environmental forces influence organizations to adopt structural arrangements similar or identical to other organizations sharing the same mission. Sometimes this pressure derives from political forces or government regulations. In other cases, organizations are compelled to copy the most successful of their peer organizations. It was not surprising in the wake of various state and federal accountability initiatives during the period from 1990 to 2005, for example, to find large school districts creating separate units devoted to educational accountability. In creating these new accountability units, many school systems turned to a few highly regarded school systems in order to copy their model. More will be said about these accountability units in the next chapter.

The desire for public legitimacy by school districts constitutes another impetus to restructuring, one related to institutional isomorphism. Hannaway (1978, p. 417) illustrates this desire with the following example:

> School districts attempt to maximize their legitimacy with the environment that gives them resources. Districts do this by offering a structure that is congruent with the social expectations and understandings about what education should be doing. Therefore, if funding agencies think that planning is important, we would expect school districts to respond by creating a planning director or an office of planning.

The remainder of this chapter discusses some of the challenges of school district organization and reorganization that face district leaders. No organizational structure is likely to continue to meet district needs without periodic adjustments. The three questions below encompass issues that school district leaders often have to consider as they weigh the costs and benefits of structural changes.

JUDGING STRUCTURAL ADEQUACY

School districts typically are organized as bureaucracies, a structural arrangement that attracted great interest during the second half of the 19th century. First adopted by large businesses that had outgrown the patriarchal organizational structures in which all authority and power were vested in a single "father figure," the bureaucratic structure soon was embraced by large urban school systems and eventually by smaller school systems.

Around the turn of the 20th century, Max Weber, a German economist and sociologist, recorded the key elements of bureaucratic structure (Gerth & Mills, 1946). The first element involves a division of labor based on functional specialization. To perform specialized functions, bureaucracies depend on hiring employees who possess specific technical qualifications. Expertise, not family ties and other connections, serve as the basis for staffing the various units into which bureaucracies are divided. The functions associated with each structural unit are to be carried out according to formalized sets of rules and regulations that apply equally to every unit member. In order to enforce the rules and regulations, bureaucratic structure calls for a hierarchical organization in which lower units are supervised by and report to higher units. Control mechanisms are necessary to ensure that employees perform their specialized functions appropriately.

Over the decades since Weber helped conceptualize bureaucratic organization, the term *bureaucracy* often has been the subject of criticism and concern. Bureaucratic organization has been associated with "red tape," rigidity, and resistance to change. Created to promote efficiency, bureaucracy for many has come to connote just the opposite (Blau & Meyer, 1971, p. 3). The impersonalization considered to be an antidote to pre-bureaucratic inbreeding and favoritism has come to be regarded as insensitivity and even heartlessness. Those who staff bureaucracies are perceived to be "bean counters" and compliance monitors rather than compassionate and caring human beings.

In recent years organization theorists have begun to challenge the notion that bureaucratic organization is inherently flawed. Adler and Borys (1996) contend that bureaucratic organization has the potential to be "enabling" instead of "coercive." The key involves the rules to which employees are subject. Adler and Borys distinguish between "good rules" and "bad rules." Good rules are those that "help committed employees do their jobs more effectively and reinforce their commitment" (p. 83).

Hoy and Sweetland (2001) applied Adler and Borys' work to schools. They developed an instrument to determine the extent to which school rules and authority serve to facilitate or impede teachers' efforts to promote learning. School organization is considered "enabling" when it facilitates problem solving, fosters cooperation, encourages collaboration, permits flexibility, spawns innovation, and buffers teachers from interruptions and complaints. School organization is regarded as "hindering" when it prevents teachers from participating in problem solving, focuses on compliance and control, denies teachers a role in decision making, inhibits adjustments based on changing circumstances, discourages constructive change, and relies on employee discipline and punishment.

School district leaders can apply Hoy and Sweetland's (2001) criteria to the structure of district as well as school operations. There is no reason why bureaucratic organization necessarily must impede effective action. Through periodic discussion with central office and school-based personnel, district leaders can learn which policies, rules, and regulations enable people to do their job well and which ones prevent them from functioning effectively. A policy, for example, that rewards people for sharing problems that they encounter in performing their responsibilities would seem to be preferable to a policy that is seen as punishing people for disclosing problems at work.

The Council of the Great City Schools (*Review of the Organizational Structure...*, 2006, p. 13) has developed a very useful set of criteria for judging the adequacy of a large school district's organizational structure. A large school district ought to have an organizational structure that

- Has an adequate number of staff members to plan, manage, coordinate, direct, implement, and evaluate programs and services.
- Controls its personnel, resources, and programs adequately.
- Has explicit reporting lines and precise locations of authority and responsibility for executing tasks.
- Strengthens professional relationships to ensure mission accomplishment.
- Is supported by job descriptions that define organizational relationships, qualifications, authority, responsibilities, functions, and accountability.
- Has appropriate span of control, a logical grouping of functions, appropriate separation of management and staff responsibilities, and consistently logical relationships among people on the same level of authority (horizontal) and up and down the scale of authority (vertical).

The preceding criteria notwithstanding, it would be a mistake to think there is "one best way" to organize a school district. When a team of experienced school district leaders was commissioned by the Council of the Great City Schools to review the organizational structure of the Los Angeles Unified School District, the second largest school system in the United States, they offered the following cautionary comment:

> The truth is that there is no perfect organizational structure; there are only temporary optimums and trade-offs. All organizations— including the LAUSD—have to move and change with a shifting environment and constantly evolving needs... (*Review of the Organizational Structure...*, 2006, p. 44)

If the above warning is valid, a school district that never restructures is unlikely to make the adjustments necessary to remain effective and efficient over time. Considered in this light, the controversial "jolt" to the San Diego City Schools occasioned by Alan Bersin's restructuring plan constituted an understandable reaction to years of declining district performance. Whether the restructuring plan was the best one under the circumstances, of course, is debatable. After three years of reforms, student achievement did improve, but many San Diego educators questioned the rapidity of change and the top-down manner in which it was introduced (Hightower, 2002, p. 88).

Bersin's restructuring plan managed to address most of the criteria endorsed by the Council of the Great City Schools. To ensure that staff members were deployed in ways that reinforced the new focus on instructional improvement, instructional leaders replaced area superintendents and peer coaches were assigned to every school in order to develop the faculty's skills in teaching literacy. Various programs and funding streams associated with teaching and learning were consolidated under the aegis of a new leader, the Chancellor of Learning. This arrangement enabled Anthony Alvarado, the first Chancellor of Learning, to direct and monitor all initiatives aimed at improving instruction, promoting literacy, and raising student achievement. With the centralization of instructional improvement efforts in San Diego came a reduction in the discretionary authority of school principals. Bersin and Alvarado believed that site-based management had not served many students well. They were unwilling to allow significant variations in practice and performance across schools to continue.

School district restructuring in the first decade of the 21st century often has involved the centralization of instructional improvement efforts. A decade earlier, however, decentralization was the preferred route to instructional improvement. David (1990, pp. 227–228) captured the essence of restructuring during this prior period:

All the restructuring districts…view the school—the locus of teaching and learning—as the appropriate organizational level for mobilizing change. Schools differ in the make-up of their staff and students, as well as in their resources and facilities, and therefore need flexibility to adapt to those differences.

The point is this—opinions change regarding the most appropriate ways to restructure school districts. The ultimate test of whether school district leaders have chosen a good organizational structure, of course, concerns the success with which the district accomplishes its mission. Every school district's mission involves student learning and academic preparation. School districts that have opted to restructure by centralizing improvement efforts probably found that leaving reforms up to school-based personnel failed to yield comparable gains across all schools.

There are, of course, a variety of reasons besides structural ones that can account for inadequate school performance. Leadership may be lacking, teachers may not possess appropriate skills, and resources may be in short supply. Still, it is hard to imagine any "cause" of low-performance that is not associated in some way with the organizational structure of a school district. When diagnosing possible relationships between structure and student achievement, school district leaders should always ask the following troubleshooting questions:

1. Do job descriptions specify how individuals at all levels are expected to contribute to teaching and learning.
2. Do control mechanisms direct action toward improved performance?
3. Are organizational units arranged in ways that promote effective cooperation and coordination?

What individuals perceive their job responsibilities to be does not always conform to what others expect them to do. A superintendent may expect a principal to spend a great deal of time in classrooms monitoring instruction and modeling good practice, but the principal may think that her primary duties are to handle student discipline and parent complaints. There are at least three "official" sources of information regarding job responsibilities: formal job descriptions, lists of evaluation criteria and standards, and employee contracts. Ideally, these sources are in alignment, but frequently they are not. Job descriptions may not have been updated in years. Changes in district priorities may not be reflected in contract language or the criteria by which people are evaluated. When professional staff are confused about what they are expected to do, the effectiveness of any organizational structure is placed at risk.

All school districts rely on four basic control mechanisms to ensure that employees stay focused on achieving district goals. These mechanisms—supervision, evaluation, rewards, and punishments—constitute the control structure of a school district. If goals are not being achieved, it may be due to problems with how one or more of these control functions is defined and carried out. If the quality and accuracy of curriculum content are important elements of a school district's improvement plan, for example, it is unwise to rely exclusively on principals' observations and evaluations of teachers. Especially at the secondary level, assessments of curriculum content coverage require the involvement of subject matter experts.

Rewarding teachers for course credits and inservice training instead of student progress, to provide another example, may not advance a school district's efforts to raise student achievement. School district leaders need to constantly review how well control mechanisms are working if they are to ensure that operations run smoothly.

The third troubleshooting question concerns the arrangement of school district departments and offices. When organizational units that rely on each other are not grouped together, the likelihood of miscommunication and coordination problems increases. In Bersin's original restructuring plan for San Diego City Schools, for instance, the special education department continued to report directly to the superintendent. This arrangement inhibited the participation of special education staff in the district's other efforts to help struggling students. When the 1998 restructuring plan was revised in 2000, the Center on Collaborative Activities was replaced by the Center for Student Support and Special Education. This new division enabled all intervention, diagnostic, assessment, and student support services to be located in the same place. Communications and community relations, which had been the focus of the Center on Collaborative Activities, were transferred to the Office of the Superintendent, a logical placement given Bersin's division of leadership responsibilities.

It is the responsibility of school district leaders to cultivate a systemic perspective on the district's organizational structure. A systemic perspective requires focusing not only on individual organizational units, but the connections (or lack of connections) between units (Senge, 1990). Only by understanding how each unit relates to and interacts with every other unit can school district leaders position themselves to propose new and more effective structural arrangements. When a school district has been especially dysfunctional, leaders frequently call on the services of outside consultants. District personnel may be more willing to share their honest opinions about connections to other units with outsiders than with district leaders.

DETECTING STRUCTURAL DILEMMAS

School district leaders who have been involved in restructuring realize that their efforts to solve one problem sometimes can generate other problems. Alan Bersin discovered this fact when he tried to push his instructional improvement model and literacy focus on San Diego high schools. Teachers and parents of children in high schools serving more affluent neighborhoods resented the focus on "basics" and the push to "de-track" science courses (Darling-Hammond et al., 2003, p. 50). Bersin's efforts to raise student achievement in the high schools ultimately fell far short of expectations because he was never able to enlist the whole-hearted support of many teachers and influential parents.

Bolman and Deal (1997, pp. 60–61) identify a variety of trade-offs that may be involved in efforts to restructure. They characterize these trade-offs as "dilemmas" rather than "problems." Problems have solutions; dilemmas do not. School leaders must make decisions regarding dilemmas knowing full well that any decision they make is likely to produce new challenges.

The decision to centralize or decentralize already has been described as involving possible trade-offs. Choosing to centralize authority may be suited to situations where resources are tight and many schools are low-performing, but such a choice can leave professional staff feeling as if their judgment is not valued. Choosing to decentralize authority can instill a sense of professionalism in front-line service providers, but the risk is that organizational priorities may not be pursued evenly across all units.

One dilemma identified by Bolman and Deal (1997) involves the choice between differentiation and integration. Differentiation entails a high degree of specialization. The more highly differentiated a school district's central office, the more likely district leaders can hire individuals with a high level of expertise and the less likely these individuals will become confused about what they are expected to do. The more central office units that are staffed by specialists, however, the greater the potential for coordination problems. As Bolman and Deal put it, "The more complex [differentiated] a role structure, with lots of people doing many different things, the harder it is to integrate it all into a focused, tightly coupled enterprise" (p. 60).

Coordination comes at a cost. When a school district organization is staffed by lots of specialists, there is a tendency for units to become "silos." People in one unit have little occasion to interact with people in other units. As a result, they may not understand what challenges are being faced by others in the district or what these individuals are trying to accomplish. It is no surprise that many school district organizations have been characterized as "loosely coupled" (Hannaway, 1978, p. 415).

Ensuring that all organizational units pull in the same direction and work cooperatively under such circumstances can be difficult.

Faced with coordination problems resulting from years of adding new programs to deal with low achievement, school leaders in Atlanta, Georgia, finally decided some structural changes were in order. A new unit was created to manage all reform-related initiatives (Mobilizing the System..., 2006). In addition, cross-functional teams were used to plan, launch, and implement all school-based reforms. Instead of a new reading or mathematics program being developed by a few curriculum specialists, this new arrangement brought curriculum specialists together with representatives from the schools and from the offices of human resources, finance, and facilities. In this way, all the possible ramifications of a project could be addressed systematically. Staffing new initiatives with individuals from all affected units greatly reduces the chances that a project will bog down because of misunderstandings, poor communications, and red tape.

Large school districts are likely to be characterized by a higher degree of differentiation than small school districts, but this does not mean that small school districts escape structural problems. Central office personnel in small districts typically undertake multiple responsibilities. For no one is this more true than the superintendent. Besides working with the school board and representing the school district in the community and at state meetings, a small district superintendent may directly supervise all central office units.

Consider the case of Eleanor Smalley, superintendent of Clarke County Schools, a rural Virginia school division with an enrollment of about 2,200 students. When the state commissioned an efficiency review of her school system, the review team found that Smalley had 11 direct reports, including the assistant superintendent, four directors, an executive secretary, and five building principals (*Clarke County School Division...*, 2006, pp. 2–14). The team offered the following recommendation: "Because of the work that necessarily occurs with the school board and community, the superintendent needs to have fewer subordinates that directly report to her" (p. 2–15). The more time a superintendent must focus on overseeing the day-to-day operations of district units, the less time a superintendent has to concentrate on "the big picture."

The suggested restructuring arrangement reduced Smalley's direct reports to eight by creating an assistant superintendent for administrative services to supervise the director of maintenance and transportation and the director of business. The assistant superintendent for instruction under the new plan supervised the director of special education. The trade-off for reducing the complexity of the superintendent's role, of course, was an increase in the complexity of the two assistant superintendents' roles. Such is frequently the nature of restructuring.

Small school districts often rely on building-level personnel to handle administrative responsibilities that would be directed by full-time central office administrators in a large district. Curriculum coordination in various subject matter areas, for example, might be delegated to school-based department chairs. Principals sometimes are assigned responsibility for staff development. When individuals occupy multiple roles, confusion and conflicts can arise regarding reporting relationships. Teachers who also function as curriculum coordinators may be unclear about when they report to their principal and when they report to their central office supervisor.

Another structural dilemma identified by Bolman and Deal (1997) concerns the degree of control necessary to accomplish the school district's mission and goals. As they put it,

When structure is too loose, people go their own way or get lost, with little sense of what others are doing. Structures that are too tight stifle flexibility and cause people to spend much of their time trying to get around the system. (p. 61)

Determining the appropriate level of control should be guided, at least in part, by performance and outcomes. It is not necessarily the case, for example, that the same degree of control is needed for all organizational units. The previous chapter referred to the decision by school district leaders in Richmond, Virginia, to place low-performing schools under a high degree of central office control. Principals in these schools were directed to use lesson plans, reading and mathematics programs, and staff development determined by the central office. As schools demonstrated their capacity to improve, the degree of control to which there were subject was reduced. High-performing schools were accorded a substantial degree of autonomy.

School district leaders stress different control mechanisms, depending on what is being controlled. If the focus is input control, leaders may concentrate on tracking how funds are allocated and spent. Another possible focus is compliance with district policies and regulations. Direct supervision becomes the preferred method of maintaining control when compliance is the primary concern. A school district may require principals regularly to observe teachers in order to ensure that instruction is guided by district curriculum standards. When the focus of control is student achievement, some school district leaders rely on rewards for schools that make significant improvements. Even students sometimes receive rewards. Other school leaders take their cue from the No Child

Left Behind Act and exercise control through the use of threats and eventual sanctions when schools fail to make adequate yearly progress. More will be said of these control options when accountability issues are discussed in the next chapter.

ORGANIZING THE SCHOOLS

Challenges exist wherever decisions have to be made, and how to organize a district's schools is no exception. While a casual observer might conclude that the organization of schools is pre-determined by the conventional division between elementary, middle, and high schools, it turns out that the matter is far more complex. School district leaders have choices to make regarding the grade-levels for individual schools, the size of schools, the focus of schools, and the sponsorship of schools. Whether and how to group schools constitutes another possible decision.

Grade-Levels   A survey of U.S. schools quickly reveals the fact that there is no universal configuration of grade-levels for elementary, middle, or high schools. There are, of course, arrangements that tend to be relatively typical—kindergarten to 5th or 6th grade for elementary schools and 9th to 12th grade for high schools, but variations are common.

One consideration involved in determining school grade-levels is financial. It is costly to operate schools with empty classrooms. Some decisions about grade-levels, therefore, are guided by the availability of existing instructional space and the cost of new construction.

Other considerations are based on educational beliefs, outcomes, and research. Concerns, for example, have grown in recent years regarding the negative impact of school transitions. When students complete their work at one school and move to another, the likelihood of academic problems increases. This is especially true of the transition from middle school to high school. The ninth grade, in particular, has been targeted as a troubled time in students' lives (Duke, Bourdeaux, Epps, & Wilcox,1998). Grades plummet and behavior problems increase. In response to these concerns, leaders in some school districts have decided to minimize the transition from 8th to 9th grade by creating secondary schools covering grades 6 or 7 through 12. One study comparing secondary and high schools in Virginia reported that 9th graders experience fewer academic and behavioral problems in 7 through12 and 8 through 12 schools (Wang, 2006). A few school systems, including Alexandria, Virginia, and St. Mary's County, Maryland, have taken a different tack. They established separate schools just for 9th graders.

Another option involves eliminating the transition from elementary to middle school. A number of urban districts, including Baltimore, Cincinnati, Cleveland, Milwaukee, New Orleans, Philadelphia, and New York, have converted elementary schools to K–8 schools. Several studies have found that students in K–8 schools out-perform their middle school counterparts (Arcia, 2007; Offenberg, 2001; Poncelet & Metis Associates, 2004). Advocates for the K–8 configuration argue that it affords greater continuity than the separate middle school experience and is far less emotionally challenging.

The desire for racial balance represents another consideration when determining school grade-levels. In the 1980s, Charlottesville, Virginia, had two middle schools, one predominantly white, the other predominantly black. To correct what he regarded as an undesirable situation, Superintendent Vincent Cibarelli decided to reorganize the two schools, forming one upper elementary school serving all 5th and 6th graders in the city and one middle school serving all 7th and 8th graders.

Other impetuses to adjustments in school grade-levels involve concerns about at-risk students. To increase the likelihood of school success for students from economically disadvantaged homes, many elementary schools have added a pre-kindergarten component to serve four-year-olds. At the other end of the spectrum, some high schools have begun to afford seniors the opportunity to commence their post-secondary studies without changing schools. By making a seamless transition from high school to the first years of college or community college, school district leaders hope to encourage more students, especially those from poor backgrounds, to continue their schooling.

Size Another choice facing school district leaders involves school size. Evidence has been building that the large size of many high schools may be contributing to academic and behavior problems (Walberg & Fowler, 1991; Kahne, Sporte, de la Torre, & Easton, 2008; Mathews, 2008). The largest high schools often exceed 4,000 students and some top 5,000 students. Schools of this size are characterized as "factories" in which students are treated impersonally and teachers struggle to maintain control. Leaders in some large urban districts, including Boston, Chicago, Denver, and New York, have initiated measures to downsize many large high schools. The Bill and Melinda Gates Foundation has helped to underwrite the cost of downsizing across the United States. There are indications that some students clearly benefit from attending small high schools, but the positive effects of downsizing have not been as great as many advocates had hoped (Kahne et al., 2008).

While improved student outcomes is the most important goal supporting the move to smaller high schools, other reasons have been offered to justify downsizing. An excerpt from the "theory of action" for the Chicago High School Redesign Initiative indicates several of these additional reasons:

> ...if a district creates small, voluntary, relatively autonomous schools and limits bureaucratic control, it will create schooling contexts where trust, coherent vision, and commitment will be more likely to take root. Such schools will also have distributed leadership and be marked by strong and vibrant professional communities, where teachers share in decision making, reflect on and share practice, and collaborate with each other. (Sporte, Correa, Kahne, & Easton 2003, p. 25)

Small schools provide opportunities to promote teacher leadership and professional learning communities. The hope, of course, is that improving working conditions for teachers eventually will pay dividends in terms of student learning. It remains to be seen whether these hopes will be realized through downsizing.

Rather than building new schools on a smaller scale, many of the districts engaged in downsizing have opted to convert large high schools into so-called multiplex schools housing several autonomous schools. One of the first and best known of these multiplex schools is the Julia Richman Education Complex in New York City. What makes Julia Richman particularly interesting is that it consists of schools covering various grade-levels and areas of focus. The six schools located in the Julia Richman complex include the following:

- Ella Baker School: pre-K through 8th grade
- PS 226M: middle school for autistic students
- Vanguard High School: "second chance" school for at-risk adolescents
- Manhattan International High School: school for newly arrived immigrants
- Talent Unlimited School: performing arts school
- Urban Academy: inquiry-based, non-graded high school

Downsizing large schools can present its share of challenges. One obvious challenge involves funding. Boston has spent millions of dollars in its effort to convert every high school into small learning communities (Steinberg & Allen, 2007). Then there is the matter of deciding how small is small. Large scale studies to guide school district leaders in answering this question are scarce. In one of the few studies of its kind, Lee (2001, p. 135) examined the effect sizes of high school enrollment on student achievement in reading and mathematics. She measured effects against the modal size for an American high school—1,201 to 1,500 students. Her analysis indicated that the optimal size for a high school was between 601 and 900 students. Achievement gains were lowest for students in high schools larger than 2,100, but they also were low for high schools enrolling fewer than 300 students.

Another challenge associated with downsizing large schools involves the stresses that can result from several schools sharing the same space. Cohabitation problems can be especially great when the schools enroll students of different ages. Duke (1995, pp. 192–195) has written about the tensions that resulted when Richmond Public Schools officials co-located a new magnet school and elite Governor's School in the same building with a revered, but declining comprehensive high school. Tempers flared as students from the comprehensive high school complained that they were denied privileges accorded students in the other two schools.

The case for small schools is far from airtight. Advocates for large schools point to economies of scale and the ability to provide a wider range of courses than small schools (Duke & Trautvetter, 2001, p. 3). A third argument concerns the likelihood that large schools will enroll a more diverse student body. Fears exist that small schools can easily become homogeneous enclaves. Finally, the greater the number of small schools in a district, the greater the challenge for central office personnel responsible for supervising schools and coordinating curriculum.

Other School-Related Choices   Two other areas where district leaders may explore options involve schools' programmatic focus and school sponsorship.

Prompted by a variety of concerns ranging from desegregation to consumer demands for more choice, some school districts have developed a variety of specialty schools. The list includes magnet schools based on a particular academic or career focus, highly selective schools for gifted students, vocational-technical academies, schools based on a particular educational philosophy, year round schools, late-afternoon and evening schools for students who are overage and lacking in the credits needed to graduate, special education centers for students who cannot be effectively mainstreamed, and alternative schools for students who have failed to adjust to conventional school environments. With options come a variety of issues, including equitable access, quality control, and funding.

Another set of options concerns school sponsorship. School districts occasionally undertake joint ventures in order to offer special schools and programs for students. These joint ventures typically involve two or more school districts that cannot afford to provide a program alone or lack sufficient students by themselves to run a school program. States frequently encourage co-sponsorship of schools by offering financial incentives. Co-sponsorship is most often used for vocational-technical schools, special education centers, and regional alternative schools.

A relatively recent development in co-sponsorship concerns middle college programs. Designed to help high school students who otherwise might not consider going to college, middle college programs typically are collaborative efforts between school districts and community colleges. Students complete their high school requirements at the same time that they begin to earn college credits.

As with any joint venture, collaboration requires careful oversight and management. If one party perceives that it is not sharing fully in the benefits, problems can arise. There are also a variety of issues requiring regular negotiation, including coordination of yearly calendars, transportation schedules, and funding. School district leaders can never assume that their responsibilities have been completed when a joint venture is launched. Successful joint ventures must be continually managed and monitored.

Grouping Schools The last challenge to be discussed concerns how schools are organized within a school district. Districts with more than a handful of schools typically find it necessary to cluster schools for coordination and supervisory purposes. The standard arrangement is to create feeder system groups, each with a high school, the middle schools sending students to the high school, and the elementary schools sending students to the middle schools. The feeder system configuration permits staff members to address issues of curriculum articulation across grade-levels, student case management and placement, planning, and professional development. In very large school systems, several feeder systems may be grouped under an area superintendent. It is important, however, that an area superintendent's span of control does not grow so great that it takes an inordinate amount of time for school-based personnel to have their concerns addressed and obtain approval for requests.

Large school districts also may cluster certain types of specialty school. All special education centers, for example, may fall under the supervision of the head of the special education department. Student services departments sometimes coordinate all alternative schools and programs for at-risk students. Districts with multiple magnet schools may assign one central office administrator to oversee their operations. Because these specialty schools receive students from and return students to regular schools, it is important for school district leaders to establish processes to ensure coordination between specialty school supervisors and regular school supervisors.

Another type of clustering derives from concerns about racial isolation. Montgomery County, Maryland, for example, has experimented with the formation of multi-high school consortia in order to prevent resegregation. Instead of having to settle for a neighborhood high school, one that may be predominantly black or white, students can choose to attend any high school in a particular consortium. Each consortium is composed of several schools offering different specialty programs. The consortia have been popular, as indicated by the fact that 5,000 of 14,000 eligible students in Montgomery County opted to attend a non-neighborhood high school in 2008 (de Vise, 2008). Despite this fact, however, a county study found that the consortia had not "reversed minority isolation nor improved socioeconomic integration" (de Vise, 2008).

One recent development with school organization involves the clustering of low-performing schools in a district. Prompted in some cases by the No Child Left Behind Act, these clusters are intended to focus leadership and resources in ways that expedite improvements in student achievement.

Equity Plus II was a clustering arrangement instituted in the Charlotte-Mecklenburg School District during the late 1990s. Of the district's 141 schools, 54 met the criteria for Equity Plus II (Charlotte-Mecklenburg, NC: Investing in Equity, 2002). The criteria included low student achievement, high teacher turnover, high student mobility, large percentage of low SES students, and significant numbers of teachers lacking proper credentials. All schools in the Equity Plus II group qualified for additional resources that translated into lower teacher-student ratios, bonus pay for teachers if students met achievement goals, and tuition assistance for teachers wanting to earn advanced degrees. Equity Plus II schools also received special consulting services, targeted professional development, instructional assistance, and help in strengthening parent involvement.

The most radical form of clustering involves creating the equivalent of a separate central office division exclusively for low-performing schools. Under the direction of a top-level district administrator, schools in the division are required to develop and implement comprehensive improvement plans. Besides receiving additional resources, these schools benefit from having a high-ranking central office administrator running interference for them. This individual sees to it that school requests are expedited and staffing needs receive priority treatment.

EXECUTIVE CONCLUSION

All school districts are responsible for a common set of functions, including operating schools, securing and allocating resources, hiring and developing employees, providing transportation and food services, and maintaining facilities. How these functions are organized and supervised, however, can vary significantly across school districts. It is the responsibility of school district leaders constantly to search for the most effective and efficient ways of organizing the schools and the system that supports them. Identifying better ways to be organized periodically results in efforts to restructure and reorganize.

One of the challenges involved in restructuring concerns how to judge the adequacy of a school system's structure. Complaints regarding bureaucratic structures are common. They range from excessive red tape to unresponsiveness to the unmet needs of those "on the firing line." According to some experts, bureaucracies can be enabling as well as constraining. If policies, rules, and regulations are well thought-out and are not excessive and if the structure facilitates cooperation and coordination, bureaucratic structures can accomplish things that might be impossible for less formal organizational arrangements to accomplish. Other structural considerations include the span of control for administrators, the mechanisms by which control is exercised, and the responsibilities assigned to organizational units and the individuals in those units.

When efforts to adjust the structure of a school district are not carefully planned, a variety of problems can arise. In some cases, though, no amount of careful planning is likely to avoid negative consequences. This is because there are certain dilemmas built into the very nature of bureaucratic organizations. These dilemmas involve decisions about whether to centralize or decentralize, differentiate or integrate functions, and tighten or loosen controls. The point is that school district leaders must be prepared to make trade-offs when restructuring. No organizational arrangement is likely to be problem-free.

Besides dealing with the organization of the central office, district leaders must consider how schools are organized and configured. School districts can vary in the grade-levels assigned to schools, school size, the focus of school programs, and school sponsorship. In addition, schools can be clustered together in various ways to facilitate coordination and supervision. A recent development involves the clustering of a district's low-performing schools for purposes of targeted improvement and resource enhancement.

Whether restructuring impacts a district's mission and student achievement is a matter of considerable debate. Certainly there are examples where restructuring does little more than symbolize the arrival of a new superintendent or the election of a new school board. In other cases, though, there is compelling evidence that restructuring contributes in important ways to improved performance, both at the district level and in schools and classrooms.

NOTE

1. The material for the opening vignette on restructuring in San Diego City Schools was derived from Darling-Hammond, L., Hightower, A.M., Husbands, J.L., LaFors, J.R., Young, V.M., & Christopher, C. (2003). *Building Instructional Quality: "Inside-out" and "Outside-in" Perspectives on San Diego's Reform*. Seattle: Center for the Study of Teaching and Policy, University of Washington.

REFERENCES

Adler, P.S., & Borys, B. (1996). Two types of bureaucracy: enabling and coercive. *Administrative Science Quarterly*, 41, 61–89.

Arcia, E. (2007). A comparison of elementary/K-8 and middle schools' suspension rates. *Urban Education*, 42, 456–469.

Blau, P.M., & Meyer, M.W. (1971). *Bureaucracy in Modern Society*, second edition. New York: Random House.

Bolman, L.G., & Deal, T.E. (1997). *Reframing Organizations*, second edition. San Francisco: Jossey-Bass.

Charlotte-Mecklenburg, NC: investing in equity. (2002). *Strategies*, 9(1), 12–17.

Clarke County School Division School Division Efficiency Review, Final Report. (2006). Tallahassee, FL: MGT of American, Inc.

Darling-Hammond, L., Hightower, A.M., Husbands, J.L., LaFors, J.R., Young, V.M.;,& Christopher, C. (2003). *Building Instructional Quality: "Inside-out" and "Outside-in" Perspectives on San Diego's Reform*. Seattle: Center for the Study of Teaching and Policy, University of Washington.

David, J.L. (1990). Restructuring in progress: lessons from pioneering districts. In R.F. Elmore & associates, *Restructuring Schools*. San Francisco: Jossey-Bass, 209–250.

deVise, D. (November 27, 2008). School consortiums assess in report. *The Washington Post*, B-5.

DiMaggio, P., & Powell, W. (1983). The iron cage revisited: institutional isomorphism and collective rationality in organizational fields. *American Sociological Review*, 48, 147–160.

Duke, D.L. (2005). *Education Empire: The Evolution of an Excellent Suburban School System*. Albany: State University of New York Press.

Duke, D.L. (1995). *The School That Refused to Die*. Albany: State University of New York Press.

Duke, D.L., Bourdeaux, J., Epps, B., & Wilcox, T. (1998). *Ninth Grade Transition Programs in Virginia*. Charlottesville: Thomas Jefferson Center for Educational Design, University of Virginia.

Duke, D.L., & Trautvetter, S. (2001). *Reducing the Negative Effects of Large Schools*. Washington, D.C.: National Clearinghouse for Educational Facilities.

Gerth, H.H., & Mills, C.W. (eds.). (1946). *From Max Weber: Essays in Sociology*. London: Oxford University Press.

Hannaway, J. (1978). Administrative structures: why do they grow? *Teachers College Record*, 79(3), 413–436.

Hightower, A.M. (2002). San Diego's big boom: systemic instructional change in the central office and schools. In A.M. Hightower, M.S. Knapp, J.A. Marsh, & M.W. McLaughlin (eds.), *School Districts and Instructional Renewal*. New York: Teachers College Press, 76–93.

Hoy, W.K., & Sweetland, S.R. (2001). Designing better schools: the meaning and measure of enabling school structures. *Educational Administration Quarterly*, 37(3), 296–321.

Kahne, J.E., Sporte, S.E., de la Torre, M., & Easton, J.Q. (2008). Small high schools on a larger scale: the impact of school conversions in Chicago. *Educational Evaluation and Policy Analysis*, 30(3), 281–315.

Lee, V.E. (2001). *Restructuring High Schools for Equity and Excellence: What Works*. New York: Teachers College Press.

LeFloch, K.C., Martinez, F., O'Day, J., Stecher, B., Taylor, J., & Cook, A. (2007). *State and Local Implementation of the No Child Left Behind Act*, Volume III. Washington, D.C.: U.S. Department of Education, Office of Planning, Evaluation and Policy Development.

Mathews, J. (May 26, 2008). Small schools rising. *Newsweek*, 42–44.

Mobilizing the system around instruction. (2006). *Strategies*, 12(1), 9–14.

Offenberg, R.M. (2001). The efficacy of Philadelphia's K-to-8 schools compared to middle grades schools. *Middle School Journal*, 32(4), 23–39.

Poncelet, P., & Metis Associates. (2004). Restructuring schools in Cleveland for the social, emotional, and intellectual development of early adolescents. *Journal of Education for Students Placed at Risk*, 9(2), 81–96.

Review of the Organizational Structure and Operations of the Los Angeles Unified School District. (2006). Washington, D.C.: The Council of the Great City Schools.

School Efficiency Review: City of Richmond Public School Division. (2004). Richmond: Commonwealth of Virginia, Office of the Secretary of Finance.

Senge, P.M. (1990). *The Fifth Discipline*. New York: Doubleday/Currency.

Sporte, S.E., Correa, M., Kahne, J., & Easton, J.Q. (2003). *A Snapshot of the First Year of Implementation*. Chicago: Consortium on Chicago School Research.

Steinberg, A., & Allen, L. (2007). On the road to reform. In S.P. Reville (ed.), *A Decade of Urban School Reform*. Cambridge, MA: Harvard Education Press, 175–192.

Walberg, H.J., & Fowler, W.J. (1991). School size, characteristics, and outcomes. *Educational Evaluation and Policy Analysis*, 13(2), 189–202.

Wang, G. (2006). *The Effect of Grade Span on 9th Grade Student Retention and a Comparison of Transition Practice Used in Secondary Schools and High Schools*. Dissertation, Curry School of Education, University of Virginia.

5

THE CHALLENGES OF ACCOUNTABILITY

NORFOLK LEARNS THE MEANING
OF "ALL MEANS ALL"[1]

It was not unusual to hear educators in Norfolk, Virginia, mouth plati-
tudes like "all children can learn" and "all means all," but when Dr. John
Simpson took over as superintendent in 1998, he was determined to make
certain that the words were translated into action. Norfolk Public Schools
(NPS) was Virginia's largest urban school system with 37,000 students
and 49 schools. Nearly 65 percent of the students qualified for free or
reduced-price meals, and 66 percent were African American. Student
performance on Virginia's Standards of Learning tests was a source of
local embarrassment.

Taking a hard look at the existing accountability measures in NPS,
Simpson concluded that goals for improvement had been identified, but
there were no consequences for failure to achieve the goals. If Norfolk
was to ensure that its students received the best education possible, people
had to be held accountable for goal attainment.

Before people could be held accountable, however, a carefully aligned
accountability system had to be developed. Individuals needed more than
goals. They needed to have a plan for working on the goals, a variety of
resources, benchmarks to guide them, and regular reviews of progress.
Simpson understood that simply telling people what they were expected
to accomplish was insufficient to produce success.

The Comprehensive Accountability System (CAS), a three-tiered arrangement by which accountability expectations were extended to every

organizational unit in the school division, became the driving force behind all efforts to raise performance in NPS. Tier 1 encompassed state and division performance indicators. They ranged from passing rates on state tests to graduation rates and data on school discipline. Tier 2 involved targets aligned to state and division indicators and applied to all schools and central office departments. Every school and department was expected to identify seven targets, three of which had to concern academic achievement. Tier 3 shifted focus from quantitative data to narrative data. Described as the "story behind the numbers," Tier 3 called on school and department representatives to explain what they did to produce the results they obtained.

The CAS operated on an annual cycle. Each school year began with a review of the past year's performance for the division as a whole and then for each school and central office department. This review served as the agenda for the School Board's summer retreat. Leading and lagging indicators were pinpointed, and gap analyses were done to understand why particular targets had not been attained. Based on these analyses and additional data, school and department targets and accountability plans for the coming school year were developed.

To ensure that accountability plans actually were executed and not just shelved, monthly benchmarking and monitoring meetings were held. In this way, mid-course corrections could be undertaken if sufficient progress was not being made. Every quarter an accountability report was made to the school board.

Principals were among the division leaders who felt the greatest pressure as a result of the new accountability system. They had been accorded considerable latitude under previous superintendents. Simpson let it be known, though, that principals were not free to do whatever they wanted. They were part of a system and therefore were responsible for contributing to the achievement of system goals. When student academic performance rose significantly in 1999, the wisdom of Simpson's approach to accountability was widely acknowledged. NPS continued to make impressive strides under the CAS, eventually winning the highly coveted Broad Prize in Urban Education.

❋❋❋❋❋

It is doubtful if many school district leaders in the United States believe that educational accountability is a passing fad. Widespread recognition of the importance of education accountability masks, however, considerable variation regarding what it means and how best to ensure it. The steps taken under John Simpson to promote accountability in Norfolk differ from those taken by many other superintendents. School district leaders confront a variety of challenges as they strive to understand the complexities and day-to-day implications of educational accountability. Before addressing some of the issues involved in operationalizing accountability, it is useful to trace the evolution of accountability in education.

EDUCATIONAL ACCOUNTABILITY—
AN EVOLVING IDEA

Long before anyone ever used the term *educational accountability*, James H. Binford, the first superintendent of Richmond (Virginia) Public Schools, provided a fascinating example of what it might mean to be accountable (Duke, 1995, p. 9). The time period was the 1870s and Richmond had just opened its first public high school. To ensure that high school teachers were meeting his academic expectations, Binford created the exam that students had to pass to earn a diploma. He personally graded each exam. The graded exams were bound and made available to the public. Such transparency might make a contemporary education leader wince.

Fast forward to the summer of 2002. Deborah Jewell-Sherman had just been appointed superintendent of Richmond Public Schools. Under Virginia's tough new educational accountability program, only five out of 55 Richmond schools had achieved full accreditation status. To attain full accreditation, at least 70 percent of a school's students had to pass Virginia's Standards of Learning tests. Jewell-Sherman was hired on the condition that the number of fully accredited schools would be dramatically increased. To hold her accountable, Jewell-Sherman's contract was performance-based. Three conditions had to be met or she would be subject to dismissal the following summer. The conditions included: (1) full accreditation, based on spring 2003 testing, for 20 of Richmond's 55 schools, (2) no more than 12 schools "accredited with warning," and (3) achievement of at least a 70 percent passing rate in third grade reading by 16 of the city's elementary schools. That she achieved these lofty targets and remained superintendent long enough to turn around the school district is ample testimony to what a dynamic and impassioned school district leader can accomplish. One cannot help but wonder what James H. Binford would have thought of her performance-based contract.

The origins of the concept of educational accountability are somewhat murky. When Lessinger (1971, pp. 62–63) attempted to track down the first public use of the term, he gave credit to President Richard Nixon:

> In his March 3rd (1970) Education Message, President Nixon stated, "From these considerations we derive another new concept: *Accountability*. School administrators and school teachers alike are responsible for their performance, and it is in their interest as well as in the interest of their pupils that they be held accountable."

It did not take long for the idea to spread. Within a year of Nixon's remarks, states and school systems began to launch accountability initiatives ranging from new systems for evaluating teachers to performance contracts with private providers. *The Washington Post* proclaimed that American education had entered "an Age of Accountability" (Lessinger, 1971, p. 64).

All movements, of course, have antecedents and precursors. Early efforts to hold educators accountable can be traced to the rise of achievement testing and curriculum standards (Heinecke, Curry-Corcoran, & Moon, 2003; Ravitch, 1995). Dating back to the late 19th and early 20th centuries, these developments foreshadowed steadily increasing interest on the part of policy makers and politicians in controlling public education and ensuring that students benefitted from their school experience. By 1968, "74 different state testing programs were operating in 42 states…. However, only 17 states used the results of their tests to help evaluate and guide instruction and only 13 states used the results to measure student progress in academic subjects" (Bowers, 1991, p. 52).

Within three decades of 1968 virtually every state would have curriculum standards and a testing program for evaluating how well students were mastering the standards. State oversight of public schools, which earlier had focused on inputs such as funding and teacher credentials and compliance with state regulations, began to shift increasingly toward school outcomes. Maryland's accountability reforms during the 1980s are illustrative:

> The implicit theory of action [behind the Maryland reforms] was that meaningful improvement was possible at low cost to the state, simply by setting standards, publishing school- and district-level results of tests of those standards, pointing out individual schools that were not scoring well…and encouraging districts to improve the limited numbers of low-scoring schools. (Stringfield & Yakimowski-Srebnick, 2005, pp. 53–54)

When Brooks (2000, pp. iii–iv) examined state accountability systems, she identified three principles that supported the most effective systems. A focus on student results was the first principle. In other words, accountability in the final analysis is not about measurement, rewards for success, and penalties for failure; it is about children learning what they need to learn. The second principle involved goal and role clarity. An effective state accountability system must specify what it can and cannot do. Recognition that accountability is a two-way street was the third principle. Schools and districts, on one hand, and the state, on the other hand, have responsibilities when it comes to accountability. Accountability is not simply a matter of states demanding results from school systems.

The passage of the No Child Left Behind Act in 2001 (NCLB) ushered in a new era in educational accountability, one in which the federal government would play a major role. Previously the federal government's role in public education focused primarily on providing resources and services to states and school systems. Dissatisfied with the results of these efforts, supporters of NCLB argued that "student achievement would only improve when educators were judged in terms of student performance and consequences were attached to the results" (Stecher & Kirby, 2004, p. xiii). The No Child Left Behind Act called on states to adopt goals by which school and district performance could be evaluated, develop measures for the goals, and implement sanctions for failure to achieve goals. The model for this accountability system was derived from business.

Around the time that the federal government was moving toward a business model of accountability, another development related to business practice was beginning to gain momentum. Legislation was adopted in a number of states to promote the development of charter schools. Supporters of charter schools maintained that the market was a much better accountability mechanism than government bureaucracy. A sponsor of Arizona's charter school legislation succinctly articulated the reasoning behind this position:

> That charter schools are in a way a test of an entirely different accountability method which is decentralized, which depends, rather than on bureaucratic rules and regulations, on first of all these being schools of choice. It's accountability that comes from the parents and the consumers. (quoted in Garn, 2001, pp. 571–572)

Markets, however, have their own problems when it comes to accountability. Some consumers have access to more and better information regarding market choices than other consumers (Garn, 2001). As a result, some consumers are in a better position to make a sound selection than other consumers. Such variation may be tolerable when choosing a refrigerator, but should differential access to information characterize the choice of a school? Critics of charter schools claim that allowing school choice to be dictated by market forces only serves to perpetuate education inequity.

Despite all the attention devoted to educational accountability over the past 40 years, the concept is far from clearly understood. As with any complex and politically charged idea, accountability means different things to different people. When it comes to answering the basic question—Who is accountable for what to whom?—the responses are likely to vary widely. One thing is certain, however. School districts have become a primary focus for educational accountability.

Confusion over accountability begins with its purpose. Are accountability measures intended for control, compliance, improvement, or all three? Each accountability purpose begs additional questions. Control of whom or what? Compliance with what? Improvement of what? Some observers distinguish between procedural accountability and consequential accountability (Heim, 1995). The former entails responsibility for how things are done; the latter for what is accomplished. And what of consequential accountability? Does it refer to an accounting of outcomes, such as what students learn, or is it more of a guarantee that students have learned what they are expected to learn?

Additional questions can be raised regarding who is to be held accountable. When it comes to student achievement, is the primary unit of accountability the school board, the superintendent, the school principal, the teaching faculty, the parents, or the individual student? It is tempting to argue that all are accountable, but should all be accountable to the same degree? And if accountability is to be reciprocal, as Brooks (2000) suggests, how should the proper level of accountability for states and the federal government be determined?

Similar questions can be raised regarding the audience for accountability. Are school district leaders accountable to taxpayers who pick up the bill for public education? To parents who entrust their children to public schools? To students whose futures depend on the quality of education they receive? Or to the state which has the Constitutional obligation to provide schooling for all?

Some of these thorny issues will be taken up in the remainder of this chapter. To guide the discussion, the following "working" definition of accountability will be used: "Accountability is the responsibility that goes with the authority to do something. The responsibility is to use authority justifiably and credibly" (Heim, 1995). The benefit of this definition is that it avoids guarantees of results, while establishing an expectation for the conscientious and competent exercise of authority. Where authority is absent, accountability should not be expected.

To help focus the following discussion, three questions will be addressed.

The Challenges of Educational Accountability

1. For what should school systems be held accountable?

2. What do school district leaders need to do to manage educational accountability?

3. What are possible negative by-products of accountability measures?

AGREEING ON ACCOUNTABILITY TARGETS

The central accountability question for school district leaders concerns what school systems should be held accountable for. The position of the author is that school systems should be held accountable for what they have authority to do. In practical terms, their authority extends to what school district leaders can control or, at least, what they can influence. To map the accountability landscape, it is necessary to consider three elements of school district operations: (1) inputs, (2) throughputs, and (3) outputs/outcomes. Each will be analyzed in terms of the control/ influence criterion.

Inputs. When most people think of inputs, they think of money, or at least what money will purchase. It is thus necessary to ask whether school district leaders control or influence the funding of public schools. While they clearly control how funds are spent, school district leaders often rely on legislative bodies and government agencies for a significant portion of their financial resources. It is legislators, agency heads, and tax payers, therefore, who must bear much of the burden of accountability for funding public education.

As for what money will purchase, responsibility rests more squarely on district leaders' shoulders. Consider teachers and school administrators, for example. Under the No Child Left Behind Act, school district leaders are expected to staff schools only with highly qualified professionals. While the precise meaning of "highly qualified" varies somewhat among the states, it typically involves possession of the appropriate credential for the assignment. Each state determines what is necessary to earn a credential in the various teaching fields as well as for school administration. District leaders in school systems located in remote or undesirable locations as well as underfunded systems are at a distinct disadvantage when it comes to recruiting and retaining highly qualified professionals. Even individuals in possession of the proper credentials, of course, can turn out to be inadequate. For this reason, district leaders also are expected to put in place effective measures for regularly evaluating professional personnel. Topics related to the recruitment, retention, evaluation, and development of professional personnel will be addressed in greater depth in Chapter 8.

Other important inputs for which school leaders are accountable are the curriculum and the materials that support it. The language in Virginia's *Standards of Quality* (2007, p. 2) is indicative of the basis upon which district curriculum accountability rests:

Local school boards shall develop and implement a program of instruction for grades K through 12 that is aligned to the [Virginia]

Standards of Learning and meets or exceeds the requirements of the [state] Board of Education.

The regulation goes on to specify all the topics that must be covered by each school district's "program of instruction."

While school district leaders typically have no choice when it comes to the core subjects that their schools must teach, they are able to select the textbooks and curriculum programs that support these subjects. Some states issue lists of "approved texts" from which district leaders can choose; other states do not. Some district leaders prefer to delegate authority for the selection of curriculum-related materials to school-based professionals. Other district leaders insist that these decisions should be made centrally to ensure program comparability across schools. District leaders in recent years have been particularly concerned with the choice of commercial programs for reading and mathematics, especially for low-performing schools. Their concern is understandable, given the cost of these programs and the potential negative consequences of a poor selection. When Deborah Jewell-Sherman opted to contract with Voyager Reading for Richmond's low-performing schools, she was careful to analyze data on the program's effectiveness. In addition, she insisted that Voyager Reading representatives engage in a long-term partnership with Richmond Public Schools. She reasoned that commercial curriculum publishers also needed to be held accountable.

Recent thinking about inputs has become more sophisticated and nuanced. Instead of assuming that inputs have the same impact on all student outcomes, the new view holds out the possibility that different inputs affect different outcomes. With regard to high schools, for example, possible outcomes include test scores, student attitudes and aspirations, and student progress toward graduation. When Grubb (2008, pp. 129–130) analyzed data from the National Educational Longitudinal Survey of the Class of 1988, he found that certain inputs like increased teacher planning time enhanced test scores, while other inputs such as teacher-student ratio affected students' rate of progress through high school. Grubb (p. 130) called for a differentiated approach to inputs, one in which efforts to "improve tests scores must focus on instructional improvement… while resources that make the school a more supportive place—fewer students per teacher, more counselors and help with academic work, [and] extracurricular activities" are concentrated on helping students progress toward graduation.

Throughputs. Throughputs refer to the products, processes, and practices that enable inputs to be converted to outputs and, eventually, outcomes. At the school level, throughputs include instruction, assessment, planning, and administration. When the Education Commission of the States (*Tools for Improving...*, 2001) commissioned an inventory of possible functions of public education for which accountability might be expected, the following list of throughputs was identified for superintendents:

Creating a shared vision
Establishing performance targets
Implementing a strategic plan
Meeting professional standards
Establishing learner-centered policies
Providing district-wide instructional leadership
Using data to improve practices
Maintaining records and reporting results
Ensuring accreditation or external quality reviews
Communication with stakeholders
Recognizing and reward performance
Building staff capacity

With so many possible functions for which a superintendent might be held accountable, it is reasonable to wonder whether there should be any limits on accountability. There are clear benefits to focus and priorities. Generating a lengthy list of functions for which district leaders are accountable can have the effect of reducing the likelihood that the most critical functions receive the attention they need. Given the mission of public education and the expectation that district leaders must ensure that all students benefit from taxpayers' investment in their schooling, it seems only reasonable that functions closely associated with effective teaching and learning should be accorded the greatest importance.

Another way to think about throughput accountability involves the goals of a school district. School district leaders are expected to develop annual and long-range goals and school boards are expected to adopt these goals. It could be argued that superintendents and school boards should be held accountable for doing everything within their authority to achieve these goals. There is one potential problem, however, with this basis for accountability. It could encourage the development and adoption of relatively modest goals. Is it better, one might ask, for leaders to set ambitious goals and sometimes fail to achieve them or to set modest goals that easily can be achieved?

Focusing efforts on specific throughput functions and on district goals are two ways to address the accountability challenge. A third way, and some would argue the preferred bureaucratic approach to accountability, centers on compliance. Many aspects of school district operations are constrained by policies, rules, and regulations. They range from prescribed maximum class sizes to the ratio of school administrators to students. District leaders are expected to ensure that employees comply with all policies, rules, and regulations. It should be added, though, that leaders also have an obligation to challenge policies, rules, and regulations when there is compelling evidence that they fail to serve the interests of students.

Outputs and outcomes. Accountability for inputs and throughputs is all well and good, but for many people, the "bottom line" when it comes to educational accountability involves student outputs and outcomes. Outputs contribute to outcomes. Grades and performance on state tests are student outputs. Graduation is an outcome. Graduation depends on earning passing grades in a prescribed set of courses and attaining minimum scores on state tests. While it might seem that only students can be held accountable for outputs and outcomes, the No Child Left Behind Act and various state accountability systems hold school district leaders accountable for aggregate outputs and outcomes as well as outputs and outcomes for designated student sub-groups.

Focusing educational accountability on standardized test results presents school district leaders with several challenges. They must ensure that students actually are taught the content on which standardized tests are based. This is largely a matter of throughput accountability. Another challenge involves the nature of the content itself. If standardized tests concentrate on relatively basic content and if teachers focus their attention primarily on getting students to pass the tests, some observers fear that students will not be exposed to enough advanced material. Others worry that the heavy emphasis on reading and mathematics performance is depriving students of a well-rounded education (Rothstein, 2009). Mastering minimal curriculum requirements is unlikely to equip students with the knowledge necessary to compete for admission to the best colleges and for high-paying jobs. It is up to district leaders to ensure that students have ample opportunities to advance beyond minimum curriculum requirements.

Besides performance on standardized tests, students must earn passing grades in order to graduate. Grades also determine a student's class ranking, which can be a factor in where the student goes to college. Many school districts have grading policies that designate the numerical value of a grade and what grade a student must earn in order to pass a course. From time to time questions arise regarding a district's grading policies. Parents, for example, may challenge a policy that requires their children to attain a higher numerical mark in order to receive an "A" than children in a neighboring school district. Other concerns involve how much homework grades should count toward a final course grade and the extent to which grades should be dependent on student attendance. It is the responsibility of school district leaders to make certain that grading policies do not place certain groups of students at a disadvantage. Basing a large portion of the final grade on homework, for example, when some students lack home conditions conducive to completing homework could be challenged as unfair.

For most school district leaders, the ultimate focus for accountability is high school graduation. Graduation has been linked to students' lifetime earning prospects and the viability of the nation's economy. Failure to earn a diploma is associated with a variety of negative outcomes including long-term economic disadvantagement and the likelihood of incarceration. Accountability for graduation has caused many district leaders to provide alternative schools, evening schools, graduation coaches, and credit recovery programs so that struggling students have the opportunity to complete high school.

THE MANAGEMENT OF ACCOUNTABILITY

The intense interest in educational accountability places a variety of demands on contemporary school districts. To address these demands, district leaders have been compelled to develop new units, create new roles, and adopt new practices. The experience of Fairfax County Public Schools offers a good illustration of how a large school system has addressed the challenges associated with managing educational accountability.

Fairfax's Department of Educational Accountability

Data is the lifeblood of accountability, and Fairfax County Public Schools already had a reputation for collecting an enormous amount of data when Dan Domenech became superintendent in 1997. Problems arose, however, whenever it became necessary to pull together data from various sources in order to facilitate analysis, planning, and action (Duke, 2005, p. 152). Data on special education students resided in once place, while minority student achievement data was located elsewhere. When Domenech announced his commitment to data-driven decision making, the handwriting was on the wall—things had to change.

Domenech and his school board had developed the divisionwide strategic targets for which the school system would be held accountable. Every school and central office unit, in turn, had targets based on the districtwide strategic targets. Domenech needed quick access to data on how each school and unit were progressing toward their targets so he could keep the school board informed and allocate additional resources when necessary. The eight cluster directors who oversaw the operations of schools in their jurisdictions pressed for a coordinated data management system that would enable them to pinpoint local academic problems promptly.

Domenech considered the various units that were charged with collecting and analyzing performance data. They included the Office of Educational Planning, the Office of Program Evaluation, the Office of Student Testing, and the Office of Minority Student Achievement. The last unit had been created in the 1980s in response to concerns from the African American community about the achievement gap between black and white students. Domenech concluded that these units should be combined to form a single department under the leadership of an Assistant Superintendent. The Department of Educational Accountability was launched in July 2001.

The mission of the Fairfax Department of Educational Accountability links the unit directly to student achievement: "We value accountability and serve as a catalyst to impact student achievement through collaboration and positive action" (Duke, 2005, p. 152). The responsibilities associated with achieving the mission encompass a wide range of functions, including testing, data analysis and dissemination, program evaluation, and strategic planning.

The Department of Educational Accountability
- Administers the Virginia State Assessment Program and the Fairfax County Public Schools Testing Program.
- Develops accountability procedures and communicates results.
- Analyzes, interprets, and reports division, cluster, school, and individual student achievement data annually.
- Conducts comprehensive program evaluations.
- Provides technical assistance in planning, testing, research, and program evaluation.
- Develops and monitors policy in the areas of testing, research, planning, and evaluation.
- Coordinates development of the Divisionwide Comprehensive Plan.
- Coordinates secondary school accreditation.
- Plans and facilitates community boundary meetings, focus groups, and task forces. (Duke, 2005, pp. 153–156)

By creating one department to integrate all school system accountability functions, Fairfax County Public Schools was able to overcome a variety of problems that had challenged division leaders. A comprehensive data management system replaced the discrete data "silos" that had previously prevented quick and easy access to performance information. In place of highly idiosyncratic school improvement plans, a standard school improvement plan format with goals tied directly to divisionwide goals and benchmarks was initiated. A schedule was created for evaluating all division programs, thereby enabling division leaders to determine if programs were contributing to the achievement of divisionwide goals. A history of Fairfax County Public Schools concluded that the Department of Educational Accountability "has provided the degree of central coordination and oversight necessary to ensure that *all* Fairfax students have a reasonable opportunity to benefit from the school system's quality programs" (Duke, 2005, p. 153).

Laying the Groundwork for Accountability

The foundation of school district accountability systems consists of measurable performance goals related to inputs, throughputs, outputs, and outcomes. Typically, student achievement goals make up a significant portion of district goals, and district goals, in turn, are used to set school goals. Examples of student achievement goals for Fairfax County Public Schools can be found in Chapter 1. In order to focus energy on achieving district and school goals, school districts often develop strategic plans. These plans are continuously reviewed and adjusted in light of progress (or lack of progress) in achieving goals.

Elmore (2007, pp. 244–245) argues that district accountability efforts should be guided by "the principle of reciprocity," which he describes as follows:

For each unit of performance I demand of you, I have an equal and reciprocal responsibility to provide you with a unit of capacity to produce that performance, if you do not already have that capacity.

The principle of reciprocity can be seen in various functions performed by Fairfax's Department of Educational Accountability, from data analysis and help in interpreting data for school-based personnel to assistance with goal-setting and benchmarking for school board members. To enhance the capacity for accountability of school-based personnel, district leaders across the United States not only have created new central office units to coordinate accountability-related activities, they have developed new roles and practices, refined traditional accountability processes, and implemented incentives.

New Roles   As a result of the No Child Left Behind Act and its focus on student performance on state standardized tests, school-based personnel are expected to analyze test data, identify areas of low-performance, and make appropriate adjustments in instruction. To facilitate this process, many school systems have assigned a test coordinator to each school. Sometimes these individuals are staff members who take on additional responsibilities. Larger schools may have full-time test coordinators. They are responsible for seeing that high-stakes state tests and local benchmark tests are administered properly and proctored, distributing test results, and helping teachers to interpret test results.

To support school-based accountability efforts, many school districts have had to expand central office units that deal with student testing, program planning and evaluation, and research. The requirements associated with the No Child Left Behind Act generated the need for a variety of roles, ranging from the coordination of data disaggregation to interpreting the myriad rules and regulations spawned by the federal legislation. District liaisons are expected to link local and state accountability offices. Parents must be kept apprised of school and district performance measures. Schools must be provided with interim (benchmark) tests aligned to state standardized tests.

Where there is data, there is technology, and the demands of technology have spawned a variety of new roles and responsibilities. Individuals are needed to handle data entry, keep systems up and running, and ensure that data systems are secure. Quality control procedures must be in place to prevent inaccurate and duplicate data from being entered into data management systems. Personnel must be trained on the use of gradebook software, spreadsheets, and curriculum management systems that link content with model lesson plans and benchmark assessments.

Many of the new central-office roles involve assisting and monitoring low-performing schools. Consider the case of Chicago, which established the Office of Accountability to coordinate efforts to improve schools on probation (Sunderman, 2001). Probationary status was based on schools having fewer than 15 percent of their students scoring at or above national norms on the Iowa Test of Basic Skills. The Office of Accountability assigned a probation team to each low-performing school and charged it with assisting the principal in developing and implementing a school improvement plan. Schools that failed to improve were subject to reconstitution. The probation manager who headed each probation team had the authority to veto the principal in matters related to curriculum and instruction.

Schools on probation in Chicago also were required to contract with an external partner for services related to school improvement. Contracts typically were funded with Title I money. Outsourcing school improvement creates additional roles related to staff and organization development and contract management. Some large school systems like Los Angeles and Philadelphia have negotiated contracts with private providers to take over operation of low-performing schools. Such arrangements require oversight by school district leaders and an accounting of how district funds are being spent and to what effect.

New Practices and Processes　Demands for greater educational accountability have given rise to a variety of new practices and processes as well as requiring the refinement of existing ones. Changes start at the top. As indicated earlier in the reference to Deborah Jewell-Sherman, superintendents increasingly are being signed to performance-based contracts. These contracts specify student achievement and school-based targets tied to adequate yearly progress. Superintendents work closely with school boards to review district performance data, establish annual performance goals, and develop strategic plans to enable district personnel to achieve the goals. There also is evidence, at least in smaller urban districts, that superintendents are spending time in schools personally monitoring progress on school goals (Hentschke, Nayfack, & Wohlstetter, 2009, p. 331).

Educational accountability efforts may begin with the superintendent, but they should not end with the superintendent. When the Council of the Great City Schools conducted an assessment of the Minneapolis Public Schools in 2004, the team offered the following observations:

> The superintendent appears to be the *only* person in the school district who is evaluated based at least in part on the district's progress in improving academic performance. No one else in the school system appears to be held accountable for districtwide academic performance.
>
> There are no consequences for anyone on staff—either in the central office or at the schools—if student achievement does not improve or if racially-identifiable achievement gaps do not narrow. (*Foundations for Success...*, 2004, p. 38)

The assessment team went on to make several recommendations for expanding accountability (*Foundations for Success...*, 2004, p. 39). They suggested that job descriptions for district and school personnel should contain references to the improvement of student achievement. A second recommendation was to make the improvement of student achievement an integral part of the personnel evaluation process. Finally, the assessment team indicated that all senior instructional staff, including area superintendents, and all principals be placed on performance contracts. The contracts for principals should be tied to academic targets negotiated on a school-by-school basis.

A primary mechanism for holding school-based personnel accountable is the school improvement plan. Annual school improvement plans, in fact, are mandated for all schools in some states. In all states, such plans are required under the No Child Left Behind Act for schools "identified for improvement." Wisconsin's guidelines are illustrative (NCLB: Requirements for school improvement plan, 2008). A school "identified for improvement" in Wisconsin must develop a two-year improvement plan within three months of being notified of its status. School improvement plans initially must be approved by the school district. Schools that fail to improve are required to submit their plans to the Wisconsin Department of Public Instruction "for review, consultation, and/or intervention."

Wisconsin goes on to specify guidelines for each school improvement plan. The plan must contain specific, annual, measurable objectives "for continuous and substantial progress by each group of students, so that they will meet Wisconsin's proficient level of achievement by 2014" (NCLB: Requirements for school improvement plan, 2008). Strategies based on scientific research must be indicated, and these can include extended day and extended school year opportunities. The role of the school district in providing financial and technical assistance has to be specified. Other components of the plan include policies and practices related to core academic subjects, provisions for professional development, and strategies for involving parents in school improvement efforts and keeping them informed regarding progress.

In its efforts to facilitate school-based accountability, the New York City school system has tried several novel approaches. Borrowing from the British practice of school inspections, New York initiated "quality reviews" in 2007. Quality reviews are conducted by visiting teams of trained inspectors and "are intended to gauge not just a school's progress, but also its ability to improve" (Archer, 2006, p. 10). Unlike some traditional school review processes, the quality reviews address classroom instruction and involve focused discussions with teachers about their work with several students.

Another accountability-related move by New York City involves the grading of schools (Gewertz, 2007) Introduced in 2007, the grades are based in part on the quality reviews of schools. They also take into account student test-score progress over time, not just test scores in a single year. Additional bases for the school grades include responses on parent, teacher, and student surveys. These surveys gather data on school environment, including safety and academic expectations. Schools that receive low grades may be subject to various sanctions including replacement of the principal.

At the district level, some school systems have linked accountability efforts to a business-based practice called a "Balanced Scorecard" (Kaplan & Norton, 1996). A Balanced Scorecard provides for tracking performance across all operations considered essential to achieving long-term success. Measurable goals for making steady progress toward the achievement of long-term targets are specified along with periodic checkpoints, benchmarks, and strategies for achieving goals. Designated individuals are held accountable for seeing that each strategy is implemented, monitored, and reported on at regular intervals. Unlike some long-range plans, a Balanced Scorecard takes an incremental approach to achieving improvement targets. This approach enables stakeholders to keep track of progress, or lack of progress, on a regular basis and permits mid-course corrections to be undertaken before too much time has been wasted moving in an unproductive direction (Archer, 2007).

To assist in their efforts to be accountable, school district leaders increasingly are relying on benchmarking performance in their districts against other districts. One form of benchmarking involves the identification of districts of comparable size. The Virginia Department of Education uses this approach to produce "Efficiency Reports" for school divisions. These reports enable school district leaders to compare expenditures, staffing, and operations and pinpoint areas where their divisions exceed and fall behind norms. Another approach to benchmarking entails the identification of exemplary school districts. By comparing their district's policies, programs, and practices with those of districts with higher levels of student achievement, district leaders can generate targets for improvement. A third type of benchmarking focuses on salaries. To compete for the best teachers and administrators, school district leaders need to know what other districts are paying personnel. Such information can be persuasive when campaigning for greater local support of public schools.

Incentives and Sanctions   Another dimension of the management of school district accountability involves incentives and sanctions. Sanctions, of course, are built into the provisions of the No Child Left Behind Act. Schools that are chronically low performing may be compelled to provide parents with the option to transfer their children to another school. Eventually low-performing schools may be reconstituted or closed if they fail to improve. School district leaders routinely replace principals of low-performing schools in the hopes that new leadership will result in dramatic turnarounds.

School districts are not immune from sanctions. Some low-performing school districts have been subjected to takeover by state authorities.

When this happens, school district leaders are typically replaced and the authority of school boards is reduced. States also may reserve the right to remove a school district's accreditation. The state of Georgia, for example, threatened to deny accreditation to Clayton County School District because of behavior by school board members that was deemed "dysfunctional" and "unethical" (Jacobson, 2008, p. 6). When a school district loses its accreditation, its students may have trouble gaining admission to college and district leaders may have difficulty acquiring supplementary resources.

While the "stick" is probably relied on more, the "carrot" is gaining popularity among district leaders as a mechanism for promoting educational accountability. The use of performance-based contracts already has been noted. Some districts rely on bonuses for personnel in schools that achieve their performance targets. The use of school bonuses is a way of acknowledging the importance of collective accountability. For schools to meet their targets, all staff members must contribute.

In 2008 Guthrie and Schuermann (p. 24) estimated that approximately 10 percent of the nation's school districts were experimenting with some form of performance pay. The researchers go on to note that the research-based support for performance pay is "slender." The landscape of educational accountability is littered with failed efforts to provide "combat pay" and other incentives for teachers in struggling schools. Guthrie and Schuermann observe that effective pay-for-performance programs must find ways to (1) ensure that measurements of performance are fair, complete, and accurate; (2) explain the program clearly to key stakeholders and gain their commitment; and (3) predict accurately the financial impact of incentives so that programs can be sustained over time. Issues related to performance pay will be examined more closely in Chapter 8.

Some school systems are even providing incentives to encourage students to attend school regularly and perform well in class and on standardized tests. Incentive programs often are funded by individual benefactors and local businesses. In 2008, Washington, D.C. schools and Harvard University joined forces to sponsor the Capital Gains program, an experiment targeting 3,300 middle schoolers (Vargas, 2009). Students can earn up to a hundred dollars every two weeks by attending their classes, behaving properly, and getting good grades.

POSSIBLE NEGATIVE BY-PRODUCTS OF ACCOUNTABILITY

If the history of education reform teaches one lesson, it is that every well-intentioned reform has the potential to spawn unintended negative consequences. Educational accountability is no exception.

Some critics focus on the harm that can result from too great an emphasis on passing standardized tests. Teachers, for example, may devote so much time to ensuring that students meet the relatively minimal standards of state tests that they neglect to cover more advanced material, thereby depriving many students of the academic challenges that will prepare them for college. This "narrowing of the curriculum" was just one of ten disturbing by-products of accountability-based testing identified by Berliner and Nichols in *Collateral Damage: How High-stakes Testing Corrupts American's Schools* (2007). Other negative consequences included:

- Administrator and teacher cheating
- Student cheating
- Exclusion of low-performance students from testing
- Misrepresentation of student dropouts
- Teaching to the test
- Conflicting accountability ratings
- Questions about the meaning of proficiency
- Declining teacher morale
- Score reporting errors

Another analysis of research on the consequences of accountability policies found evidence of increased dropout rates for marginalized students, the perpetuation of racist practices for language-minority students, increased teacher demoralization, and the erosion of teachers' professional identity (Webb, 2005). Concerned district leaders worry that the present climate of high-stakes testing and complex accountability measures will make it harder to attract and retain talented teachers and administrators to work in schools, especially chronically low-performing schools.

Duke and Tucker (2003, pp. 85–90) found many of the forementioned negative consequences when they investigated the implementation of Virginia's educational accountability program in the late 1990s and early 2000s. They also detected a troubling trend related to the triaging of students. Interviews with high school administrators indicated that students were being grouped based on the likelihood that they would pass the state tests. So-called "bubble students," those students deemed to be close to passing state tests, received considerable teacher attention. Meanwhile students who were judged to have little chance of passing state tests were left mostly to fend for themselves. Triaging students may seem like a rational response in a world driven by testing, but it is hardly consistent with the democratic mission of public schools.

A study of six large county school districts in Florida found that schools were employing a different strategy in order to "game" the accountability system implemented by the state (Figlio & Getzler, 2002). According to researchers, schools tended to reclassify low-income and previously low-performing students as disabled at significantly higher rates following the introduction of high-stakes state testing. Reclassification removed these students from a school's aggregate test-score pool, thereby increasing the odds that the school would not be labeled as failing. While such reclassification practices have become less likely under the provisions of the No Child Left Behind Act, they indicate the lengths that school districts may be willing to go in order to avoid state sanctions.

Booher-Jennings (2006) warns of another way that test-driven accountability may place certain students at a disadvantage. The No Child Left Behind Act permits states to designate the minimum number of students required for a particular sub-group's test scores to be reported. There is considerable variation in the size of this number across the states. In a variation on test-based triage, Booher-Jennings observes that students in small (and therefore unreported) sub-groups may receive less instructional assistance than students in sub-groups whose scores must be reported (p. 760). In one Texas elementary school that she studied, Booher-Jennings found that teachers actually had designated the students whose scores counted as "the accountables." When she examined Houston schools, she found that an average of 16 percent of special education students and 11 percent of African American students were not counted in their schools' test-score reports because they had not been enrolled in their school for a full academic year. Texas allowed such students to be excluded from school student achievement reporting. Schools with high student mobility rates are obviously likely to enroll many newcomers. If these students receive less instructional assistance because their scores are not counted, schools may be harming the very students who are most dependent on the public schools.

Efforts to promote educational accountability may have a negative impact on teachers as well as students. When researchers tracked 11 years of accountability efforts in the Baltimore City Public School System, they found that some schools were punished for very small variations in year-to-year test scores (Stringfield & Yakimowski-Srebnick, 2005). The faculties of these schools reacted with bitterness and cynicism, hardly the dispositions necessary to facilitate continued school improvement.

Researchers who investigated how school accountability systems functioned in Maryland, Kentucky, and the city of San Francisco reported, not surprisingly, that low-performing schools in each system were expected to implement school improvement plans that conformed to external guidelines (Mintrop, MacLellan, & Quintero, 2001). These guidelines, however, proved to be so extensive and complicated that the resulting plans often overwhelmed school personnel. Instead of focusing improvement efforts, the plans typically incorporated so many objectives that teachers did not have a clear sense of priorities. Not only were they resentful, but teachers grew less inclined to initiate their own improvement efforts. If the result of externally driven accountability efforts is to undermine school-based initiative to improve, the value of such efforts must be questioned.

It is up to school district leaders to monitor the accountability process closely in order to ensure that the kinds of negative by-products noted above are prevented or, at least, kept to a minimum. This, of course, is not simple or easy. Sunderman (2001, p. 512), for example, observes that "accountability policy is in a constant state of flux as states and districts develop and change their systems in response to local conditions." She goes on to point out that accountability policies are subject to political and institutional influences that are highly variable. In the spring of 2009, for example, the federal government announced that it would begin to permit multiracial students to identify each of their racial identities. While such a move enables students to acknowledge their true racial heritage, it makes it harder to track the progress of traditional sub-groups under the No Child Left Behind Act. The challenge for school district leaders is to preserve the benefits of educational accountability despite constantly evolving policies and practices, and guard against unintended negative consequences.

EXECUTIVE CONCLUSION

School district leaders operate in an environment where accountability is expected. What educational accountability actually means, however, is open to interpretation. Definitions range from accounting for the expenditure of public funds to ensuring that all students achieve at high levels. District leaders are variously held accountable for the quality of "inputs" such as instructional personnel and curriculum programs, "throughputs" including the processes by which schools are run and students are taught, and "outputs" such as scores on standardized tests and promotion rates. Provisions governing accountability are contained in the complex regulations and policies of the No Child Left Behind Act as well as state and local accountability systems.

Two primary responsibilities of school district leaders involve determining who should be held accountable for what and ensuring that district personnel have the capacity to exercise accountability. Capacity building has led many districts to develop special central office units devoted to coordinating accountability functions. These functions range from collecting and analyzing performance data to setting district improvement targets. Accountability demands also have given rise to a variety of new roles, many of them associated with monitoring and assisting low-performing schools. Accountability provisions at the federal, state, and local levels entail both incentives and sanctions. Whether these mechanisms are effective in promoting accountability is open to debate.

Accountability measures have the potential to produce negative as well as positive consequences. Among the unintended by-products of contemporary accountability programs are cheating by school personnel and students, narrowing of the curriculum, demoralization of teachers, and the triaging of students. School district leaders are challenged to make certain that accountability measures work for the benefit of students, not to their detriment.

NOTE

1. Material for this vignette was drawn from Megan Gillespie, "All Means All: Maintaining Success in Norfolk's Public Schools," an instructional case published in 2005 by the Darden Graduate School of Business Administration, University of Virginia.

REFERENCES

Archer, J. (February 21, 2007). District tracking goals with "Balanced Scorecards." *Education Week*, 10.

Archer, J. (May 17, 2006). British inspectors bring instructional focus to N.Y.C. *Education Week*, 10.

Berliner, D.C., & Nichols, S.L. (2007). *Collateral Damage: How High-stakes Testing Corrupts America's Schools*. Cambridge, MA: Harvard Education Press.

Booher-Jennings, J. (2006). Rationing education in an era of accountability. *Phi Delta Kappan*, 87(10), 756–761.

Bowers, J.J. (1991). Evaluating testing programs at the state and local levels. *Theory into Practice*, 30(1), 52–60.

Brooks, S.R. (2000). *How States Can Hold Schools Accountable*. Seattle: Center on Reinventing Public Education, University of Washington.

Duke, D.L. (2005). *Education Empire: The Evolution of an Excellent Suburban School System*. Albany: State University of New York Press.

Duke, D.L. (1995). *The School That Refused to Die*. Albany: State University of New York Press.

Duke, D.L., & Tucker, P.D. (2003). Initial responses of Virginia high schools to the Accountability Plan. In D.L. Duke, M. Grogan, P.D. Tucker, & W.F. Heinecke (eds.), *Educational Leadership in an Age of Accountability*. Albany: State University of New York Press, 69–96.

Elmore, R.F. (2007). *School Reform from the Inside Out*. Cambridge, MA: Harvard Education Press.

Figlio, D.N., & Getzler, L.S. (2002). Accountability, ability, and disability: gaming the system. Working paper 9307. Cambridge, MA: National Bureau of Economic Research.

Foundations for Success in the Minneapolis Public Schools. (2004). Washington, D.C.: The Council of the Great City Schools.

Garn, G. (2001). Moving from bureaucratic to market accountability: the problem of imperfect information. *Educational Administration Quarterly*, 37(4), 571–599.

Gewertz, C. (November 14, 2007). N.Y.C. district issues "value added" grades for schools. *Education Week*, 6.

Grubb, W.N. (2008). Multiple resources, multiple outcomes: testing the "improved" school finance with NEL588. *American Educational Research Journal,* 45(1), 104–144.

Guthrie, J.W., & Schuermann, P.J. (October 29, 2008). The question of performance pay. *Education Week,* 24–26.

Heim, M. (1995). Accountability in education. Unpublished paper submitted to the Hawaii Department of Education.

Heinecke, W.F., Curry-Corcoran, D.E., & Moon, T.R. (2003). U.S. schools and the new standards and accountability initiative. In D.L. Duke, M. Grogan, P.D. Tucker, & W.F. Heinecke (eds.), *Educational Leadership in an Age of Accountability.* Albany: State University of New York Press, 7–35.

Hentschke, G.C., Nayfack, M.B., & Wohlstetter, P. (2009). Exploring superintendent leadership in smaller urban districts. *Education and Urban Society,* 41(3), 317–337.

Jacobson, L. (March 26, 2008). Loss of accreditation looming in Georgia for troubled district. *Education Week,* 6.

Kaplan, R.S., & Norton, D.P. (1996). Using the Balanced Scorecard as a strategic management system. *Harvard Business Review,* Reprint 96107.

Lessinger, L.M. (1971). The powerful notion of accountability in education. In L.H. Browder (ed.), *Emerging Patterns of Administrative Accountability.* Berkeley, CA: McCutchan, 62–73.

Mintrop, H., MacLellan, A.M., & Quintero, M.F. (2001). School improvement plans in schools on probation: a comparative content analysis across three accountability systems. *Educational Administration Quarterly,* 37(2), 197–218.

NCLB: Requirements for school improvement plan. (2008). Downloaded from Wisconsin Department of Public Instruction website: http://dpi.wi.gov/oea/sirequire.html

Ravitch, D. (1995). The search for order and the rejection of conformity: standards in American education. In D. Ravitch & M.A. Vinovskis (eds.), *Learning from the Past.* Baltimore: The John Hopkins University Press, 167–190.

Rothstein, R. (January 28, 2009). Getting accountability right. *Education Week,* 36,26.

Standards of Quality as Amended. (2007). Richmond, VA: Virginia Department of Education.

Stecher, B., & Kirby, S.N. (2004). *Organizational Improvement and Accountability.* Santa Monica, CA: Rand.

Stringfield, S.C., & Yakimowski-Srebnick. M.E. (2005). Promise, progress, problems, and paradoxes of three phases of accountability: a longitudinal case study of the Baltimore City Public Schools. *American Educational Research Journal,* 42(1), 43–75.

Sunderman, G. (2001). Accountability mandates and the implementation of Title I schoolwide programs: a comparison of three urban districts. *Educational Administration Quarterly,* 37(4), 503–532.

Tools for Improving Education Accountability Systems. (2001). Denver: Education Commission of the States.

Vargas, T. (March 22, 2009). Cash incentives create competition. *The Washington Post,* C-1, C-6.

Webb, P.T. (2005). The anatomy of accountability. *Journal of Educational Policy,* 20(2), 189–208.

6

THE CHALLENGES OF INSTRUCTIONAL IMPROVEMENT

INSTRUCTIONAL LEADERSHIP MUST BEGIN AT THE TOP[1]

When retired Air Force major general John Fryer took the helm of the public schools in Duval County, Florida, the large school system that included Jacksonville had experienced years of declining performance. A local blue ribbon commission had gone on record as claiming that the school system lacked vision, direction, and high-quality academic standards.

After sizing up the impediments standing between Duval schools and improved student achievement, Fryer concluded that the school system had to concentrate on improving teaching and learning. The job of focusing resources and energy on teaching and learning could not be left, however, to principals alone. Instructional leadership, Fryer believed, had to begin with the superintendent.

Realizing that Duval educators did not share a common understanding of effective instruction, Fryer set to work developing a specific vision of what high-quality instruction should look like. The result was a model that identified pedagogical strategies that teachers should rely on to raise student achievement. These strategies were linked to content standards, curriculum materials, and pacing guides.

Once the instructional vision was in place, Fryer focused on building the commitment and capacity of professional personnel to implement the vision. This step required extensive professional development at the school level. Relying on his belief in the chain of command, Fryer understood that principals had to embrace the instructional vision first in order to be able to provide appropriate direction for their faculties.

The third component of Fryer's plan involved the development of mechanisms to provide performance data to all levels of the school system. Without data, teachers could not identify student strengths and weaknesses, principals could not spot areas in need of instructional improvement, and central office administrators could not determine which schools required assistance. In short, accountability depended on data.

The last component of instructional improvement derived from the recognition that the process had to be continuous. Fryer made certain that provisions were in place to ensure regular examination and fine-tuning of instructional practices and programs.

Evidence that Fryer's plan was having an effect did not take long to emerge. Within two years, the number of schools receiving low grades under Florida's performance grading system began to decline. Student achievement in reading, writing, and mathematics rose steadily in absolute terms and relative to student achievement in most comparison districts.

✳✳✳✳✳

All school systems need to focus on instructional improvement, but not necessarily for the same reasons. Some school systems like Duval County are compelled to reverse years of declining student achievement and reduce the attending public criticism. Other school systems need to ensure that hard-won gains are sustained over time. They cannot afford for school personnel to become complacent. Even relatively high-performing school systems must embrace continuous instructional improvement if they are to move from "good to great." Each year brings new knowledge about what constitutes effective instruction, new content that students are expected to learn, new students with new needs, and new teachers and administrators. There simply is no excuse for any school system to assume that the challenges of instructional improvement can be put to rest.

IMPEDIMENTS TO HIGH-QUALITY INSTRUCTION

School district leaders over the years have understood that high-quality instruction can never be assumed. In the opening chapter of his excellent account of John Fryer's efforts to improve teaching and learning in Duval County, Supovitz (2006, pp. 7–10) identifies five obstacles that often block the path to high-quality instruction. First is the sheer complexity of the contemporary school district. Promoting high-quality instruction is but one of a multitude of pressing issues that competes for the attention of district leaders. The second obstacle is the lack of coherence that often characterizes the various components of school systems. Programs and initiatives are developed at different times for different purposes, leaving district leaders to figure out how all the pieces fit together. Supovitz's third obstacle involves "the deeply rooted culture of teacher autonomy over instructional decision making" (p. 9). Teachers believe, quite justifiably, that no one understands the instructional needs of their students as well as they, and they often recoil when outsiders attempt to tell them how to teach.

Perhaps teachers would be more inclined to embrace overtures to improve instruction if there were incentives for doing so, but typically there are not. Lack of incentives is the fourth obstacle. The situation may be beginning to change, however, as the previous chapter indicated. The fifth obstacle to high-quality instruction is the very nature of teaching itself. Supovitz (2006, p. 10) observes that instruction is "inherently nonroutine, complex, and therefore difficult to manage and support." The vagaries of instruction lead many district leaders to back away from direct efforts to influence how teachers teach.

Supovitz is by no means the only observer to recognize the challenges associated with instructional improvement. When the Council of the Great City Schools commissioned a study comparing urban districts that had made impressive gains in student achievement with districts that had yet to make such gains, several important differences were identified (Snipes, Doolittle, & Herlihy, 2002). The policies and practices of the central offices of low-performing districts were not strongly connected to desired changes in teaching and learning. Responsibility for instructional improvement in these districts was left largely to the schools, and the schools received multiple and conflicting expectations regarding curriculum content and instruction. These problems were traceable, in part, to the lack of consensus among key stakeholders regarding district priorities and an overall strategy for instructional improvement.

The impediments to high-quality instruction, of course, do not reside entirely in the central office. Payne (2008, p. 81) lays much of the problem at the school's doorstep. He notes, for example, that teachers often are skeptical about the ability of some students to learn. Teachers also may not be open to new and better ways to teach. School-based staff development frequently fails to address instructional improvement in a sustained and systematic way. Many teachers struggle to establish the classroom structure and order necessary for productive learning. Teachers in many cases also lack adequate knowledge of the content they are assigned to teach. These problems are exacerbated by inadequate instructional supervision by school administrators and high rates of teacher turnover.

Taken collectively, the combination of these district-based and school-based obstacles results in what has been variously referred to as a lack of coherence or alignment. Newmann, Smith, Allensworth, and Bryk (2001, p. 299) provide a useful operational definition of *instructional program coherence*: "a set of interrelated programs for students and staff that are guided by a common framework for curriculum, instruction, assessment, and learning climate and are pursued over a sustained period." This common framework combines specific expectations for what students are to learn and how they are to be taught and assessed. Provisions for assisting struggling students are spelled out. Instructional program coherence also is characterized by the allocation of resources in ways that advance the common framework.

The absence of instructional program coherence is easy to detect. Efforts to improve instruction are isolated and idiosyncratic. Curriculum content is relatively unstable over time, and student assessments are constantly changing. Teachers tend to "do their own thing" and rarely explore opportunities to coordinate instruction. School administrators make little effort to hold teachers accountable for instructional program coherence or provide professional development that focuses on developing and implementing a common framework for curriculum, instruction, and assessment. Weak instructional program coherence, not surprisingly, has been associated with low levels of student achievement (Newmann et al., 2001).

The term *alignment* frequently is used to describe the relationship between what students are expected to learn and the material on which they are tested. If instructional improvement ultimately is measured by student achievement, it obviously is difficult to achieve measurable gains when teachers are not teaching material to which students will be exposed on standardized tests.

Alignment can also refer to other dimensions of instruction. Problems can arise, for example, when curriculum content is not aligned across grade-levels. Or when two teachers of the same subject and grade-level cover very different material. Instructional interventions may be poorly aligned with the needs of struggling students. The criteria by which teachers are evaluated may not match the elements of effective instruction or the district instructional model. Professional development for teachers may address issues other than district instructional priorities.

Opinions vary regarding why coherence and alignment problems exist. In a study of the impact of a new state reading policy on one California elementary school, Coburn (2001) found that teachers reconstructed "policy messages" based on their interactions with each other and the principal. Reading policy related to the state's commitment to a "balanced" approach to reading instruction was interpreted, adapted, and even transformed during the process of implementation. The state-approved reading series was used in various ways depending on how teachers "made sense" of the state's intentions, their own beliefs about reading, and the principal's communications regarding the new reading series. Some teachers opted not to use the new series at all.

Darling-Hammond (1997, pp. 210–260) observes that efforts by school district leaders to promote coherence and alignment may be perceived negatively by teachers as the standardization of teaching. She distinguishes between standards, which are necessary to guide practice, and standardization of instruction, which many teachers resent and resist because they consider it demeaning and anti-professional.

High rates of teacher and principal turnover also can undermine coherence and alignment. Every time a new principal arrives, the possibility for a shift in instructional focus arises. Understandings of curriculum alignment can be disrupted with the hiring of every new teacher. These problems are especially acute in low-performing schools because turnover rates typically are high.

Yet another reason for coherence and alignment problems can be traced to factors outside school systems. The policy and political contexts in which public education is conducted are restless. Just as local educators begin to feel they have a grasp of what students are expected to know, changes may be promulgated in curriculum guidelines and evaluation instruments.

Given this book's focus on district leaders, it is only fair to ask whether central office personnel contribute in significant ways to coherence and alignment problems. Based on an in-depth examination of district-school relations in Chicago, Milwaukee, and Seattle, the answer is yes (*A Delicate Balance...*, 2005). The three-year foundation-supported qualitative study zeroed in on the actions of mid-level district staff to facilitate instructional improvement.

The major finding was that district-wide instructional policies and mandates in the three urban school systems had little impact on improving instruction. Determining why this was the case led researchers to identify a number of contributing factors. Teachers' voice and expertise were not tapped during the process of policy development and implementation. The intense focus on raising scores on standardized tests appeared to deflect attention away from actually improving instruction. Principals had so many non-instructional responsibilities that they struggled to promote instructional policies and mandates. Mid-level central office personnel might have picked up the slack, but for various reasons they did not. Consequently key ingredients in instructional improvement such as focused professional development and curriculum coordination often were lacking. Teachers and principals felt unsupported and complained that district leaders failed to recognize the unique circumstances of their individual schools.

Was John Fryer's success in improving instruction in Duval County an anomaly? Are most school district leaders destined to be disappointed when they press for high-quality, research-based classroom practice? What can districts do to build school-based capacity for continuous instructional improvement? These and related questions will be taken up in the remainder of the chapter.

The Challenges of Instructional Improvement

What can school district leaders do to improve instruction, especially in low-performing schools?

What provisions are needed to help students who experience difficulties learning required content?

What district policies can help to support high-quality instruction?

IMPROVING INSTRUCTION WHERE IT'S NEEDED MOST

All students have a right to high-quality instruction. They are required by law, after all, to attend school. Students in low-performing schools are especially vulnerable to instruction that is less than ideal. School district leaders have a special obligation to do all they can to ensure that these students receive the best instruction possible.

The failure of low-performing schools to provide sound instruction cannot be blamed on a lack of research regarding the components of teaching effectiveness. A large knowledge base on the keys to good instruction exists. Students benefit, for example, from clear goals and directions, structured lessons, opportunities to apply what they learn, constructive and frequent feedback, and encouragement (Bransford, Brown, & Cocking, 1999). Advances in cognitive learning research stress the importance of challenging assignments, high expectations, and instruction in strategies for learning. Payne (2008, p. 94) notes that good instruction also depends on contexts characterized by protected and extended (when needed) instructional time, teacher collaboration and collective responsibility, academic press combined with social support for students, program coherence, and qualified teachers.

The existence of knowledge regarding effective instruction, of course, does not ensure that educators are aware of this knowledge. When evidence surfaces that teachers are unaware of best instructional practices or when they are unwilling to implement these practices, it is necessary for principals and district leaders to get involved. This is what happened in Duval County. To improve academic performance, a framework was developed that specified alignment of instruction and assessment with state curriculum guidelines (Supovitz, 2006, p. 41). Common expectations were developed by course and grade-level. To promote literacy, model classrooms were established at each grade-level to exemplify best practices in teaching reading, phonics, and writing. A similar approach was adopted for mathematics. The framework included additional provisions, such as tutoring and extended learning time, for struggling students.

The Duval framework was designed for all schools in the large system. Some school district leaders, however, prefer to concentrate instructional improvement efforts on their lowest performing schools. Such was the case in Richmond, Virginia. As associate superintendent for accountability and instruction, Deborah Jewell-Sherman realized that raising student achievement depended on helping all teachers in low-performing schools focus on literacy. To this end she contracted with an outside firm to acquire benchmark tests aligned to Virginia's Standards of Learning in language arts and other subjects. Teachers administered these tests periodically during the school year in order to identify content with which individual students were struggling. After examining a variety of supplementary reading programs, she elected to partner with the Voyager program. In addition to materials and software, Voyager provided ongoing teacher training. The Voyager reading program was made available to struggling readers in special summer sessions designed to help students catch up to their peers.

When Jewell-Sherman became Richmond's superintendent, she continued her efforts, focusing on aligning lessons with the Virginia Standards of Learning. Teachers and curriculum specialists spent summers developing lesson plans and identifying supporting materials based on the state standards. Principals were expected to monitor instruction to ensure that teachers were implementing the lessons.

The aligned lessons paved the way to curriculum consistency, but without high quality instruction, the road to higher achievement would remain rocky. Jewell-Sherman and her associate superintendent, Yvonne Brandon, undertook a thorough review of best practices in teaching low-achieving students. Eventually they decided on an instructional model that included the introduction of new material using direct instruction, guided practice, the assignment of homework, an opportunity to begin homework during class, time for student questions, and a concluding activity that tied the current lesson to previous learning. Jewell-Sherman and Brandon realized that many teachers would resist the imposition of a common instructional model, but they also understood that struggling students benefitted from highly structured lessons. Dramatic improvements in student achievement across Richmond's numerous low-performing schools confirmed the wisdom of Jewell-Sherman and Brandon's approach.

In the cases of Duval County and Richmond, district leaders elected to create their own research-based instructional models to guide improvement efforts. Other school systems have chosen to adopt or adapt ready-made school reforms that include instructional components. The range of options has expanded greatly since the early 1980s. Slavin (1998, pp. 1300–1302) divides ready-made school reforms into two basic designs: (1) systemic reforms that apply to all schools and involve changes in assessment, accountability, standards, and governance, and (2) school-based reforms that focus on creating a model school and then exporting the model to interested school systems. He goes on to identify three variations on the second reform design: organizational development models, comprehensive reform models, and single-subject innovations.

Organizational development models, such as Sizer's (1992) Essential Schools model and Levin's (1987) Accelerated Schools model, require that school staffs get involved in developing school improvement programs based on certain principles. Comprehensive reform models are more prescriptive and include Slavin's Success for All program (Slavin, Karweit, & Madden, 1989). Schools that adopt comprehensive reform models are provided with instructional materials, teachers' manuals, staff development training, and evaluation instruments. Single-subject models focus on one curriculum area and , often, a particular grade or cluster of grades. Reading Recovery is such a model, and it targets emerging readers, typically first graders.

Another school reform classification scheme comes from a Rand study of New American Schools (Bodilly, pp. 297–298). Three designs are identified: core designs, comprehensive designs, and systemic designs. Core designs, such as Expeditionary Learning, focus on school partnerships and changes in core elements of schooling, including instruction, student grouping, assessment, and curriculum. Comprehensive designs go beyond core elements to address school governance, staffing, and relationships with youth service providers. Systemic designs, as the name suggests, target entire school systems, not just individual schools.

Research on the adoption of ready-made reforms has yielded a variety of cautionary advice. Lee (2001, p. 75), for example, concluded from a study of high school reforms that "the simultaneous implementation of many restructuring reforms...did not increase either effectiveness or equity." Questions have been raised regarding the wisdom of trying to scale-up whole-school reforms from original sites to other schools in a given school system (Viadero, 2001). Datnow (2000) warns that reforms that do not include some degree of local participation face formidable implementation obstacles. An in-depth study of school improvement efforts in three elementary schools found that the more teachers were engaged in school-level restructuring, the less likely were there to be instructional improvements in classrooms (Elmore, Peterson, & McCarthey, 1996).

Regardless of whether school district leaders elect to adopt, adapt, or create programs to improve instruction in low-performing schools, the ultimate success of the initiative will depend to a great extent on the school system's capacity to support improvement efforts. Individual schools, especially schools that are chronically low performing, simply lack sufficient resources to get the job done alone.

The problem in some school systems is that low expectations begin at the top. Payne (2008, p. 75) illustrates this point by drawing on a study conducted by students at a Philadelphia high school. The student researchers found that teachers lacked leadership to go out and secure the necessary resources to undertake improvements. According to Payne, "By failing to provide what the school needed to function, higher-ups were sending a signal. It didn't make sense for teachers to have high expectations in a [district] context where they knew the environment didn't have the resources it would take to do the job" (p. 75).

What, then, do district leaders need to do in order to build the capacity of low-performing schools for instructional improvement? Studies of successful efforts to improve instruction identify a variety of important actions related to instructional leadership, access to student achievement data, appropriate instructional materials, targeted professional development, and staffing adjustments (Orr, Berg, Shore, & Meier, 2008; Payne, 2008; Quint, Akey, Rappaport, & Willner, 2007; Spillane & Thompson, 1997; Supovitz, 2006).

A school's capacity for instructional improvement may depend on:

Instructional leadership

Access to student achievement data

Appropriate instructional materials

Targeted professional development

Staffing adjustments

Without capable and committed instructional leadership in schools, it is unlikely that efforts to improve instruction will succeed. Responsibility for recruiting and placing principals rests squarely on the shoulders of district leaders. As the pool of prospective principals has become shallower, some district leaders have developed in-house leader development programs that identify promising staff members and provide them with the training to function as instructional leaders. This means ensuring that principals understand the elements of effective instruction and know how to determine the extent to which these elements are present in classrooms. Some states and universities have created special programs to train "turnaround specialists," experienced administrators with the skills to guide teachers in low-performing schools through the process of instructional improvement. Regardless of the source of instructional leadership, it is essential that district leaders provide ongoing support for principals charged with improving instruction. Without such support, principals can easily become isolated and their improvement efforts can be neutralized.

The effectiveness of instruction depends to a great extent on teacher awareness of student learning. Such awareness, in turn, depends on access to timely assessment data. Mention already has been made (in Chapter 5) of the value of benchmark or interim tests based on the curriculum standards upon which state standardized tests are based. Given periodically during the school year, these tests provide an indication of particular aspects of the required curriculum with which students are struggling, thereby enabling teachers to re-teach material in a timely and targeted manner. District leaders have a role to play in seeing that benchmark and interim tests are either developed locally or purchased from commercial providers.

As helpful as benchmark and interim tests can be, they are no substitute for sound classroom assessment (Chappuis, Stiggins, Arter, & Chappuis, 2004). It is up to district leaders to see that principals and teachers understand the principles of sound classroom assessment and that these principles are embedded in their practice. School-based educators must appreciate the fact that assessment is an on-going process, not something that happens only at the end of every grading period.

It goes without saying that high-quality instruction is difficult without the availability of high-quality instructional materials. In identifying the school district responsibilities that have a direct impact on teaching and learning, Supovitz (2006, pp. 200–202) notes that districts are expected to select textbooks, develop lesson plans tied to curriculum standards, provide pacing guides and scope-and-sequence frameworks, and monitor promising new instructional products. School-based personnel typically lack the time, resources, and often the expertise to conduct

systematic examinations of instructional materials. When decisions regarding textbooks, reading programs, mathematics programs, and other
curriculum-related products are left to individual teachers and schools,
the possibility of potentially harmful disparities between schools arises.
By overseeing and coordinating the selection of instructional materials,
especially in low-performing schools, district leaders can ensure that
teachers have a common set of tools to raise student achievement.

Having high-quality instructional materials, of course, does not
ensure that teachers know how to use them. A crucial component of
capacity-building, therefore, involves targeted and ongoing professional
development aligned to instructional programs and materials. So-called
"drive-by" workshops where teachers are exposed to content for a day
and then are expected to implement the content in a consistent and effective manner are of little value to low-performing schools. Instead,
what is needed is sustained training on adopted instructional practices
tied to the needs of students (Garet, Porter, Desimone, Birman, & Yoon,
2001). Sustained training provides opportunities for teachers to try new
programs and practices, share their experiences, correct implementation problems, and systematically refine their skills and understandings.
This kind of professional development usually requires the involvement
of central office personnel, though it may be delivered on a school-by-
school basis.

Although the primary audience for targeted professional development to improve instruction may be teachers, it is vital that principals be
included. A large scale study of three urban school districts found that
delivering instruction-related professional development to principals
constituted an effective first-step toward instructional improvement for
teachers (Quint et al., 2007). It stands to reason that, if principals are
expected to monitor, supervise, and evaluate classroom instruction, they
need to know what teachers need to know regarding instructional practice.
Once again, the responsibility for principals' professional development
logically lies with school district leaders.

Timely and targeted professional development is essential to instructional improvement, but it is not a panacea. Under certain circumstances,
staffing arrangements may not support high-quality instruction. Large
class sizes, for example, may undermine efforts to upgrade instruction
for struggling students. In other cases, teachers may be assigned to teach
content for which they are not qualified. Professional development is
unlikely to compensate for lack of basic training. School district leaders
have important roles to play in staffing low-performing schools.

One critical role involves finding the resources to reduce class sizes
in low-performing schools. Smaller classes increase the likelihood that

struggling students will receive more individual assistance and reduce the likelihood of classroom management problems. School districts that have experienced success in turning around low-performing schools often adopt flexible staffing policies that allow district leaders to allocate extra teachers on an "as needed" basis (Duke, 2005, p. 123).

Another promising staffing practice involves teacher looping. This arrangement enables a teacher or team of teachers to work with the same group of students for two consecutive years, thereby increasing the likelihood that teachers understand the needs of individual students. While most looping occurs in elementary school, it may be worthwhile to consider looping between elementary and middle or between middle and high school. The trauma of transition from one school to another can be eased when students already know some of their teachers.

Besides lower class sizes and looping, low-performing schools also can benefit from the involvement of educators with specialized credentials. A national study of Title I schools (Stullich, Eisner, McCrary, & Roney, 2006, p. 52) indicated that large percentages of Title I schools reported a need for technical assistance with a variety of challenges:

Improve quality of teachers' professional development (80%)
Get parents more engaged in their child's education (74%)
Address instructional needs of students with IEPS (71%)
Improve students' test taking skills (70%)
Analyze assessment results to understand student's strengths and weaknesses (68%)
Identify or develop detailed curriculum guides, frameworks, pacing sequences, and/or model lessons aligned with state standards (62%)
Develop or revise school improvement plan (62%)
Address problems of truancy, tardiness, discipline, and dropouts (57%)
Address instructional needs of LEP students (49%)

In a study of efforts to help low-performing schools in New York City, Orr and colleagues (2008, p. 687) found that district leaders assigned various specialists and instructional coaches to lead instructional improvement efforts. State and regional agencies also deployed school improvement specialists to help with the turnaround process. The proliferation of additional personnel presented some challenges, however. The researchers reported that the delivery of extra assistance was "fragmented (typically focused on one part of the school's problems), uncoordinated, and difficult to use collectively because of scheduling, funding, and oversight differences" (p. 687). Low-performing schools have enough obstacles to overcome without adding coordination problems involving the very people assigned to provide help.

San Diego experienced some success in improving elementary reading when Alan Bersin (superintendent) and Anthony Alvarado (chancellor of instruction) used resources obtained from downsizing the central office to provide 100 certified and trained literacy peer coaches for low-performing schools (Hightower, 2002, p. 85). A year later 200 additional coaches were deployed. Coaches worked with principals and faculty members to design and implement professional development activities aligned to the district's newly adopted Literacy Framework. Coaches spent four days a week at their schools and a fifth day at the district's Institute for Learning receiving advanced training in coaching strategies and best instructional practices related to literacy.

Coaches in San Diego were assigned to schools based on the schools' needs. Not all low-performing schools have identical needs. One school may require a specialist trained to diagnose the reading problems of English language learners and a school-community liaison who is fluent in Spanish, while another school may need the services of a mathematics specialist and an additional special education teacher. School district leaders should avoid personnel allocation formulas that treat every low-performing school the same. Customized approaches to assigning additional staff that take into account the specific needs of individual schools are most likely to yield positive results.

SPECIAL PROVISIONS FOR STRUGGLING STUDENTS

No matter how much instruction is improved in low-performing schools, some students still are likely to experience difficulty learning particular content. It is therefore essential that district leaders ensure that schools have the capacity to address learning problems. Since students encounter a variety of learning problems, it is unlikely that any one intervention will meet the needs of all struggling students. A continuum of interventions is recommended for every school and school system.

A good illustration of a continuum of interventions is the arrangement adopted for secondary students in Hartford, Connecticut (Blankstein, 2004, pp. 239–243). Referred to as the "Pyramid of Intervention," the set of services consists of nine levels. The first four levels constitute early intervention programs designed to help at-risk students before they get into serious academic difficulties. Level one is a summer transition program intended to prepare rising ninth graders for the challenges of high school. Level two involves the placement of every ninth and tenth grader in an interdisciplinary teaching team. By working with the same group of roughly 100 students, the four core teachers on each team can coordinate efforts to assist struggling students. Tutored study halls constitute the third level of intervention. All ninth graders are required to attend these study halls, thereby ensuring that students have supervised opportunities to complete homework, prepare for tests, and receive help. The study halls are staffed by full-time tutors who also are members of the ninth grade interdisciplinary teams. Level four of the "Pyramid of Intervention" is the 15-day identification system. After the 15th day of school each fall, interdisciplinary teams are expected to identify students who are beginning to fall behind in their school work and implement appropriate assistance.

Level five involves struggling students being pulled out of class in order to receive one-on-one and small-group help from full-time tutors. If these tutorial sessions are insufficient, students are required to attend after-school study sessions, the sixth level of intervention.

The last three levels target students who are at serious risk of not graduating. Level seven consists of credit recovery opportunities. Thanks to the fact that Hartford high schools operate on block schedules, students who fail to earn a half-credit in the fall semester can recover that half-credit in the spring semester. Summer school provides additional opportunities for credit recovery.

When the first seven levels of intervention have not worked, students may be placed in the Success Team. Parental permission is required. The Success Team offers students a smaller learning environment together with counseling services and intensive tutoring. Students enter and exit the Success Team at the beginning of a marking period.

The last level of intervention is the LIFE Program. Designed for a small number of students, it functions as an alternative school combining academic work and counseling with service learning and vocational education. If students are unable to earn a diploma, the hope is that they will receive sufficient training to find gainful employment.

To address the varied needs of students who experience academic difficulties, a continuum of interventions should consist of certain critical components. These include provisions for extended learning time, both in class and outside of class, and access to specialists. Alternative learning environments, including self-contained programs and team-based options, should be available for students who do not function well in conventional settings. At the high school level, credit recovery programs are important to reduce the number of dropouts. These programs may be operated in the late afternoon, evenings, and summer.

Regardless of how a continuum of interventions is configured, the regular classroom remains the first line of defense against learning problems. Through early detection of problems and timely delivery of assistance, many academic difficulties can be addressed before they become serious impediments to educational progress. It is this concern for early detection and timely intervention that prompted the promotion of "response to intervention" (RTI) for early childhood literacy instruction. RTI resulted from a provision in the re-authorized Individuals with Disabilities Education Act (IDEA) of 2004. School systems are allowed to allocate up to 15 percent of their federal IDEA funds to pre-referral services in order to reduce the over-representation of certain groups of students in special education and minimize the number of unnecessary referrals for special education. Pre-referral services, however, must involve scientifically-based academic and behavioral interventions.

School district leaders must understand the conditions under which classroom teachers are most likely to provide effective instructional interventions. These conditions are characterized by five essential elements: (1) awareness that a student is experiencing difficulty, (2) accurate diagnosis of the causes of difficulty, (3) the competence to provide a focused intervention, (4) the commitment to provide a focused intervention, (5) and the willingness to persist with the intervention and make appropriate adjustments (Duke, 1998). Let us briefly examine each of these elements.

Payne (2008, p. 110) notes that it is often difficult for minority students to ask for help because they do not want to reinforce the stereotype of academic weakness. Veteran teachers have learned that extending an invitation to struggling students to ask for help when they need it often produces few takers. Teachers obviously must be aware that students need help in order to provide timely and targeted assistance. If teachers wait until an end-of-unit test is given in order to identify struggling students, the students may have fallen far behind their peers. School district leaders can promote timely awareness of students' need for help by providing training in questioning strategies, classroom assessment, and self-regulated learning (Chappuis et al., 2004).

Awareness that students need help, of course, does not mean that teachers necessarily understand *why* students need help. To provide effective assistance, the causes of students' difficulties must be diagnosed. Accurate diagnoses may depend on close observation of students at work, private discussions with students, and regular error analyses of student quizzes, tests, and other assignments. Because the potential sources of learning problems are varied and complex, classroom teachers may require the services of experts in order to pinpoint the reasons why some students experience academic problems. District leaders are obliged to see that the services of trained experts are available to teachers.

The third ingredient in effective intervention is instructional competence. Classroom teachers need to know how to assist students when they struggle with reading, mathematics, processing information, analysis of abstract concepts, problem solving, inferential thinking, and a host of other cognitive operations. While certain academic difficulties may require referral to a specialist, it is generally preferable to provide assistance in the context of the regular classroom. In many school districts, staffing arrangements allow specialists to work in tandem with regular education teachers. By demonstrating how to assist students, specialists increase the likelihood that teachers will acquire greater competence in instructional intervention.

Competence, of course, does not guarantee that teachers are willing to provide instructional interventions when students need them. Some teachers believe that it is not their responsibility to help struggling students. They are quick to refer struggling students to Title I teachers, special education teachers, and other specialists. Overcoming the tendency to refer learning problems to others may require re-culturing schools and creating an expectation that all teachers can provide struggling students with timely and targeted help. School administrators should encourage teachers to meet with students to develop assistance plans.

Persistence constitutes the fifth element of effective instructional intervention. One-time assistance without any follow-up may be insufficient to ensure that a student moves forward in a content area. Teachers should be prepared to monitor struggling students in order to be certain that their problems have been addressed successfully.

There is validity to the oft-stated assertion that low-performing schools are turned around one student at a time. Classroom teachers represent the best defense against academic problems. This does not mean, of course, that teachers are on their own when it comes to helping students. There is much that schools and school districts can do to bolster and augment classroom-based interventions. The previous section, for example, noted the importance of reduced class size. It is clearly easier for teachers to detect learning problems and deliver assistance when classes are relatively small. Coordinated professional development aimed at increasing teachers' repertoire of instructional interventions also is important. In the next section, we shall look at some of the policies that district leaders promulgate to promote and support high-quality instruction for all students.

POLICIES SUPPORTING HIGH-QUALITY INSTRUCTION

To support school-based efforts to improve instruction, school district leaders adopt a variety of policies. Reference already has been made to policies regarding class size, intervention continuums, staffing, alignment, and standard instructional models. In this section, additional policies will be discussed. They include policies concerning challenging curriculum content and student grouping, homework, increased instructional time, and required assistance for struggling students.

Challenging Content and Student Grouping

Improving instruction is unlikely to benefit students if what they are taught is of little value. Aware that the content of many low-level and basic courses is "dumbed down" and irrelevant, school district leaders are making a determined effort to expose all students to a challenging curriculum. When Eric Smith was superintendent of Charlotte-Mecklenburg School District, for example, he gained national attention by directing middle school guidance counselors to tear up the schedules of 8,000 middle school students and re-assign them to advanced courses. He reasoned that the black-white achievement gap would never be closed unless African American students studied alongside white students in challenging courses. During his six years at the helm, the number of African American students taking college-level courses rose 450 percent (Johnson, 2002). The result was a substantial narrowing of the achievement gap and an increase in the percentage of African American students attending college.

Mention already has been made of Dan Domenech's efforts in Fairfax County to open access to Advanced Placement and International Baccalaureate courses. While a number of school districts have taken the same course of action and allowed any student to enroll in these courses, Fairfax was one of the first districts to require that every student in an AP or IB course had to take the external, end-of-course exam. In this way, teachers are compelled to help all students, not just hand pick some students to take the exams and leave the rest to struggle.

Eliminating low-level courses and opening access to advanced courses are two indirect strategies for raising the quality of instruction. A somewhat more direct approach involves policies that govern the use of homogeneous grouping. For years researchers have known about the potential dangers of homogeneous grouping (Duke & Canady, 1991, pp. 46–54; Good & Brophy, 1987, pp. 128–134; Weinstein, 2002, pp. 103–104). Students who are assigned to low groups tend to remain in low groups. Their continued presence in these groups becomes a self-fulfilling prophecy. They receive less challenging lessons and begin to think of themselves as lacking the academic ability of their classmates in high groups.

When researchers at the University of Virginia (Duke et al., 2008) studied the instruction-related policies of a stratified random sample of

21 Virginia school divisions, they found that 16 divisions had policies designed to address the potential negative effects of homogeneous grouping. The policies covered such matters as the circumstances under which homogeneous grouping can be used, diversity of group membership, pull-out programs, and who is responsible for the oversight of grouping practices. The grouping policy of the Danville Public Schools constitutes a representative example (Duke et al., 2008, pp. 13–14):

> The principal shall have the responsibility for pupil assignment in accordance with board regulations. The teacher shall have the responsibility for grouping within the classroom to meet the needs of individual pupils. Grouping decisions shall be based on mastery of instructional objectives. Grouping should be as flexible as possible with provision for altering the grouping as often as necessary to fit the specific purpose involved. Acceleration in the learning of all students is desirable. Strategies will be employed to encourage racial and gender balance in all classes.

Danville's policy acknowledges that teachers may have to employ grouping practices, but it goes on to indicate that groups should not become permanent placements for students. The policy further calls for review of group make-up to ensure racial and gender balance. The benefit of accelerating student learning is recognized, thereby reminding school personnel of the importance of moving students out of low groups as soon as possible. Though unstated in the Danville policy, it should be stressed that, when grouping is used, instruction in all groups should reflect best teaching practices.

In no aspect of public education have the potential adverse effects of homogeneous grouping received more attention than special education. As a result of the Education of All Handicapped Law of 1975 (Public Law 94-142), students with disabilities had to receive educational services in the "least restrictive environment." The law came about in part because parents of disabled students believed their children were not exposed to the quality of content and instruction that their peers received in regular education classrooms. Too often special education students were pulled out of regular classes for large portions of each school day or assigned exclusively to self-contained classes.

Since 1975 school district leaders have made a concerted effort to "mainstream" many special education students for all or most of each school day. Special education teachers often work in tandem with regular education teachers, thereby ensuring that disabled students do not miss instruction received by their peers. Regular education teachers also have been exposed to professional development aimed at improving their ability to address the needs of special education students.

Homework

Many teachers believe that homework is an integral part of good classroom instruction. Parents have come to expect homework to be assigned on a regular basis. Some researchers, Cooper (1989) among them, however, have questioned whether all homework is beneficial. Concerns related to the purposes for which homework is assigned, the amount of homework, and the evaluation and grading of homework have led school district leaders to develop policies governing homework.

Homework may be assigned for a variety of purposes, ranging from opportunities to practice skills introduced in class to punishment for inappropriate behavior. Some purposes are more defensible than others. If teachers want students to regard homework as helpful, for example, its use as a form of punishment makes little sense. The purposes for which homework generally is assigned include practice, preparation, and extension (Eddy, 1984). Practice assignments provide opportunities for students to reinforce newly acquired skills and knowledge. Preparation assignments involve activities such as background reading and library research that provide students with information needed for upcoming lessons. Extension assignments require students to draw on previous learning in order to complete a creative or academic project that requires more time than is available in class. When homework involves tackling new material for which students are unprepared, its value may be limited. Unless students have ready access to assistance, such assignments can lead to frustration and avoidance.

Other homework issues concern the amount of homework assigned for particular subjects and grade-levels and the length of time students are expected to spend completing homework. Most educators expect the amount of homework to increase as students get older. Older students, however, often have after-school commitments that interfere with their ability and willingness to complete large amounts of homework. The previously mentioned study of instruction-related policies in Virginia found that four of the 21 school divisions implemented policies specifying the amount of time students at various grade-levels were expected to spend on homework (Duke et al., 2008, pp. 15–16). Arlington's policy was the most extensive:

Grade K: maximum of 15 minutes plus an additional minimum of 15 minutes of reading or being read to
Grade 1: maximum of 20 minutes plus an additional minimum of 20 minutes of reading or being read to

Grade 2: maximum of 30 minutes plus an additional minimum of 20 minutes of reading or being read to

Grade 3: maximum of 45 minutes plus an additional minimum of 20 minutes of reading or being read to

Grade 4: maximum of 60 minutes plus an additional minimum of 30 minutes of reading or being read to

Grade 5: maximum of 60 minutes plus an additional minimum of 30 minutes of reading or being read to

Grade 6–8: maximum of 20 minutes a night for each course for a total of 90 minutes a night plus an additional minimum of 30 minutes of reading

Grade 9–12: maximum of 30 minutes a night for each course for a total of three hours a night with the understanding that some advanced-level courses may require additional time to complete particularly the reading components of those courses

The evaluation and grading of homework is a third area where school district leaders sometimes develop policy. Homework that is assigned but not evaluated is unlikely to be useful. Students need feedback on their homework in order to identify areas in need of assistance. Reviewing homework also alerts teachers to material that they may need to re-teach. While few question the importance of providing feedback on homework, some educators worry about the impact of homework grades (Duke & Canady, 1991, pp. 87–89). Their concerns focus on students whose home environments may not be conducive to completing assignments. Is it fair to grade homework when some students go home to well-maintained study areas, computers, and parents who are willing and able to help with assignments, while other students lack these advantages? Grading homework also may encourage students to copy assignments rather than completing homework on their own.

If homework is to be graded, it is incumbent upon school district leaders to ensure that needy students have access to assistance and places where they can complete assignments. Some schools provide homework "hotlines" and websites where struggling students can get help after school hours. Other schools set up "homework centers" during lunch, free periods, and after school. To prevent students from receiving too much homework at one time, school-based educators sometimes coordinate schedules so that homework for certain subjects is assigned only on specific days of the week. Given forethought and careful planning, there is no reason why homework cannot support and augment classroom instruction without placing any particular group of students at a disadvantage.

Increased Instructional Time

For decades, American educators treated instructional time as a constant while they varied content depending on the academic track to which students were assigned. Concerns over both educational excellence and equity, however, have led contemporary educators to regard time as a variable, even as they make concerted efforts to ensure that all students are exposed to the same content.

International comparisons of student achievement have found that U.S. students are exposed to less instructional hours per year than students in countries where achievement is higher (Gewertz, 2008). While students in the United States averaged 799 instructional hours per year, students in South Korea, Japan, the Netherlands, and Finland averaged 1,079, 926, 911, and 861 instructional hours respectively.

Within the United States, variations in time spent in school also are great. A 2006 study reported that the average U.S. student spends 1,161 hours a year in school; although not all of this time involves instruction (Gewertz, 2008, p. 14). When various urban school districts were examined, the number of hours a year that students spent in school ranged from 1,274 in Houston, Texas, to 914 in Chicago. Chicago students spent the equivalent of eight weeks less time in school than the national average.

The length of summer vacation for U.S. public school students also presents a challenge to equity-minded district leaders. Research conducted at Johns Hopkins University found that disadvantaged students lose important ground over the summer in comparison with their better-off peers (Alexander, Entwisle, & Olson, 2007). The researchers estimated that, by the time students reach ninth grade, two-thirds of the achievement gap between disadvantaged and better-off students could be traced to "summer learning loss."

A major catalyst for rethinking how schools use time was the 1991 federal legislation that created the National Education Commission on Time and Learning (Public Law 102-62). One impetus for the commission was growing awareness of the achievement gap between American students and students in other industrialized nations. Many observers believed that this gap was traceable, in part, to the fact that students in many other countries were exposed to more instructional time than their American counterparts. When the National Education Commission on Time and Learning issued its report, *Prisoners of Time*, in 1994, evidence was provided to back up this belief. While high school students in the U.S. were estimated to spend 1,460 hours over four years receiving instruction in core academic subjects, their peers in Japan, France, and Germany spent 3,170, 3,260, and 3,528 hours respectively (*Prisoners of Time*, 1994, p. 24).

The commission report followed up its analysis of how U.S. schools lagged behind schools elsewhere in hours of academic instruction with a set of recommendations for state and district policy makers. The recommendations included the following:

- State and local boards work with schools to redesign education so that time becomes a factor supporting learning, not a boundary marking its limits.
- Schools provide additional academic time by reclaiming the school day for academic instruction.
- Keep schools open longer to meet the needs of children and communities.
- Teachers be provided with the professional time and opportunities they need to do their job.

An important step for school district leaders who recognize the challenges associated with improving time use in schools involves evaluating the effectiveness of daily school schedules and yearly calendars. *Prisoners of Time* (1994) urged schools to adopt flexible scheduling such as that provided in block schedules:

A more flexible time schedule is likely to encourage greater use of team teaching, in which groups of teachers, often from different disciplines, work together with students. Greater flexibility…will also make it easier for schools to take advantage of instructional resources in the community…and to work effectively with emerging technologies. (p. 31)

One flexible scheduling option that has proven helpful for elementary schools with significant numbers of low-performing students is the parallel block schedule (Duke & Canady, 1991, pp. 38–39). Developed by R. Lynn Canady, this schedule separates instructional staff into base teachers and extension-center teachers. While base teachers work with small groups of students on critical subjects like reading and mathematics, extension-center teachers provide large-group instruction. This arrangement makes it possible to provide struggling students with additional instructional time.

Block scheduling also has become popular in middle and high schools. By reducing the number of classes each day and increasing the length of time for each class, teachers are provided with more uninterrupted time for in-depth lessons. Another option involves modifying a traditional 6 or 7-period daily schedule so that certain challenging courses such as Algebra I can be allocated two consecutive periods for struggling students.

Revising the daily schedule is important for planning as well as instructional purposes. Teachers need time during the regular school day to meet and analyze data, coordinate lessons, and discuss students in need of assistance. School district leaders should encourage principals to develop schedules that provide such opportunities.

Besides revising the regular daily schedule, some school districts allocate resources to support an extended school day for students in need of additional assistance. Several states, including Massachusetts, New Mexico, and New York, provide funds to enable selected low-performing schools to add additional minutes to the school day and additional days to the school year (Glod, 2008). Washington, D.C.'s superintendent, Michelle Rhee, funded a 14-week Saturday Scholars program for students at risk of not passing end-of-year tests in reading and mathematics. Like Rhee, some district leaders prefer to concentrate additional learning time for struggling students in the weeks leading up to the administration of standardized tests in the spring. Other district leaders choose to operate extended days throughout the school year.

Another way to obtain additional instructional time involves rethinking the annual school calendar. When educators at J.E.B. Stuart High School in Fairfax County, Virginia, expressed a commitment to raise student achievement in their perennially low-performing high school, Dan Domenech, the superintendent, endorsed their request for an expanded school year (Duke, 2005, pp. 127–129). By adopting a 242-day calendar, Stuart was able to run two summer sessions. This benefitted students who needed extra time to acquire language proficiency in English. It also helped students who, for whatever reason, had fallen behind in the number of credits needed to graduate. Students who did not complete required coursework by the end of spring semester were allowed to finish their work in the summer. Others who spent their freshman year in noncredit classes for English language learners were able to earn academic credits during the summer to make up credit deficits, thereby enabling them to graduate on time. Summer session also was used to operate two academies: one for students with strong academic potential who, with additional preparation, could succeed in high-level classes and one designed to improve the behavior and study skills of struggling students.

For districts that have not adopted year-round schedules, summer school constitutes a popular vehicle for increasing learning time. An added benefit involves reducing the likelihood of learning loss over the protracted summer break. When districts sponsor summer school, a policy may be required to address the need for summer courses to be comparable in content and difficulty to courses given during the regular school year (Duke et al., 2008, p. 23). Summer school also can provide an opportunity for teacher training. When Richard Wallace was Pittsburgh's superintendent, he arranged for teachers to learn new methods for helping students by working under the tutelage of master teachers in summer school classes for at-risk students.

Recognizing the relationship between dropping out of school and credit deficiency, it is important for school district leaders to consider various ways that students can make up the credits needed to obtain a diploma. Besides several self-contained programs noted earlier in the discussion of a continuum of interventions and special summer school programs such as the one at Stuart High School, there is the option to extend the time period available to students who want to earn a diploma. The Boston Public Schools, for example, adopted a policy that grants high school students a fifth year in which to complete the coursework needed to graduate. Efforts such as these are crucial if the high number of dropouts in the United States is to be significantly reduced.

Required Assistance for Struggling Students

One of the more controversial issues concerning low-achieving students involves policies that require these students to participate in assistance programs. Critics of such policies argue that required participation is unlikely to yield benefits (1) when students are unmotivated to succeed and (2) when students have competing commitments after school and during the summer.

Proponents, however, argue that school districts are obliged to do everything in their power to ensure that students successfully complete their K–12 education and graduate. To this end, some districts have adopted policies that require failing students to take advantage of assistance programs. With the school system's blessing, Mel Riddile, principal of Stuart High School, mandated that all students with a D or an F grade in a core course had to attend after-school tutoring sessions until their grades improved. Arrangements were made for a late bus run to accommodate students who stayed after school.

When assistance programs are not compulsory, students often fail to take advantage of them. Beginning in the fall of 2000, school districts in New York were required to implement Academic Intervention Services (AIS) for under-performing students. The intent was to help students who did not score well on state tests. AIS teachers work with students individually and in small groups to help them master skills in core academic areas and acquire test-taking strategies. When a study was conducted in 2003 to determine how AIS was working, however, researchers reported that teachers experienced difficulties getting students to show up when before-school and after-school AIS programs were strictly voluntary (Killeen & Sipple, 2004, p. 19).

In some cases, the focus of remediation efforts is summer school. A good example of a district policy permitting administrators to require summer school attendance comes from Rockingham County, Virginia (Duke et al., 2008, p. 23):

> The division superintendent may require students who are educationally at risk to take special programs of prevention, intervention, or remediation in summer school if the superintendent determines that remediation of the student's poor academic performance, literacy passport test performance, if applicable, performance on the Standards of Learning assessments in grades three, five or eight, or promotion necessitates the student's attendance in summer school.

When Mecklenburg County Public Schools (Virginia) took the step of requiring summer school for students who failed the newly instituted state Standards of Learning tests, district leaders first needed to gain the support of the local juvenile court judge. Unless he was willing to back up district action by supporting possible prosecution, district leaders believed the policy of requiring summer school was unlikely to be effective.

EXECUTIVE CONCLUSION

Efforts to ensure educational equity are unlikely to succeed unless school district leaders focus on ensuring that all students receive high quality instruction. Accomplishing this goal, however, presents its share of challenges. The world of the school district leader is filled with a complex array of obligations that easily can divert leaders from instructional oversight. Without instructional leadership from the central office, it is unlikely that improving instruction, especially for low-achieving students, will receive adequate attention in the schools. The key to effective instruction across all schools in a system is agreement about what constitutes good instruction and leadership aligned behind a district-wide effort to make certain that good instruction takes place in every classroom.

As the case of Duval County illustrates, there is much that school district leaders can do to promote good instruction. They can see that a viable and research-based instructional model is developed and implemented. They can ensure that the content of instruction reflects state and local curriculum guidelines. They can make certain that teachers receive the proper training in instructional practices and that school administrators understand how to monitor and evaluate classroom instruction. Additional efforts by district leaders to develop capacity for instructional improvement include providing access to student achievement data, seeing that up-to-date instructional materials are available, and staffing schools in ways that support effective teaching.

Despite these initiatives, it is likely that some students will not experience academic success, at least not initially. For this reason, district leaders also must make provisions for assisting struggling students. Since there is no evidence that any one intervention works equally well with every student in need of help, it is best for school districts to implement a continuum of interventions, ranging from preventive measures and in-class assistance to alternative schools for students who do not function well in conventional learning environments.

Central office instructional leadership also may involve the promulgation of policies that support effective teaching and learning. These policies should address such issues as homework, student grouping, increased time for instruction, and required assistance for needy students.

NOTE

1. The material for the opening vignette was drawn from the very detailed account of reform in Duval County in J.A Supovitz, *The Case for District-based Reform* (Cambridge, MA: Harvard Education Press, 2006).

REFERENCES

Alexander, K.L., Entwisle, D.R., & Olson, L.S. (2007). Lasting consequences of the summer learning gap. *American Sociological Review,* 72(3), 167–180.

Blankstein, A.M. (2004). *Failure Is Not an Option.* Thousand Oaks, CA: Corwin.

Bodilly, S. (1996). Lessons learned. In S. Stringfield, S. Ross, & L. Smith (eds.), *Bold Plans for School Restructuring.* Mahwah, NJ: Erlbaum, 289–324.

Bransford, J.D., Brown, A.L., & Cocking, R.R. (eds.). (1999). *How People Learn.* Washington, D.C.: National Academy Press.

Chappuis, S., Stiggins, R.J., Arter, J., & Chappuis, J. (2004). *Assessment FOR Learning.* Portland, OR: Assessment Training Institute.

Coburn, C.E. (2001). Collective sense making about reading: how teachers mediate reading policy in their professional communities. *Educational Evaluation and Policy Analysis,* 23(2), 145–170.

Cooper, H. (1989). *Homework.* New York: Longman.

Darling-Hammond, L. (1997). *The Right to Learn.* San Francisco: Jossey-Bass.

Datnow, A. (2000). Power and politics in the adoption of school reform models. *Educational Evaluation and Policy Analysis,* 22(4), 357–374.

A Delicate Balance: District Policies and Classroom Practice. (2005). Chicago: Cross City Campaign for Urban School Reform.

Duke, D.L. (2005). *Education Empire: The Evolution of an Excellent Suburban School System.* Albany: State University of New York Press.

Duke, D.L. (1998). School leadership and the hard work of helping individual students to learn. In O. Johansson & L. Lindberg (eds.), *Exploring New Horizons in School Leadership.* Umea, Sweden: Centrum for Skolledarutveckling, 35–57.

Duke, D.L. & Canady, R.L. (1991). *School Policy.* New York: McGraw-Hill.

Duke, D.L., Tucker, P.D., Higgins, J., Lanphear, L., Levy, M.K., & Salmonowicz, M.J. (2008).

Are local policies supporting instruction becoming standardized? *Leadership and Policy in Schools*, 7(1), 1–29.

Eddy, Y. (1984). Developing homework policies. *ERIC Digest*. Identifier ED 256473.

Elmore, R.F., Peterson, P.L., & McCarthey, S.J. (1996). *Restructuring in the Classroom*. San Francisco: Jossey-Bass.

Garet, M.S., Porter, A.C., Desimone, L., Birman, B.F., & Yoon, K.S. (2001). What makes professional development effective? Results from a national sample of teachers. *American Educational Research Journal*, 38(4), 915–945.

Gewertz, C. (September 24, 2008). Consensus on learning time builds. *Education Week*, 1, 14–18.

Glod, M. (February 4, 2008). Finding time for success. *The Washington Post*, B1–B2.

Good, T.L., & Brophy, J.E. (1987). *Looking in Classrooms*, 4th ed. New York: Harper and Row.

Hightower, A.M. (2002). San Diego's Big Boom: systemic instructional change in the central office and schools. In A.M. Hightower, M.S. Knapp, J.A. Marsh, & M.W. McLaughlin (eds.), *School Districts and Instructional Renewal*. New York: Teachers College Press, 76–93,

Johnson, D. (May 5, 2002). School chief works fast, furious. *The Washington Post*, C5.

Killeen, K.M., & Sipple, J.W. (2004). The implementation of Academic Intervention Services (AIS) in NYS: implications for school organization and instruction. Unpublished paper.

Lee, V.E. (2001). *Restructuring High Schools for Equity and Excellence*. New York: Teachers College Press.

Levin, H.M. (1987). Accelerated schools for disadvantaged students. *Educational Leadership*, 44(6), 19–21.

Newmann, F.M., Smith, B., Allensworth, E., & Bryk, A.S. (2001). Instructional program coherence: what it is and why it should guide school improvement policy. *Educational Evaluation and Policy Analysis*, 23(4), 297–321.

Orr, M.T., Berg, B., Shore, R., & Meier, E. (2008). Putting the pieces together: leadership for change in low-performing urban schools. *Education and Urban Society*, 40(6), 670–693.

Payne, C.M. (2008). *So Much Reform, So Little Change*. Cambridge, MA: Harvard Education Press.

Prisoners of Time. Report of the National Education Commission on Time and Learning. (1994). Reprinted by the education Commission of the States, Denver, CO.

Quint, J.C., Akey, T.M., Rappaport, S., & Willner, C.J. (2007). *Instructional Leadership, Teaching Quality, and Student Achievement*. New York: MDRC.

Sizer, T. (1992). *Horace's School*. New York: Houghton Mifflin.

Slavin, R.E. (1998). Sand, bricks, and seeds: school change strategies and readiness for reform. In A. Hargreaves, A. Lieberman, M. Fullan, & D. Hopkins (eds.), *International Handbook of Educational Change*. Dordrecht, The Netherlands: Kluwer, 1299–1313.

Slavin, R.E., Karweit, N.L., & Madden, N.A. (1989). *Effective Programs for Students at Risk*. Boston: Allyn & Bacon.

Snipes, J., Doolittle, F., & Herlihy, C. (2002). *Foundations for Success*. Washington, D.C.: The Council of the Great City Schools.

Spillane, J.P., & Thompson, C.L. (1997). Reconstructing conceptions of local capacity: the local education agency's capacity for ambitious instructional reform. *Educational Evaluation and Policy Analysis*, 19(2), 185–203.

Stullich, S., Eisner, E., McCrary, J., & Roney, C. (2006). *National Assessment of Title I, Interim Report, Volume I: Implementation of Title I*. Washington, D.C.: Institute of Education Sciences, U.S. Department of Education.

Supovitz, J.A. (2006). *The Case for District-based Reform*. Cambridge, MA: Harvard Education Press.

Viadero, D. (November 7, 2001). Whole-school projects show mixed results. *Education Week*, 1, 24–25.

Weinstein, R.S. (2002). *Reaching Higher*. Cambridge, MA: Harvard University Press.

7

THE CHALLENGES OF SCHOOL SAFETY

HOW SAFE ARE DANVILLE'S SCHOOLS?[1]

Most school systems do not face a school safety crisis, but that does not mean that local residents are not concerned about student safety. When district leaders in Danville, Virginia, wanted to learn more about how various stakeholders felt about school safety and student behavior, they enlisted the services of a university-based research group. The superintendent and school board planned to develop a comprehensive approach to school safety based on the results of the external assessment.

When the assessment was conducted in 1999, Danville schools enrolled approximately 7,000 students. Half the students qualified for free or reduced-price lunch. White and African American students were evenly divided and made up the vast majority of the total school enrollment.

The researchers first interviewed school administrators and school resource officers. Elementary administrators expressed "moderate" concern for bullying, strangers on campus, and fighting. Secondary administrators and school resource officers indicated a number of "serious" safety concerns, including verbal abuse of teachers, strangers on campus, fighting, alcohol use, and drug use. "Moderate" concern was indicated for fighting, sexual harassment, theft, bullying, gangs, racial tension, and vandalism.

Teachers next were surveyed. Almost one in four teachers regarded student absenteeism and class cutting as the most serious problems related to school safety and student behavior. Other "serious" concerns included verbal abuse of teachers, fighting, and bullying.

Ninth grade students also were asked to complete a survey on school safety. About 10 percent of the responding students indicated that they were subjected to bullying at school. Approximately one in ten students reported being in a fight at school. Eight percent of the ninth graders admitted to using a drug while at school, and 4 percent indicated that they had consumed alcohol at school.

After analyzing these data and a variety of other information, the research team shared several observations with district leaders. The team agreed that Danville Public Schools did not face a school safety "crisis." Safety-related issues were identified, but opinions varied within and across stakeholder groups as to which issues were "serious." Both educators and students expressed fear that an "over-reaction" to safety concerns could result in "prison-like" school conditions that would be counter-productive.

In an effort to reduce safety-related concerns without turning Danville schools into harsh environments, the research team offered a variety of recommendations. Most of the suggestions involved preventive measures. Students, for example, should receive training in how to recognize and report suspicious behavior. Special education teachers who deal with behavior disorders should conduct teacher inservice programs on how to handle troubled students. To help engage students in constructive activities, the research team recommended that district leaders initiate a campaign to involve every middle and high school student in at least one extra-curricular activity.

Several recommendations focused on interventions. The team suggested that the school system develop an alternative school for students who were unable or unwilling to benefit from a conventional learning environment. Because of concerns about truancy, the team urged district leaders to work with local law enforcement officials and community leaders to develop an initiative aimed at checking on out-of-school students.

One important lesson from the external assessment was that school safety and student behavior are multifaceted issues requiring a range of responses. No single approach is likely to address all concerns effectively.

*****

There was a time when issues related to school safety and student behavior were considered to be primarily the province of principals and teachers. As the frequency and severity of problems have increased, however, it has become necessary for school district leaders to play a greater role in ensuring that students learn and teachers teach in orderly environments. Before examining some of the challenges associated with maintaining orderly environments, it is instructive to consider how concerns over school safety and student behavior have evolved over the past half century.

A PERSISTENT AND EVER-CHANGING CONCERN

Anyone who believes that school safety concerns originated with the shootings at Columbine High School on April 20, 1999, needs to read a history of public education in the United States. Educators in the 1950s worried that juvenile delinquency and gang activity would spill over from the streets into school yards and corridors. The 1960s brought a host of new concerns, including racial tensions in desegregating schools, student protests and demonstrations, and drug use. Acts of violence and vandalism garnered headlines in the 1970s; although these serious problems were limited to a relatively small number of schools. Drug use displaced "lack of discipline" at the top of the list of concerns on the 1986 Gallup Poll of the Public's Attitudes toward the Public Schools (Elam & Gallup, 1989, p. 42). For the first time in over a decade, respondents to the Gallup Poll did not regard student disrespect and disruptive behavior as their chief concern.

When President George H.W. Bush convened an Education Summit of Governors at the University of Virginia in the fall of 1989, school safety was very much on the minds of participants. Among the eight national education goals that emerged from the historic meeting was the following goal:

By the year 2000, every school in the United States will be free of drugs, violence, and the unauthorized presence of firearms and alcohol and will offer a disciplined environment conducive to learning. (National Education Goals Panel, 1995, p. 13)

In response to the targets set by the nation's governors at the Education Summit, school district leaders around the nation revised codes of student conduct, developed crisis management plans, established "zero tolerance" policies regarding drugs, alcohol, weapons, and violence, and initiated a variety of interventions aimed at helping troubled students. That these measures were unable to prevent the Columbine tragedy and killings at other schools is less a statement about the inadequacy of school districts' responses to safety concerns than a commentary on the availability of weapons and the culture of violence that surrounds many young people.

In an effort to describe trends in school safety over a 50-year period, the author (Duke, 2002, p. 13) identified these five developments:

- Expansion of the range of concerns associated with school safety
- Expansion of the types of school-based responses to safety concerns
- Expansion of the role of government and the courts in matters related to school safety
- Growing politicization of school safety
- Growth in the knowledge base regarding school safety

To appreciate how the range of school safety and discipline concerns has expanded, one need only compare a list of school rules in 1960 and in 2010. In 1960, it was unlikely that there would have been any reference to drug use, bomb threats, or acts of violence. Sexual harassment and hazing certainly existed, but they were not acknowledged in most codes of student behavior. School administrators in 1960 did not have to deal with student use of cell phones or with limiting student access to the internet. The advent of widespread school desegregation during the 1960s ushered in an era of racial tension and conflict between white and African American students. Later, organized gang activity, once largely limited to neighborhoods, spread to campuses, bringing with it the potential for violence. Gang members laid claim to "turf" in schools and on school grounds. Non-gang members who were caught wearing gang colors were subject to beatings.

Student victimization of other students clearly has escalated since 1960, but so, too, have incidents in which school employees victimize students and students victimize school employees. It is not unusual today to open a newspaper and read about a teacher charged with molesting a student or a student caught abusing a teacher.

With the expansion of the range of concerns associated with school safety has come, not surprisingly, an increase in the range of school-based responses to safety concerns. There was a time when matters involving student conduct and school safety were resolved between teachers and students. If the problem was particularly serious, the principal would be involved. Unconstrained by regulations and formalized school discipline plans, educators were relatively free to exercise their discretion when it came to handling student behavior problems.

Contemporary educators must contend with a complex array of policies, procedures, and practices related to discipline and safety. Discipline plans typically identify a range of acceptable sanctions, including counseling, parental involvement, detention, suspension, referral to an alternative program, and expulsion. The traditional response to increasing behavior problems was to promulgate more rules and harsher punishments. Realizing that this approach often has proven to be counter-productive, educators today try to understand what conditions give rise to misconduct and threats to school safety. These efforts often lead to the realization that academic frustration and negative teacher-student relations can contribute to disruptive and destructive behavior. The first line of defense against discipline and safety problems, therefore, may be a focus on providing academic assistance for struggling students and improving relations between teachers and students.

One major reason for the growing complexity of school safety efforts has been the increased role of government and the courts. School personnel in the past enjoyed considerable discretion when it came to handling student behavior. They operated under the principle of *in loco parentis*, meaning that they exercised the authority granted to parents in dealing with children. This authority began to erode during the 1960s when a variety of court decisions established the fact that students have rights, including the right to assemble, the right to express their beliefs, and the right to due process when their access to an education is threatened. The rights of students with disabilities, including serious behavior disorders, came under the protection of the federal government with the passage of Public Law 94-142 in 1975.

The focus on student rights began to be displaced in the late seventies by legislation and court decisions aimed at protecting students and school employees (Duke, 2002, pp. 21–22). Bills were passed by states as well as the federal government to control drugs, alcohol, and weapons on campus. Government funding became available for a host of interventions, special programs, and training related to school safety. The courts upheld the authority of school officials to mete out various forms of punishment, but they also served notice that disciplinary practices must not discriminate against any particular group of students. With the increased role of government and the courts, predictably, came more oversight and paperwork for local educators.

The increasing role of state and federal government in protecting students bespeaks the growing politicization of school safety. People vary considerably in their explanations for the perceived increase in unsafe schools. Consider the aftermath of a school shooting incident. Some individuals indict the lack of strict gun control laws. Others blame parents for failing to exercise greater control over their children. Still others decry the isolation and alienation of troubled teenagers.

Invariably special interest groups form around particular explanations for school safety problems. These groups compete to have their explanations accepted, knowing that gaining such acceptance places them in a good position to influence the determination of a solution. It is in the best interests of a special interest group like the National Rifle Association, for example, to discredit arguments that school violence is attributable to the availability of weapons to young people. Similarly, it is in the best interests of teacher organizations to downplay the role of ineffective teaching in the etiology of school behavior problems.

There also is an economic component to the politicization of school safety. Elsewhere the author (Duke, 2002, p. 23) has noted in this regard,

> Education is big business in the United States. Initiatives designed to make schools safer, whether they involve hiring more school resource officers, building smaller schools, or installing electronic surveillance equipment, carry hefty price tags. Contention typically arises when decisions must be made concerning the allocation of public funds.

The fifth trend involves the expanding knowledge base on school safety. Scholars representing a variety of disciplines have devoted considerable effort to understanding the causes of and cures for youth violence, disruptive behavior, school failure, substance abuse, and other safety-related concerns. Education researchers have zeroed in on behavior disorders, classroom management strategies, and crisis management plans. Much of the research related to school safety has focused on identifying the conditions that give rise to disruptive, violent, and self-destructive behavior in young people. It is important for district leaders to understand that some of these conditions are the result of factors that educators can control or, at least, influence. These factors include the quality of school leadership, teaching effectiveness, student supervision, the availability of assistance for troubled students, the level of training and preparedness for handling emergencies, and the design and condition of school facilities.

This chapter addresses some of the aspects of school safety and student behavior on which district leaders can have the greatest impact. The questions below are used to focus the discussion.

The Challenges of School Safety

1. How can school district leaders provide a well-balanced approach to school discipline and safety?

2. What responsibilities must school district leaders undertake to promote safe and orderly schools?

3. In what areas of school discipline and safety should district leaders expect to encounter controversy and conflict?

A BALANCED APPROACH TO DISCIPLINE AND SAFETY

Schools must be rule-governed organizations, but they need not be prisons. Educators understand that learning is not facilitated when order is achieved through threats and punitive measures. Rules are no substitute for relationships, nor is coercion preferable to caring. Working with principals and teachers, school district leaders should strive to implement a balanced approach to school discipline and safety, one that promotes responsible behavior as well as discourages irresponsible behavior.

A balanced approach to discipline and safety involves measures designed for (1) problem intervention, (2) problem prevention, and (3) problem management (Duke, 2002, pp. 18–21).

Problem intervention measures focus on dealing effectively with discipline problems and other threats to school safety that actually have occurred. The goal is "to minimize the negative impact of these acts and ensure that they do not recur" (Duke, 2002, p. 19). Examples of intervention measures include the following:

Type of Measure	Examples
Direct communication	Warning, direct order
Counseling	Behavior contracts, therapy
Behavior modification	Coordinated plan for reinforcing appropriate behavior
Punishment	Loss of privileges, detention, work detail, in-school suspension, expulsion
Alternative placement	Alternative education program, homebound instruction
Parental involvement	Parent-teacher conference

Intervention measures vary in their effectiveness, depending on such factors as student motivation and the consistency with which the intervention is applied. It is of little value to negotiate a behavior contract with a student and then fail to monitor the student's compliance with contractual expectations. Suspension is unlikely to be an effective deterrent to chronic absenteeism. Because no single intervention is likely to be effective with every student or for every disciplinary offense, district leaders should encourage schools to develop a continuum of interventions. Interventions should be evaluated on a regular basis to determine whether certain interventions are failing to correct discipline and safety problems.

It is always preferable to prevent problems from occurring in the first place. To develop problem prevention measures, educators must understand the causes of inappropriate and dangerous behavior. Educators know, for example, that students who experience academic frustration are more likely than successful students to engage in behaviors that are harmful to themselves and others.

One traditional measure intended to prevent problems are school rules. Rules are important because they inform students about what they are expected to do and not to do. It is essential for young people to learn how to function in rule-governed organizations in order for them to succeed later in life. School districts usually require every school to have a code of student conduct or list of rules. In some districts, the same set of rules is required of every school; in other districts, the development of rules is left largely to school-based personnel. Rules often are accompanied by specified punishments for particular rule violations.

Educators must be careful to establish rules that are reasonable and enforceable. Too many rules can overwhelm those charged with enforcement, invite inconsistent discipline, and encourage students to try and "beat the system." The mere presence of rules and punishments, of course, is no guarantee that students will behave appropriately. Rules must be enforced consistently, and punishments must be applied fairly. Even then, some students still may choose to act out. To supplement rules and punishments, a range of preventive measures is necessary. Several examples appear below:

Type of measure	Example
Rules	Clear statements of how students should/should not behave
Punishment	Loss of privileges, detention, work detail, in-school suspension, expulsion
Instructional assistance	Tutoring and other forms of targeted help for students who struggle academically
Special skills training	Anger management
Affective education	Self-esteem enhancement, emotional intelligence training
Values education	Character education
Positive reinforcement	Incentives/privileges for appropriate behavior
Parent education	Parenting skills classes

Many preventive measures require considerable training for school staff. District leaders can assist by securing the resources to support staff development. They also can see to it that preventive measures are evaluated periodically to determine their effectiveness in reducing discipline and safety problems.

The third component of a balanced approach to school safety and discipline is problem management. Problem management presumes that disruptive behavior and threats to safety, no matter how comprehensive the preventive measures, are unlikely to be completely eliminated. Various mechanisms therefore should be in place to ensure that, when problems do arise, their impact on students, staff, and school operations is minimized. Mis-handling an incident has the potential to spiral downward, leading to worse problems and placing additional individuals in harm's way. A critical element in problem management is a comprehensive crisis management plan for every school. District leaders are expected, and in many states required, to see to it that such plans are in place and that district personnel are trained to handle serious threats to safety. Some of the key measures associated with problem management are listed below:

Type of measure	Example
Specialized personnel	Deans of students, school resource officers, crisis counselors
Team troubleshooting	Rumor monitoring, data analysis, early detection of troubled students, threat assessment
Surveillance	Video cameras on buses and in poorly supervised areas of schools
Conflict resolution measures	Ombudsman, peer mediation
Environmental design	Sub-dividing large schools into smaller units, improved lighting, controlled access to school
Contingency planning	Development of crisis management plans, practice drills

Tragic events in recent decades demonstrate that schools no longer are sanctuaries of safety. Criminal acts that used to occur "in the streets" have moved into school classrooms and corridors. District leaders, even those in seemingly safe and secure suburbs, cannot afford to assume that their schools are immune to violence, vandalism, and self-destructive behavior. By implementing measures for problem intervention, prevention, and management, district leaders can reduce the likelihood of serious problems and ensure that school personnel are prepared to handle discipline and safety problems when and if they do occur.

DISTRICT RESPONSIBILITIES

The front lines in efforts to ensure school safety are schools and classrooms, but this does not mean that substantial central office support is not essential. There is much that district leaders must do to underwrite efforts by school administrators and staff to address discipline and safety concerns. Among the most important safety-related responsibilities are: (1) developing and implementing policies related to school safety, (2) collecting and analyzing school safety data, (3) handling hearings and appeals related to student discipline, (4) coordinating relations with local law enforcement agencies, (5) supervising the crisis management and contingency planning process, (6) overseeing the placement of disruptive and dangerous students, and (7) ensuring that school facilities are safe. Let us take a closer look at each of these responsibilities.

School Safety Policies

A review of the *Parent-Student Handbook* (2004) for the Los Angeles Unified School District (L.A.U.S.D.)reveals an extensive list of safety-related policies. They include "zero tolerance" policies regarding alcohol, tobacco, drugs, and firearms; a policy requiring "safe school plans" that address violence prevention, emergency preparedness, traffic safety, and crisis intervention; and policies related to improper relations between school district employees and students. Additional policies define and prohibit sexual harassment, control visitors to school campuses, and specify the offenses that will result in mandatory expulsion. These offenses include possession of a firearm, brandishing a knife at another person, unlawfully selling a controlled substance, committing or attempting to commit a sexual assault or committing a sexual battery, and possession of an explosive device.

The *Parent-Student Handbook* goes on to present a variety of policies related to student conduct and the maintenance of an orderly learning environment. There are policies pertaining to student dress codes, truancy, student demonstrations, and student searches. Finally, the handbook addresses several environmental safety matters, including asbestos management and pest control.

In addition to the more obvious aspects of school safety where policies would be expected, there are an increasing number of less obvious matters that reveal just how complex has become the protection of students. School districts, for example, are responsible for student safety from the time students arrive at school bus stops to the time they are returned to these points. Policies govern student conduct on school buses and during field trips, at school-sponsored events, and during summer programs. School districts have policies related to the disciplining of special education students, bullying, hazing, hate crimes, the use of corporal punishment, and the degree of discretion that can be exercised by school administrators when meting out punishment. Protecting students also entails policies related to access to students by non-custodial parents and monitoring of potential child abuse and neglect.

There is no question that the proliferation of safety-related policies has contributed greatly to the growing complexity of school district leadership. Failure to have a policy can lead to charges of contributory negligence. Once policies have been promulgated, district leaders must ensure that school personnel are aware of them, that any training related to the policies is provided, and that the policies are implemented consistently and in a manner that does not discriminate against any particular group of students. Policies that fail to achieve their intended goals should be re-evaluated and adjusted.

School Safety Data

It is the responsibility of school district leaders to see that data on student discipline and school safety is collected, analyzed, and used to guide improvement efforts. As the author (Duke, 2002, p. 134) contends, "When members of the school community lose track of school safety data, they diminish their capacity to identify problems, set improvement goals, and celebrate successes." School districts are required to compile certain kinds of school safety data, including weapons violations, acts of violence, suspensions, and expulsions. Other kinds of data also can be of value in monitoring and evaluating school discipline and safety.

Most schools document disciplinary referrals in some way. It is not necessarily the case, however, that referral data is systematically and regularly reviewed. Such reviews can indicate the most and least frequent disciplinary offenses and the teachers who account for the most and least referrals. This information can help to pinpoint staff development needs and set improvement goals. Referral data also can reveal times of the day and the week when problems are most likely to arise.

School districts that have established data warehouses and that require all safety and discipline-related incidents to be reported are in a good position to track trends over time and identify growing problems that need focused attention. Broward County (Florida) routinely compiles and analyzes school safety data. Table 7.1 contains data for the three-year period from 2004 to 2007 (Blasik, 2007, p. 7).

Table 7.1
Number and Percentage of Total Incidents by Type of Incident, 2004–2005 through 2006–2007

Type of Incident	2004–2005		2005–2006		2006–2007	
	n	%	n	%	n	%
Crimes Against Persons	4,700	51.0	4,240	54.1	6,242	64.2
Battery	1,036	11.2	889	11.3	1,244	12.8
Bullying/Harassment[a]	—	—	—	—	871	9.0
Fighting	2,603	28.3	2,471	31.5	2,937	30.2
Homicide	0	0.0	0	0.0	0	0.0
Kidnapping	0	0.0	2	<0.1	1	<0.1
Robbery	35	0.4	22	0.3	32	0.3
Sexual Battery	13	0.1	12	0.2	11	0.1
Sexual Harassment	252	2.7	198	2.5	274	2.8
Sexual Offense/Other	256	2.8	194	2.5	258	2.7
Threat/Intimidation	505	5.5	452	5.8	614	6.3
Property Offenses	796	8.6	543	7.0	492	5.1
Arson	28	0.3	24	0.3	11	0.1
Breaking & Entering/Burglary	64	0.7	102	1.3	74	0.8
Motor Vehicle Theft[b]	6	0.1	—	—	—	—
Larceny/Theft ($50+/$100+)[c]	450	4.9	264	3.4	264	2.7
Vandalism ($100+/$1,000+)[c]	248	2.7	153	2.0	143	1.5
Alcohol/Tobacco/Drug Offenses	864	9.4	812	10.4	725	7.5
Alcohol	105	1.1	74	0.9	81	0.8
Drug[d]	462	5.0	506	6.5	392	4.0
Tobacco	297	3.2	232	3.0	252	2.6
Other Offenses	2,854	31.0	2.245	28.6	2,259	23.2
Disorderly Conduct[b]	1,262	13.7	—	—	—	—
Disruption on Campus-Major[e]	—	—	801	10.2	827	8.5
Trespassing	153	1.7	129	1.6	110	1.1
Weapons Possession	527	5.7	445	5.7	491	5.1
Unclassified/Other Major	912	9.9	870	11.1	831	8.6
Grand Total	**9,214**	**100.0**	**7,840**	**100.0**	**9,718**	**100.0**

[a] Bullying/Harassment was added as a SESIR incident in 2006–2007.
[b] Motor Vehicle Theft and Disorderly Conduct were removed as SESIR incidents in 2005–2006. Motor Vehicle Theft is currently reported under Larceny/Theft
[c] In 2005–2006 the value criteria were raised for reporting Larceny/Theft ($50 to $300) and Vandalism ($100 to $1,000) as SESIR incidents.
[d] Includes both DRD (Drug Sale/Distribution-Excluding Alcohol) and DRU (Drug Use/Possession-excluding Alcohol) for 2005–2006 and 2006–2007.
[e] Disruption on Campus-Major was added as a SESIR incident in 2005–2006.

A quick glance at the data in Table 7.1 reveals a steady increase in incidents involving crimes against persons. Other major categories of safety-related problems appear to be declining. District leaders reviewing this data might decide to concentrate efforts on addressing fighting, battery, and intimidation. Without regular incident reports like the one from Broward County, district leaders can only guess at where to focus safety initiatives.

Incidents involving rule violations are one kind of data that needs to be monitored. Threats are another. A relatively recent addition to school safety measures involves student threat assessment. Cornell and Sheras (2006) recommend that every school have a threat assessment team that can respond quickly when threats are reported. They go on to provide a seven step process to guide student threat assessment, including evaluating the threat and determining whether the threat is transient or substantive. Transient threats may be handled with a reprimand and parental notification, while substantive threats demand more concerted actions, possibly involving notification of potential victims and involvement of Law enforcement agencies.

Another valuable kind of data involves the location of safety-related problems. Astor, Meyer, and Behre (1999), for example, gave students and teachers in five high schools maps of their schools and asked them to identify the locations and times of the most violent acts in and around the school. By locating the most dangerous areas of schools and school grounds, school and district leaders can deploy personnel more effectively to prevent problems.

The most useful school safety data often comes from students. They frequently are aware of impending fights, troubled classmates, drug-related activity, and the presence on campus of gangs. Principals who are successful in maintaining safe and orderly schools find ways to tap student knowledge and monitor rumors.

School district leaders may not be involved directly in the collection of school-based safety data, but they must create the expectation that principals will regularly collect and review data. District leaders, in turn, are responsible for analyzing data across all schools in order to identify pervasive problems and develop strategies to address them. If gang activity is found in most schools, for example, district leaders may need to provide appropriate staff development for school personnel and enlist the assistance of local law enforcement agencies. As the spokespersons for school systems, district leaders also are responsible for sharing school safety data with the public. Not only does the public need to know how safe their schools are in order to assist schools in addressing threats to safety, they have a right to know. Concealing safety problems from local citizens is almost never an appropriate course of action.

Hearings and Appeals

Unlike the justice system where provisions are made to separate the functions of police, jury, and judge, schools often assign all three functions to the same individual, typically the principal or assistant principal. Failure to separate these functions sometimes leads to challengeable judgments and questionable sanctions. Because public education is a right protected by the Constitution, any action that threatens a student's access to an education requires due process. When a student faces expulsion for an act deemed threatening to his classmates, he is entitled to a hearing. District leaders are responsible for providing a hearing process in which the student or his advocate presents his side of the story. Depending on the results of the hearing and the severity of the sanction, the student also may be granted an appeal. Final action on expulsion from school, the most severe sanction, typically requires action by the school board.

School districts, of course, are subject to state and federal laws, including laws related to civil rights. There is considerable evidence to indicate that a disproportionate number of African American students are expelled each year from public schools (Fenning & Rose, 2007). It is therefore possible that African American students, or students from other minority groups, may challenge expulsions and other serious disciplinary actions such as placement in a special program on the grounds that they have been victims of discrimination. School district leaders must monitor disciplinary actions to determine whether such claims are valid.

Relations with Local Law Enforcement Agencies

Most of the most serious threats to school safety constitute criminal acts. Educators are not police officers. When crimes are committed in and around schools, it is essential that local law enforcement personnel be involved. The need for close working relations between school district leaders and local law enforcement agencies does not end, however, with intervention to deal with criminal acts. Local police and sheriff's offices also can play an important role in preventing safety problems.

Some school district leaders convene regular meetings with representatives of law enforcement agencies to share information. Local police, for example, may be able to alert school personnel about gang-related activities that could impact schools. Regular contact between districts and police departments also provide opportunities to review and fine tune contingency plans for handling various emergencies. Research on effective school-police partnerships indicate that these initiatives are characterized by community awareness and support, counseling services for students, and adequate support services for teachers and administrators (Brady, Balmer, & Phenix, 2007, p. 474). Just deploying police officers into schools, in other words, is not enough. Their presence must be accompanied by other measures designed to involve, train, and support stakeholders.

Having close working relations between school districts and police departments can lead to coordinated programs aimed at reducing safety threats and preparing students and staff members to handle emergencies. When Danville Public Schools experienced an increase in high school absenteeism, for instance, district and police officials worked out an agreement whereby police officers would pick up truants and deliver them to a central, district-operated truancy center for processing. This initiative succeeded in substantially reducing absenteeism as well as youth-related crimes during school hours.

Larger school systems may maintain their own security unit, but many districts prefer to retain the services of school resource officers from local law enforcement agencies. When school resource officers are assigned to schools, it is important for district leaders and police officials to agree on their responsibilities. Are school resource officers (SROs), for example, expected to provide in-class instruction, make arrests, report criminal activities, and be present during on-campus interrogations? Figure 7.1 provides an example of a Memo of Understanding between Danville Public Schools and the Danville Police Department (Duke, 2002, pp. 197–198). The memorandum of understanding (MOU) carefully spells out the roles and responsibilities of both school officials and law enforcement officers.

Crisis Management and Contingency Planning

One of the greatest safety-related challenges for district leaders concerns emergency preparedness. Developing a comprehensive crisis management plan (CMP) for the district and for each school is essential, but insufficient alone to ensure a reasonable level of preparedness. District and school personnel must be trained on how to implement CMPs. Community members must be informed. Students must be drilled in how to respond during emergencies. The steps that need to be taken to handle various crises must be specified. When new personnel are hired, they must be apprised of the CMP.

MEMORANDUM OF UNDERSTANDING (MOU)

The following MOU is a joint understanding of the Danville Police Department and the Danville Public School System concerning the position of a School Resource Officer or a D.A.R.E. Officer working with the Danville Public School System.

CHAIN OF COMMAND

All Danville Police Officers working in the position of a school Resource or D.A.R.E. Officer will be under the command of the Captain of Patrol in his everyday activities. However, each officer working as either an SRO or D.A.R.E. Officer will be assigned to a specific Captain at the Police Department for days off, vacation days, evaluation purposes, etc. If the Captain of Patrol cannot be located for one reason or another, the chain of command would be followed with the Assistant Chief being next, and then the Chief of Police.

LAW ENFORCEMENT'S ROLES AND RESPONSIBILITIES

All officers working as either SRO or D.A.R.E. Officer will first and foremost be a law enforcement (LE) Officer on campus. He or she will wear the uniform in accordance with the policy of the Danville Police Department, which will include their duty weapons. All officers will act as role models to all students in their everyday activities. Each officer will have the responsibility to be a resource to the school administrators, teachers, parents and students for conference or counseling, and present specialized educational programs such as Class Action, D.A.R.E. Core lessons, etc. The SRO/D.A.R.E. Officer will implement reactive m4ethods of SRO policing; reporting procedures, police reports, arrests, intervention, and respond to calls on campus. The SRO/D.A.R.E. Officers will gather intelligence information on gangs, burglaries, juvenile crimes, etc. The SRO/D.A.R.E. Officer will determine whether law enforcement action is appropriate and will take action as required. As soon as possible the SRO/D.A.R.E. Officer will make the principal of the school aware of the situation or action. The SRO/D.A.R.E. Officer will assist the principal in developing plans and strategies to prevent and/or minimize dangerous situations on or near the campus. The SRO/D.A.R.E. Officer will be responsible to fill out and maintain a copy of all School Safety Assessments, which will be filled out twice within a school year. Recommendations concerning school safety issues will be forwarded to the school principal as soon as possible. I twill also be the responsibility of the SRO/D.A.R.E. Officer to fill out a student Incident Report on each incident and send this form to the Department of Criminal Justice Services each month as ordered in the policy of Danville Police Department. The SRO/D.A.R.E. Officer will be consistent and fair, use good judgment and discretion, show respect for students and faculty, and show sincere concern for the school community.

SCHOOL'S ROLES AND RESPONSIBILITIES

It will be the responsibility of the principal of each school where a School Resource Officer or D.A.R.E. Officer works, to inform him or her as to problems occurring in and around their school. However, no SRO/D.A.R.E. Officer shall be used for regularly assigned lunch room duties, bus duties, hall monitors, etc. If there is a problem area, the officer may assist the school until the problem is solved. It will be the responsibility of all faculty members to report all violations of the law to SRO/D.A.R.E. Officer. This will assist the officers with the type of programs that they need to emphasize as well as assist the police with problems that occur after school hours. It will be the responsibility of the principal to assist the officers working their schools in school safety assessments as required by HB 1851. This will be done twice within a school year. All school administrators and police officers will work together to make a safe school environment conducive to learning.

TIME LIMIT OF REVIEW

The Memorandum of Understanding will be reviewed by the Police Department and the Danville Public School System every two years.

Figure 7.1 Danville Public Schools and Danville Police Department.

The Virginia Department of Education's Resource *Guide for Crisis Management in Schools* (1998) identifies 29 different situations that are likely to require crisis management planning:

Accidents at school
Accidents to and from school
Aircraft disaster
Allergic reaction
Angry parent/employee/patron
Assault by intruder
Bomb threat
Bus accident
Chemical spill
Childnapping/lost child
Death
Disaster (tornado, bomb)
Disaster preventing dismissal
Fighting
Fire/arson/explosives
Gas lead
Hostage/armed
Injury
Intruder/trespasser
Life-threatening crisis
Perceived crises

Poisoning
Power failure/lines down
Rape
Shooting/wounding
Suicide/threats
Vandalism
Weapons situation
Weather

Plans for responding to these situations are likely to involve some degree of overlap. Generally speaking, there are two kinds of CMPs, those that call for evacuation and those that call for lockdown. A bomb threat requires all students and staff members to leave the building. An armed intruder necessitates a lockdown. The implementation and coordination of CMPs calls for a Crisis Management Team (CMT). The central office and every school should have a designated CMT. The members of the CMT receive special training, above and beyond that provided for all personnel. Each CMT member has specific responsibilities during particular emergencies. It is up to district leaders to make certain that every school has a CMT and that CMT members receive the necessary training to handle various emergencies.

District leaders' responsibilities do not end with the implementation of CMPs. Depending on the nature of the crisis, the superintendent or her designee may need to coordinate crisis response and serve as the official spokesperson for the school system. Once a crisis has ended, district leaders should conduct a thorough after-crisis review to determine what components of the CMP worked well and what components did not work well. Such a review after the Columbine shootings, for example, revealed the fact that police officers did not possess a map of the school. As a result, they were unable to pinpoint the location of the cafeteria and other locations where students had been shot.

Placement of Dangerous and Disruptive Students

When individual students have been deemed to pose a threat to their classmates and teachers, it is the responsibility of district leaders to determine whether an alternative placement is warranted. In some cases, of course, district personnel initially may be unaware of a student's potential to cause harm. Unless the student actually has been convicted of a crime, police may be prevented from officially notifying district authorities of any dangerous activities in which the student has been involved. When district and local law enforcement representatives meet on a regular basis, however, it is often possible for threat-related information to be shared "informally."

When the reason why a student is disruptive or dangerous is related to a confirmed disability, the school district is required by law to place the student in an appropriate educational setting. Expulsion is not an option. While special education laws permit students with disabilities to be suspended, a suspension of more than ten days is considered to be a change of placement (O'Reilly & Green, 1992, pp. 164–166). As a consequence, students must be accorded due process, including a review of the student's Individual Education Plan (IEP).

In an effort to address the educational needs of students who pose a threat to their classmates, larger school systems frequently operate alternative schools and programs. These alternatives typically are staffed with specialists who are prepared to handle disruptive behavior. Another option, especially for smaller school systems, involves paying tuition so that troubled students can attend a privately operated program. A third possibility is placing the student on homebound instruction. The decision of where to place disruptive and dangerous students ultimately must be made by the central office. Superintendents typically establish a committee to review student cases and recommend placements. Parents, of course, have the right to challenge alternative placements recommendations.

Safe Facilities

Another area where district leaders are expected to be responsible involves the safety of school facilities, including permanent structures, portables, and school grounds. Ensuring safe facilities starts on the drafting table. District leaders should work closely with architects and designers to make certain that new and renovated facilities are designed in ways that reduce the likelihood of safety problems (Duke, 2002, pp. 170–176). Safety-related design measures include corridors that are wide enough to accommodate traffic flow, elimination of difficult-to-supervise areas, good lighting and ventilation, and adequate access for students with physical disabilities. Areas where students are dropped off and picked up should be designed so that bus zones are separated from drop-off points for students arriving in automobiles and on foot. School grounds must be free of obstacles that obstruct supervision and inhibit effective security.

Maintaining facilities represents another dimension of school safety. District leaders along with school-based personnel are expected to see that repairs and upgrades are made in a timely manner so that students and staff members are not placed at risk. Facilities, especially older structures, may require asbestos and lead paint removal, frequent monitoring for mold and mildew, and improvements to heating and cooling systems. While it is tempting to skimp on preventive maintenance, particularly during times when resources are in short supply, doing so often leads to greater expenditures in the long run and increases the likelihood of facilities-related accidents.

Access to facilities and surveillance represent additional safety challenges for school and district leaders. Regardless of whether schools are located in high-crime areas or tranquil neighborhoods, access to schools and school grounds needs to be controlled to prevent intruders from going undetected. Locating offices near entrances, placing alarms on doors in poorly supervised areas, installing electronic surveillance equipment, requiring students and staff members to have identification badges, and stationing official "greeters" at school entrances are some of the ways that school districts are controlling access to schools. In schools with a record of weapons offenses, portal-style and hand-held metal scanners may be employed. Facilities safety has become a highly specialized field requiring the involvement of experts. Arrangements to retain the services of these individuals are best made by the central office.

SCHOOL SAFETY CONTROVERSIES

Everyone agrees that students and staff members should learn and teach in safe and orderly schools, but opinions vary as to how best to achieve safety and order. Consider the preceding discussion of controlled access and surveillance. Critics argue that surveillance equipment constitutes an invasion of privacy. The use of metal detectors at school entrances may be challenged because it causes the inflow of students to back up, thereby increasing the likelihood of disruptions. Locking school doors can violate fire codes.

This section examines several aspects of school discipline and safety where district leaders can expect differences of opinion and possible controversy. These include discriminatory disciplinary practices, zero tolerance policies, student searches, and what to do with troubled students.

Discriminatory Practices

Mention already has been made of concerns that a disproportionate number of African American students receive severe punishments in many schools. The same also is true for Hispanic students. Why these students should be more likely to receive severe punishments such as suspension and expulsion is open to debate. One position is that minority students growing up in impoverished homes fail to acquire the social skills needed to conform to behavioral expectations in schools (Casella, 2003). Others contend that the "fear of losing control in the classroom on the part of educators, rather than an actual threat of dangerousness," results in educators over-reacting to minor misconduct by students from backgrounds that are different from their own (Fenning & Rose, 2007, p. 537). Pressure to meet mandated requirements for academic achievement also may compel teachers and administrators to quickly remove from classrooms students perceived to pose a threat to the maintenance of orderly learning environments. Little effort may be made to try and understand why certain students seem inclined to act out.

It is impossible for school districts to fulfill the mission of educational equity if district leaders allow certain groups of students to receive a disproportionate number of suspensions and expulsions. Furthermore, there is little evidence that these severe punishments are effective in meeting the needs of *any* students (Mayer, 1995; Sugai & Horner, 2002). Rather than supporting the removal of students, district leaders need to encourage school-based personnel to create more caring and less punitive learning environments.

Fenning and Rose (2007) suggest four steps that need to be taken to reduce the likelihood of discriminatory disciplinary practices. Step one calls for a continuous review of discipline data to determine what infractions result in severe punishments. District leaders should be especially vigilant regarding any tendency for certain groups to receive suspensions for relatively minor, nonviolent offenses. Step two requires the formation of collaborative, school-based discipline teams. An important function of these teams, made up of teachers and administrators, is to clarify behavioral expectations. School personnel can reduce the likelihood of discriminatory discipline by reaching agreement about what constitutes inappropriate conduct and disruptive behavior.

The third step in the Fenning and Rose (2007) prescription involves professional development designed to promote "cultural competence." It is critical that teachers and administrators from backgrounds that differ from their students' backgrounds understand the norms and values of all groups of students. Step four entails the development of proactive school policies. Proactive policies focus on teaching students how to handle conflict and potentially dangerous situations rather than punishing them for inappropriate behavior. The overall message of these measures is clear—the cause of school discipline and safety is vitally important, but it does not justify discriminatory practices and highly punitive learning environments.

Zero Tolerance Policies

Few aspects of school safety have generated as much concern and controversy as so-called zero tolerance policies. Intended to address the most serious threats to safety, including bringing weapons to school and physical assault, zero tolerance policies call for immediate suspension and eventual expulsion, following due process procedures. By eliminating administrative discretion in cases involving zero tolerance offenses, these policies have resulted in a number of questionable actions.

Consider the case of "look alike" weapons. A student in northern Virginia was not allowed to graduate because a water pistol was spotted on the back seat of his car in the school parking lot. The water pistol turned out to be a prop for a school play. A first grade South Carolina boy who kissed a classmate was accused of sexual harassment and suspended. A fourth grade student from Henrico County, Virginia, brought an unopened can of "Billy Beer" (President Jimmy Carter's brother had a novelty beer named after him and it became a collector's item) to show-and-tell at school and was suspended because of a zero tolerance policy for alcohol on campus. The student and her parents had to participate in an alcohol prevention class in order for the young student to be reinstated. Cases such as these demonstrate the limitations of zero tolerance policies. It is ironic that no such draconian policy obtains in a court of law. Mitigating circumstances and the merits of each case must always be taken into account.

The problem with zero tolerance policies is perhaps most apparent when it comes to students who get into fights at school. When students are caught fighting and the school has a zero tolerance policy for fighting, typically all involved students are suspended. This means that a student who is attacked by another student cannot defend himself without risking suspension and eventual expulsion. Discouraging a student from defending himself could result in serious injury. The fairness of such a policy has to be questioned.

School district leaders are responsible for the safety of staff and students, but they also are expected to make certain that individuals are treated fairly and with compassion. Where zero tolerance policies are in effect, district leaders should do everything in their power to see that the policies are applied only to the most serious threats to safety. This means clarifying what should be done about such "gray area" acts as bringing aspirin to school and defending one's self against an assailant.

Student Searches

Many matters related to school discipline and safety cannot be left to the discretion of school-based personnel. These matters involve laws and civil rights. District leaders are expected to see that appropriate policies that reflect these laws and civil rights are adopted and implemented. A good illustration of an aspect of school safety requiring a uniform policy concerns student searches.

Periodically the courts weigh in on the subject of student searches. In 2009 the case of a 13-year-old girl who was strip-searched at her Arizona school made it all the way to the U.S. Supreme Court. The case considered "where to draw the line between protecting student privacy rights and allowing school officials to take steps to ensure a safe environment" (Robelen, 2009, p. 1). The search was prompted by the belief that the girl had prescription-strength ibuprofen in her possession, thereby violating the school system's anti-drug policy. The high court eventually ruled against school authorities, contending that such an intrusive search was unjustified given the clear lack of serious threat to other students (Barnes, 2009, p. A-1).

The issue of student searches turns out to be multi-faceted and complex. Drug-testing of students, for example, is considered to be a form of search, since it entails an invasion of privacy. Then there are searches involving lockers, backpacks, and automobiles. The clearest statement by the courts regarding searches was provided in the 1985 case, *New Jersey v. T.L.O.* (Dowling-Sendor, 1997). The court determined that school officials should not be held to the same standard—"probable cause"—as police authorities. Two criteria had to met, however, for a school-based search to be warranted:

1. The search must be justified at its inception. In other words, reasonable suspicion that the search will reveal evidence of a violation must exist prior to beginning the search.
2. The search must be conducted in "a way that is reasonably related in scope to the facts that justified the search to begin with." (Dowling-Sendor, 1997, p. 18)

The second criterion means that school officials need to take into consideration such matters as the age and gender of the student and the nature of the violation before conducting their search. Strip-searching a kindergartner to locate a quarter she supposedly had stolen, for example, would be unwarranted.

District leaders are obliged to specify not only the circumstances that warrant student searches, but also the procedures by which searches are to be conducted. A good example of a policy that addresses various aspects of student searches is contained in the *Parent-Student Handbook* for Los Angeles Unified School District (2004). The policy includes provisions for the use of metal detectors in conducting searches.

Student Searches

The 4th Amendment of the United States Constitution protects individuals from unlawful searches. However, the law allows school officials to conduct searches of students under certain limited circumstances.

A. *Searches Based on Reasonable Suspicion*
   If a student has engaged in conduct that causes an administrator to have *reasonable suspicion* that the student has committed, or is about to commit, a crime or has violated statutory laws or school rules, the administrator may conduct a search of that student. The administrator must:
   - Be able to articulate the reason for his or her suspicion and the facts and/or circumstances surrounding a specific incident.
   - Be able to reasonably connect the student to a specific incident, crime or rule or stature violation.
   - Have relied on recent, credible information from personal knowledge and/or other eyewitnesses.
   - Ensure that a search based on reasonable suspicion is not excessively intrusive in light of the student's age and gender and the nature of the offense.

When conducting a student search based on reasonable suspicion, school officials must adhere to the following practices:
   - Conduct the search only if there are clear and specific reasons for suspicion and there are facts that connect the student to a specific incident or misconduct.

Jackets, purses, pockets, back packs, bags, and containers in the student's possession may be searched to the extent reasonably necessary.
Under no conditions may a body or strip search be conducted.
Only school officials of the same sex as the student being searched may conduct the search.
Searches based on reasonable suspicion must be conducted in a private area where the search will not be visible to other students or staff (except for a school administrator or designee witness, also of the same sex).

B. *Random Metal Detector Searches*
   California courts and the California Attorney General's Office have approved the use of random metal detector searches for weapons. Random use of metal detectors is appropriate only if:

- The method of selection of students to be searched is genuinely random.
- Students selected to participate in random metal detector searches are selected without regard to personally identifiable characteristics such as race, gender, surname, group affiliation, or past history of misconduct (i.e. selection is *random*).
- The searches are minimally intrusive.
- School officials provide parents and students with advanced and detailed notice of the random metal detector search procedures.

If, as a result of a metal detector search, *reasonable suspicion* arises that a particular student may have a weapon, school officials may conduct a search of that student, in a private area, in accordance with the above guidelines for reasonable suspicion searches.

The L.A.U.S.D. policy follows the guidelines laid out in *New Jersey v. T.L.O.* While the policy allows searches of students' backpacks and coats, it specifically forbids body or strip searches. Searches must be conducted in a private area by a school official of the same sex as the student. With regard to the use of metal detectors, school officials are expressly prevented from "profiling" students. Searches using metal detectors must be based on reasonable suspicion and conducted in a completely random manner. Advanced notice of random searches must be provided to students and parents.

With regard to locker searches, the courts have provided school officials with greater latitude than they have regarding body searches. Lockers are regarded as school district, not student property. Drug-sniffing dogs may be used in conducting locker searches. When it comes to using dogs for body searches, though, school officials must possess a high level of reasonable suspicion (Duke, 2002, p. 216).

Unlike lockers, automobiles are not district property. Unless weapons or contraband are in plain view, school officials probably should avoid searching automobiles. If reasonable suspicion exists that an automobile contains an unlawful substance or a weapon, a prudent policy would be to have school officials detain the student driver until the student's parents and law enforcement authorities arrive on the scene. Because district policies are always subject to challenge in the courts, district leaders are advised to have all school discipline and safety policies reviewed by legal counsel prior to formal adoption by the school board.

Handling Troubled Students

Opinions vary greatly regarding how best to handle students who are prone to disrespect and disruption. These are students who are not violent, but who have a track record of substantial misconduct and who often make it difficult for teachers to teach and classmates to learn. In many cases, they are capable of performing well academically.

Advocates of behavior modification strategies suggest that rewarding disruptive students for behaving appropriately can be an effective intervention, one that is clearly preferable to punishing them for misbehaving (Duke, 2002, pp. 77–79). Critics, however, point out that such approaches send the wrong message to other students who behave appropriately day in and day out. Kohn (1996, pp. 32–36) notes that students should obey school and classroom rules because it is the right thing to do, not because they stand to be rewarded.

The matter of whether or not to use rewards as a strategy for handling troubled students illustrates a dilemma that district leaders frequently confront. Should they opt for a course of action that is ethically correct or one that has been shown to be effective? It may be unfair to reward disruptive students when they do not disrupt, but overlook students who always behave appropriately. Yet, what if this approach succeeds in reducing disruptive behaviors? Perhaps the best strategy is the one where educators "develop a reasonable balance between proactive and reactive consequences" (Walker, Colvin, & Ramsey, 1995, p. 142). As is the case for any policy, district leaders should always consider possible unintended as well as intended outcomes.

Another area of controversy concerns the use of drugs to control the behavior of troubled students. Antipsychotic drugs (tranquilizers), antidepressants, and stimulants have been used to control various behavior disorders while young people are in school. There is evidence that drug therapy can be effective, but it is by no means a panacea. Breggin (2000) points out that some drugs can have an effect opposite of what is intended. Antidepressants, for example, may cause some young people to feel invincible, thereby causing them to behave in dangerous ways. Violent behavior has been linked to the use of certain stimulants like Ritalin (Breggin, 2000, pp. 138–140). And what about the message that drug therapy conveys to young people? Aren't we trying to discourage drug dependency? Once again, district leaders may be called on to steer a course between what is right and what is effective.

In some cases, troubled students pose a greater threat to themselves than to their classmates. Are school personnel obliged to take steps to prevent students from harming themselves? In May 1995 a U.S. District Court in Tampa ruled that a Florida school district was partly to blame for the suicide of a 13-year-old student (Portner, 1995). The student tried to hang himself in the school's restroom the day before he took his life. When he was found, the school administrator read passages from the Bible to the student, but did not notify the student's mother or take any other action. The court determined that the administrator had failed to exhibit "reasonable care" in handling the incident. Poland (1994, p. 184) observes that the key issue in cases of suicide is not whether the school *caused* the suicide, but whether the school took reasonable steps to prevent it. District leaders are obliged to see that school-based personnel understand what is entailed in these "reasonable steps."

The business literature is full of advice regarding the importance of a focused mission for organizations that aspire to greatness. Many school district leaders probably would like nothing more than to be able to focus exclusively on the academic development of young people. Unfortunately, young people do not leave their psychological issues, dysfunctional beliefs, and emotional problems at home when they come to school. It is imperative that school personnel are prepared (1) to recognize when students are struggling with both academic and non-academic challenges and (2) to offer appropriate assistance or, if the challenges are too great, see that assistance is provided by specialists. For many troubled young people, school offers the only opportunity to receive the help they need to overcome their problems.

EXECUTIVE CONCLUSION

Most schools are reasonably safe and disciplined environments, but that does not mean that they are immune from periodic disruptions and threats to student safety. Over the years, the sources of disruptions and the types of safety threats may have changed, but the need for educators to be vigilant and prepared for emergencies has remained constant. The challenge for district leaders is to promote vigilance and preparedness without inducing panic or creating prison-like schools.

Efforts by district leaders to ensure school safety do not occur in a vacuum. They take place in environments characterized by competing opinions about how best to achieve order and address threats to safety. Special interest groups, politicians, and the courts have weighed in on issues related to student discipline and school safety. Actions by district leaders increasingly are constrained by legal mandates and legislation. At the same time, district leaders are able to draw on a growing knowledge base related to effective ways of addressing school discipline and safety.

The key to safety preparedness is a balanced approach involving measures designed for problem intervention, problem prevention, and problem management. Experience has shown that no single focus can ensure that schools run relatively smoothly. A continuum of interventions enable school personnel to correct or improve inappropriate and dangerous behavior. Preventive strategies focus on eliminating the conditions that can give rise to disruptive and dangerous behavior. Problem management measures aim to reduce the likelihood that periodic threats and disruptions get out of hand, thereby creating more serious problems.

While school-based personnel shoulder most of the duties related directly to maintaining safe and orderly environments, district leaders are expected to undertake a number of important safety-related responsibilities. These include the development and implementation of policies related to school safety, the collection and analysis of school safety data, the handling of hearings and appeals related to discipline, the coordination of relations with local law environment agencies, the supervision of crisis management and contingency planning for emergencies, the placement of disruptive and dangerous students, and the maintaining of safe school facilities.

In fulfilling these responsibilities, district leaders should be prepared to encounter a variety of challenges and controversies. Among the sources of possible conflict are discriminatory disciplinary practices, zero tolerance policies, student searches, and the handling of troubled students. One reason why addressing these conflicts can be so difficult is that district leaders may be compelled to choose between doing what they think is ethically correct and doing what they believe to be effective.

NOTE

1. The material in this vignette was taken from a report by the Thomas Jefferson Center for Educational Design at the University of Virginia. Entitled "School Safety in Danville, Virginia: A Needs Assessment," the report was written and presented by the author in January, 2000.

REFERENCES

Astor, R.A., Meyer, H.A., & Behre, W.J. (1999). Unowned places and times: maps and interviews about violence in high schools. *American Educational Research Journal*, 36(1), 3–42.

Barnes, R. (June 26, 2009). Student strip search illegal. *The Washington Post*, pp. A-1, A-8.

Blasik, K. (2007). *Districtwide Summary of Incidents. 2004–05 through 2006–07*. Ft. Lauderdale, FL: Broward County Public Schools.

Brady, K.P., Balmer, S., & Phenix, D. (2007). School police partnership effectiveness in urban schools. *Education and Urban Society*, 39(4), 455–478.

Breggin, P.R. (2000). *Reclaiming Our Children*. Cambridge, MA: Perseus Books.

Casella, R. (2003). Punishing dangerousness through preventive detention: illustrating the institutional link between school and prison. In J. Wald & D.J. Losen (eds.), *New Directions for Youth Development*. San Francisco: Jossey-Bass, 55–70.

Cornell, D., & Sheras, P. (2006). Guidelines *for Responding to Student Threats of Violence.* Longmont, CO: Sopris West.

Dowling-Sendor, B. (1997). A search of last resort. *The American School Board Journal,* 18–19.

Duke, D.L. (2002). *Creating Safe Schools for All Children.* Boston: Allyn & Bacon.

Elam, S.M., & Gallup, A.M. (1989). The 21st Annual Gallup Poll of the Public's Attitudes toward the Public Schools. *Phi Delta Kappan,* 71(1), 41–53.

Fenning, P., & Rose, J. (2007). Overrepresentation of African American students in exclusionary discipline. *Urban Education,* 42(6), 536–559.

Kohn, A. (1996). *Beyond Discipline: From Compliance to Community.* Alexandria, VA: Association for Supervision and Curriculum Development.

Mayer, G.R. (1995). Preventing antisocial behavior in the schools. *Journal of Applied Behavior Analysis,* 28(4), 467–478.

National Education Goals Panel. (1995). *Building a Nation of Learners 1995.* Washington, D.C.: U.S. Government Printing Office.

O'Reilly, R.C., & Green, E.T. (1992). *School Law for the 1990s: A Handbook.* New York: Greenwood Press.

Parent-Student Handbook, 2004–2005. (2004). Los Angeles: Los Angeles Unified School District.

Poland, S. (1994). The role of school crisis intervention teams to prevent and reduce school violence and trauma. *School Psychology Review,* 23(2), 175–189.

Portner, J. (May 17, 1995). Florida district is partially responsible for student's suicide, U.S. judge rules. *Education Week,* 9.

Resource Guide for Crisis Management in Schools. (1998). Richmond, VA: Virginia Department of Education.

Robelen, E.W. (April 29, 20009). Strip-search case testing the balance between privacy, student safety. *Education Week,* 1, 14–15.

Sugai, G., & Horner, R.H. (2002). Introduction to the special series on positive behavior support in schools. *Journal of Emotional and Behavioral Disorders,* 10(1), 130–135.

Walker, H.M., Colvin, G., & Ramsey, E. (1995). *Antisocial Behavior in School: Strategies and Best Practices.* Pacific Grove, CA: Brooks/Cole.

8

THE CHALLENGES OF STAFFING SCHOOLS

RECRUITING AND RETAINING TALENTED TEACHERS FOR PHILADELPHIA[1]

When Paul Vallas accepted the position of Chief Executive Officer of the School District of Philadelphia (SDP) in July of 2002, he understood that the system required a lengthy list of reforms in order to raise student achievement. The accomplishment of those reforms, in turn, would require a highly qualified team of educators. Without capable teachers, meaningful improvements in teaching and learning were doubtful.

Building a talented army of teachers for the massive school district (214,350 students) would require new thinking across a broad spectrum of human resource operations. Bright new teachers had to be recruited, and then their working conditions needed to be good enough to ensure that most of them would stay in the district. Existing staff as well as newcomers would require continuing professional development in order to address the needs of students.

To move forward with his staffing initiative, Vallas turned to Thomas Hanna, a Philadelphia principal with a proven record as a turnaround specialist. Using a project management approach frequently found in private industry, but rarely used in public education, Hanna built a team to develop a set of recommendations for Vallas. Less than six months after Vallas' arrival, he received the report from Hanna's group. Entitled "The Three R's Retention, Recruitment, and Renewal: A Blueprint for Action" (or "The Blueprint" for short), the report contained recommendations regarding a variety of issues related to the staffing of Philadelphia's public schools.

Based on an analysis of the backgrounds of teachers who stayed in the district, Hanna's group concluded that a small number of local colleges accounted for a significant percentage of veteran teachers. To reduce turnover rates, the report recommended targeting these colleges for extensive recruitment efforts. To improve the diversity of the teaching force, the report suggested more recruiting efforts at historically black colleges and universities.

The report acknowledged that Philadelphia was not perceived to be an attractive place to teach. With help from an expert in multicultural communications, Hanna's group suggested that the school district host on a regular basis "getting to know you" weekends for sophomores, juniors, and seniors at targeted colleges. At these sessions, the advantages of working in Philadelphia would be stressed. To further enhance recruitment efforts, the report urged the district to offer signing bonuses, tuition reimbursement, and higher starting salaries (adjusted to match the 50th percentile of salaries for districts surrounding Philadelphia).

Hanna and his colleagues realized that recruitment alone would not solve Philadelphia's staffing problems. Conditions in the schools had to be sufficiently favorable to cause teachers to want to stay in Philadelphia. Since many new teachers left after their first or second year, the report called for a support system for new teachers. New teachers would be assigned a "coach" to help them adjust to the realities of the classroom. An Office of Alternative Certification would be established to support teachers who still needed to complete certification requirements.

Instead of continuing the arrangement whereby new teachers could only be hired after more senior teachers in the district had an opportunity to fill vacancies, Hanna's group insisted that principals be accorded more control over teacher hiring. A vote of teachers at a school and the principal's recommendation would replace the previous procedure if this controversial recommendation was accepted.

Vallas was pleased with the report and took steps to implement its various suggestions. By 2004, district officials were able to report increased teacher applications, including applications from minority candidates. The hiring timeline was moved up to enable recruiters to "sign" new teachers before other school districts could lure them away. Coaches were hired to assist and encourage new teachers.

While the initial impact of the report was encouraging, Philadelphia's staffing problems continued. In March of 2004, the Education Law Center lodged a complaint that high-poverty schools in Philadelphia continued to be staffed by high proportions of uncertified teachers. The complaint went on to blame the district's collective bargaining agreement with the teachers union for problems associated with the assignment of teachers.

*****

School district leaders readily acknowledge that there are few goals that cannot be achieved with the right collection of talented professionals. Very little can be accomplished, on the other hand, when schools are staffed by poorly trained and burned-out individuals. High-performing school districts devote considerable time, energy, planning, and resources to recruiting a steady stream of talented professionals. But they do not stop there. Additional challenges must be faced. What must be done to retain talented professionals and ensure that they do not become complacent, but continue to grow? What steps must be in place to address incompetent and unprofessional practice? How can district leaders make certain that schools have the leaders they need to keep improving? This chapter focuses on the challenges associated with staffing schools.

THE CHALLENGING WORLD OF HUMAN RESOURCES

One of the assumptions upon which many district leaders operate is that it is difficult to change schools and districts unless there are changes in the people who work in them. Put differently, either district leaders *change* people or they change *people*. Bringing new people on board takes time, so districts also must have the capacity to develop existing staff members. The No Child Left Behind Act helped to spotlight a problem about which district leaders long have been aware. Many public schools are not staffed by a full complement of highly qualified professionals. The legislation required states to clearly articulate the criteria for determining what constitutes a "highly qualified" teacher and then see to it that only individuals who met the criteria staff schools. This requirement has posed an enormous challenge for many school systems, especially those serving large numbers of poor students.

It is unclear whether the lofty intent of the No Child Left Behind Act has been achieved. Jacob (2007) doubts that teacher quality in urban school systems has changed much as a result of the legislation. He notes that states are accorded great latitude when it comes to determining whether experienced teachers demonstrate competence. Some states, for example, allow experienced teachers to become "highly qualified" by taking short professional development courses or participating in other activities of dubious value. One state permits teachers to complete a self-assessment in order to demonstrate subject knowledge competence.

Estimates of marginally qualified and unqualified public school teachers vary, depending on when the study was done and what definition of "qualified" is used. A national survey of school staffing issues during the 2003–2004 school year, for example, found that 19.2 percent of urban schools and 14.4 percent of suburban schools filled teacher vacancies with "less than fully qualified teachers" (National Center for Education Statistics, 2006). Many urban (42.4%) and suburban (30.0%) schools were compelled to fill vacancies with short or long-term substitutes. The supply of qualified teachers was particularly limited in mathematics, special education, biology, and English as a Second Language.

A 2008 study by Education Trust (Sawchuk, p. 6) found that students in high-poverty schools are about twice as likely as those in more affluent schools to be taught by teachers who lack certification or academic majors in their subject matter area. Urban schools are more likely to be staffed by unqualified teachers than suburban schools, according to a rigorous study of schools in New York State (Lankford, Loeb, & Wyckoff, 2002, p. 44). The researchers also reported that nonwhite students are four times as likely as white students to be taught by an unqualified teacher.

Some critics of school staffing are unlikely to be silenced by efforts to hire more teachers with proper credentials. These individuals question the quality of teacher preparation programs and the persons who choose to enter the teaching profession. Programs like Teach for America have attracted a following because they purposely seek talented applicants who do not major in education. Even possession of an advanced degree fails to predict gains in student achievement (Murnane & Steele, 2007, p. 23). One of the few teacher characteristics that consistently predicts student outcomes is academic ability, "as measured by verbal aptitude scores and undergraduate college selectivity (Murnane & Steele, 2007, p. 23). Presumably school districts that seek Teach for America educators concur with this finding.

Additional criticisms of school staffing concern the race, ethnicity, and gender of teachers hired to staff public schools. Many schools that serve large numbers of nonwhite students have faculties made up of disproportionately large percentages of white teachers. Black male teachers are particularly under-represented, accounting for just 2 percent of the nation's 4.8 million teachers (Thomas-Lester, 2009, p. B-1). Several studies have concluded that minority students benefit from being taught by teachers of the same minority (Meier & Juenke, 2005, pp. 218–223).

Recruiting and selecting a diverse and talented pool of educators may be important, but these measures are insufficient alone to ensure that all students receive high quality instruction. A major problem concerns retention. The neediest schools and school districts typically have the highest teacher turnover rates (Johnson, Berg, & Donaldson, 2005, p. 9). High-poverty schools often are staffed by large percentages of first-year teachers who may possess considerable energy and enthusiasm, but who lack the experience and expertise to reach large numbers of struggling students. The 2003–2004 Schools and Staffing Survey (National Center for Education Statistics, 2006) reported that 20.3 percent of teachers in urban schools had three or fewer years of experience, while 17.6 percent of their suburban counterparts were in their first three years of teaching. Urban teachers also were reported to be less likely than suburban teachers to stay at one school for an extended period of time.

When Monk (2007, p. 159) investigated staffing problems for rural schools, he found that they were less likely than schools in general to employ teachers with a Master's degree or higher. He also reported on research that indicated rural schools were only about half as likely as schools in urban areas to employ teachers who had graduated from top-ranked colleges and universities.

Blame for staffing problems in many public schools is widely distributed. Communities and their elected representatives are faulted for not providing competitive salaries and affordable housing for teachers. Teacher unions are criticized for defending incompetent teachers, preserving seniority rules, and fighting pay-for-performance programs. School district leaders also must share the blame when they do not insist on placing the most skilled educators in the neediest schools and when they under-fund continuing staff and professional development. University-based teacher educators can be culpable when they fail to offer rigorous and relevant instruction or screen out weak candidates.

Because school district leaders cannot be assured that every staff member, even those with appropriate credentials, is capable of performing at a high level, they must see that procedures are in place to monitor, supervise, and evaluate staff. These procedures, of course, are unlikely to be implemented effectively without skilled school administrators. Recruiting, retaining, and developing school-based leaders therefore constitutes one of the most important responsibilities for district leaders. One indication of the growing importance of school administrators is the fact that their numbers have been steadily increasing relative to the number of classroom teachers (Darling-Hammond, 1997, p. 193).

Staffing central offices with capable professionals poses many of the same problems as staffing schools. This chapter, however, concentrates on the challenges associated with staffing schools with highly qualified teachers and administrators. These challenges can be captured in three questions that district leaders must be prepared to answer.

The Challenges of Staffing Schools

1. What must be done to recruit and retain highly qualified teachers?
2. What steps are necessary to ensure that teachers are contributing to the mission of the school district?
3. What must be done to provide capable leaders for schools?

THE RELENTLESS QUEST FOR TALENTED TEACHERS

In their book, *Reframing Organizations*, Bolman and Deal (1997, pp. 102–103) discuss a perspective on organizations that focuses on "human resources." Unlike other perspectives including the structural, political, and symbolic, the human resource perspective stresses the symbiotic relationship between organizations and their employees. To use Bolman and Deal's words, "People and organizations need each other: organizations need ideas, energy, and talent; people need careers, salaries, and opportunities" (p. 102). They go on to note that, when the fit between individuals and organizations is good, individuals find their work meaningful and satisfying, while the organization gets the talent and support needed to accomplish its mission. When the fit is bad, both individuals and organizations are prevented from meeting their needs.

School district leaders, like the leaders of any organization, must devote considerable time, energy, and resources to (1) attracting individuals who are likely to serve well the district's mission and (2) making certain that these individuals receive the care and concern necessary to keep them focused and satisfied. Ensuring a good fit between individuals and organizations begins, in other words, before people are hired and extends through their tenure in the organization.

Recruitment

The first challenge, then, is to recruit talented teachers who have the potential to address the needs of a school district's students. As any human resource department administrator knows, this challenge involves far more than placing an advertisement in a newspaper or on-line. Consider the steps called for in Philadelphia's "The Blueprint" (described in the opening vignette). The report recommended identifying the teachers who remained for long periods of time in the school system and then determining where they went to college. When district personnel administrators found that a majority of teachers attended colleges in the Philadelphia metropolitan area, they were able to focus their recruitment efforts on a relatively small number of colleges.

School district leaders in Philadelphia also were interested in increasing the number of minority teachers in the system. The student body, after all, was predominantly African American. It is important for African American students to see role models of their own race. A second recruitment initiative therefore concentrated on historically black colleges and universities.

Because competition for talented prospects can be keen, "The Blueprint" recommended reaching out to college sophomores and juniors as well as students getting ready to graduate. College students were invited to weekend gatherings where they learned about the ambitious goals for Philadelphia schools. To encourage college students to consider a career with the School District of Philadelphia, various incentives were offered. These included signing bonuses, competitive starting salaries, and tuition reimbursement. To overcome the school district's negative image, a communications expert was assigned to develop an attractive sales pitch based on the many benefits of locating in Philadelphia.

School district leaders no longer can afford to assume that highly qualified teachers will beat a path to their doorstep. As in the case of Philadelphia, they must think about recruitment as a comprehensive and continuing campaign to find talent. When the Council of the Great City Schools (2000) surveyed 57 large urban school districts, a variety of recruitment strategies were found to be in use. These strategies included providing routes to certification (65%), sponsoring job fairs (65%), offering on-the-spot contracts (62.5%), using technology to reach a wider pool of applicants (37.5%), and offering monetary signing bonuses (25%).

While tangible incentives such as bonuses, relatively high entry-level salaries, and housing allowances can enhance recruitment efforts, district leaders should not lose sight of the role of intangible motivators. Many new teachers express a desire to make the world a better place (Paynter, 2003). Researchers at Johns Hopkins University (Stotko, Ingram, & Beaty-O'Ferrall, 2007, p. 43) suggest that recruitment strategies should include the following:

> promotional materials with altruistic themes and photos; opportunities for applicants to interact closely with recruiters who are successful...educators themselves; timely follow-up; information on mentoring and peer coaching programs for new teachers; videotapes and printed materials that profile student success stories; student recruiters; and information on quality of life issues...

Strategies such as those listed above may be especially useful in attracting talented teachers to chronically low-performing schools. These schools desperately need highly qualified, energetic, and compassionate teachers if they are to raise student achievement. Former Chicago CEO Arne Duncan (2009) attributes the success of efforts to turn around low-performing Chicago schools to the replacement of entire staffs with highly motivated and skilled teachers. To ensure that talent flows to the neediest schools, district leaders may have to permit principals of these schools to make choices from the applicant pool before other principals do so.

Recruitment, of course, is only one piece of the staffing puzzle. Steps must be taken to ensure that the teachers who are selected are a good match for the schools to which they are assigned. Most college-based teacher preparation programs undertake a generic preparation that presumably equips graduates to teach in any setting, but some question the validity of such claims (Stotko et al., 2007, p. 41). Research on candidates for teaching positions in urban school systems suggests, for example, that certain beliefs and characteristics are keys to effectiveness in these settings (Stotko et al., pp. 40–41). Teachers well-suited for urban teaching are persistent, flexible, and unwilling to give up on students. They are willing to work with others to meet the needs of their students, and they are constantly involved in professional development.

Knowing what characteristics and beliefs to look for in candidates is one important aspect of the selection process. Who is involved in the selection process also is important. District leaders understand that school-based personnel should have a voice in teacher selection. It is unrealistic to expect new teachers to be a good match for their assigned schools if principals and teachers in those schools are denied a role in the selection process. District leaders, of course, must oversee the selection process to ensure that selections are made in accordance with legal requirements and mission-based commitments, such as faculty diversity.

Retention

A teacher hired is not necessarily a teacher retained for the long-haul. Teacher turnover, as indicated earlier, is a persistent problem for schools, especially low-performing schools. Drawing on data from the School and Staffing Survey conducted periodically by the U.S. Census Bureau for the National Center for Educational Statistics, Ingersoll (2001) challenged the belief that better recruitment efforts alone can solve district staffing problems. He found that the early departure of large numbers of qualified teachers was more likely to account for staffing problems than a shortage of qualified applicants. Furthermore, turnover was traced to teachers pursuing other jobs and to job dissatisfaction. The message to school district leaders and human resource departments is clear—recruitment by itself will not ensure that students are taught by highly qualified teachers. Conditions in the schools that drive off good teachers also must be addressed. When Ingersoll (2003) combed through the School and Staffing Survey data in order to pinpoint reasons why teachers leave their jobs, he found five major contributing factors. They included poor salary (61%), poor administrative support (32%), student discipline problems (24%), poor student motivation (18%), and lack of faculty influence (15%).

The cost of high teacher turnover can be substantial, thereby depriving district leaders of badly needed resources. When the National Commission on Teaching and America's Future (Barnes, Crowe, & Schaefer, 2003) undertook a study of the real cost of teacher turnover in five districts of different sizes, it found that the cost of a teacher leaving a small, rural district exceeded $4,000. Chicago lost almost $18,000 for each teacher who left.

The key to retaining talented teachers for Philadelphia leaders in the opening vignette was working conditions in the schools. To provide as much support as possible for new teachers, "The Blueprint" called for every new teacher to be assigned a coach. An Office of Alternative Certification also was established to assist teachers who needed to complete their certification requirements.

Teacher retention is a multi-dimensional issue involving induction processes, instructional and non-instructional assignments, teacher support and assistance, school leadership and working conditions, opportunities for growth and advancement, and compensation. Particular items from this list may be more important for some teachers than for others. A comprehensive approach to retention, therefore, is essential.

Veteran teachers joke sometimes about the "orientation" to their first teaching job—they were given a copy of the teacher's manual, a set of keys to their classroom, and a pat on the back. Most school district leaders today recognize that new teachers require a more thorough and constructive set of induction experiences. The complexities of the manual must be explained and discussed. Expectations for new teachers have to be reviewed and clarified. Formal induction programs often extend well into the school year and sometimes beyond. New teachers frequently are provided with inservice training on the district instructional model and content-based programs.

District induction efforts sometimes are complemented by state requirements. Among the 22 states that mandate some type of district induction process, all require that new teachers be assigned a mentor (Olson, 2008, p. 19). Other induction components include performance assessment (14 states), professional development (11 states), observation and reflection (9 states), orientation sessions (8 states), and individual growth plans (5 states).

As with most personnel strategies, induction programs can be done poorly or well. Experts agree that a one-time orientation session before the beginning of school is unlikely to accomplish much. Many first-year teachers decide to leave their school or even the teaching profession because they feel isolated and unsupported. Assigning a mentor to a new teacher can be an antidote to these negative feelings, but only if the mentoring program is carefully designed. Important design considerations include paid teacher mentors with experience in the subject their mentees are assigned to teach, release time for mentors, and two-year mentoring arrangements for beginning teachers (Snipes & Horwitz, 2007, p. 7).

There are clear indications that district leaders can do a great deal to ensure that new teachers get the support they need to thrive. In one study comparing the experiences of first-year language arts teachers in two different school districts, researchers found that beginning teachers in one district fared much better than their counterparts in the other district. The first district had greater success because of "a cohesive policy environment around the language arts" together with administrators who agreed on a broad vision for the language arts and "professional development opportunities generally focused on frameworks for the teaching of reading and writing that were consistent with this larger vision" (Grossman, Thompson, & Valencia, 2002, p. 140). The second district lacked a coherent approach to reading and the language arts, which resulted in hit-and-miss inservice training, inadequate supervision, and teacher confusion regarding priorities. The researchers concluded that school districts can play important roles in the lives of new teachers when they attend to the "tasks they assign to new teachers, the resources they provide, the learning environments they create, the assessments they design, and the conversations they provide" (p. 141).

How new teachers are assigned can have an especially great bearing on their decision to continue teaching. Teacher folklore is full of all-too-true stories of beginners who were assigned the most challenging groups of students, multiple preparations, and onerous extra-curricular duties. Such thoughtless staffing decisions are unfair to new teachers and their students. If experience and expertise are worth anything, it is the most talented veteran teachers who should be assigned to the students who struggle to learn. No other profession reserves its toughest cases for novices. Ideally, highly skilled veterans would view assignment to challenging classes as an honor, official recognition of their expertise as teachers. For such a perspective to become the norm, many school systems would need to be "re-cultured." It goes without saying that district leaders would have to take the initiative in any such effort.

A report for the Council of the Great City Schools (Snipes & Horwitz, 2007, p. 9) notes that urban school districts often serve as training grounds for new teachers who eventually move on to more affluent and less troubled districts. The authors urge district leaders to consider addressing policies that enable experienced teachers to avoid challenging schools. One suggestion is to cap the percentage of inexperienced teachers that can be hired at any one school. Alternatively, the percentage of experienced teachers allowed to transfer from low-performing schools in a given year can be limited by district policy.

Another dimension of teacher retention strategy involves assistance and support for teachers. Programs for new teachers already have been referenced. Experienced teachers also benefit from similar efforts. The quality of work life for all teachers can be enhanced, for example, when district leaders promote collaboration and idea-sharing among teachers. One mechanism for achieving these ends is a professional community (PC). Related terms include "professional learning communities" and "communities of practice." Coburn and Russell (2008, p.205) state that a PC, as a reform strategy, "aims to encourage teachers to share ideas, discuss teaching strategies, and work together in planning, teaching, and advising in an effort to reduce isolation, facilitate stronger professional connections, and foster positive changes in instructional practices." Key characteristics of a PC include shared norms and values, trust, collective responsibility, and openness to new ways of doing things. These building blocks result, ideally, in the "deprivatization of practice."

When Coburn and Russell (2008) investigated teacher collaboration in eight elementary schools in two school districts, they discovered various ways that district policy can support greater networking and cooperation among teachers. Policy, for example, can impact teacher access to expertise and the quality of professional interactions among teachers. The researchers warn, however, that teacher collaboration can be inhibited when schools and school systems undertake too many initiatives at one time.

Protecting teachers' time so they can focus on a reasonable number of objectives is an important element in job satisfaction. Teachers are likely to be less inclined to remain at a school where they are constantly pressed to tackle multiple initiatives. They also are apt to experience "reform fatigue" when new initiatives in which they have invested considerable energy are allowed to decline when a change in leadership occurs.

The quality of school leadership is a key factor in teachers' decisions to remain at a school or leave. Principals are in a position to control or influence many aspects of teachers' jobs and working conditions that ultimately have a bearing on retention. Consider the matter of teacher assignments. Principals may determine that a teacher must undertake an out-of-field assignment because of an unexpected resignation or last minute change in enrollment. A comprehensive review of research on teacher job satisfaction, however, found that an out-of-field assignment "unnecessarily increases many teachers' dissatisfaction with their jobs by making the work difficult day to day and diminishing the likelihood that they can feel pride in the accomplishments" (Johnson et al., 2005, p. 57).

When teachers do not feel supported by their principals, they are more likely to consider leaving. Support, of course, can assume many forms, ranging from encouragement and recognition for work well done to desirable room assignments and help in expediting purchase orders. Treating teachers with respect and valuing their voices when it comes to important decisions are two of the most important manifestations of principal support for teachers. When Ingersoll (2003, pp. 74–82) asked teachers how much influence they exercised with regard to a variety of key school-based decisions, most indicated that they had little or no influence over such matters as the assignment of non-teaching duties, the allocation of school space, the selection of administrators, teacher hiring, and the school schedule. The areas where they felt they exercised the most influence were limited largely to what went on in their own classroom.

Research underscores the role of leadership—or lack of leadership—in teachers' decisions to remain at or leave a school. Over one-third of the teachers in one large study (Luekens, Lyter, Fox, & Chandler, 2004) reported that they transferred to another school because of their dissatisfaction with support from administrators.

There is much that principals can do to create desirable working conditions for teachers. Recognizing and celebrating teacher successes, for example, is important, especially for veteran faculty members. All too often their contributions are taken for granted because school leaders focus most of their attention on newcomers. One important form of recognition that has received considerable interest in recent years involves distributed leadership, providing capable teachers with opportunities to exercise leadership responsibilities (Mayrowetz, 2008). Distributed leadership also addresses another teacher retention strategy, promoting growth and advancement. Facing new challenges such as chairing a program review team and serving as a mentor for new teachers offers veteran teachers a chance to develop new skills and understandings. In the process, school and district leaders also get an opportunity to identify teachers who have the potential to become administrators.

Some school districts have formalized distributed leadership by adopting career ladders. These arrangements enable teachers to qualify for a variety of leadership roles, thereby creating opportunities to boost their salaries. Linking distributed leadership and teacher pay, however, can give rise to controversy and conflict. When Fairfax County Public Schools experimented with a career ladder and merit pay during the period from 1982 to 1993, district leaders ran into resistance from teachers and taxpayers (Duke, 2005, pp. 94–104). Teacher union representatives questioned the instrument used to evaluate teachers and the skill-level of evaluators. A group of African American teachers brought suit against the school system on the grounds that the new evaluation system and career ladder discriminated against minority teachers. Taxpayers registered concern over the price tag for the program when they discovered a large percentage of Fairfax teachers qualified for advancement on the career ladder.

Career ladders are designed, in part, to provide incentives for teachers to remain in the teaching profession. By exposing teachers to leadership opportunities, however, career ladders actually can cause some teachers to abandon the classroom for fulltime administrative positions. An alternative that keeps talented teachers teaching is pay-for-performance. Since linking teachers' salaries to student achievement and other outcomes also constitutes a control mechanism for keeping educators focused on district priorities, a discussion of pay-for-performance will be taken up in the next section.

Opinions vary greatly regarding the relationship between teacher salaries and teacher mobility. Some experts question whether modest hikes in salary will result in greater teacher retention. Hanushek, Kain, and Rivkin (2004), for example, estimated that salary increases would need to range from 25 to 40 percent in order to convince highly qualified teachers to stay in high-needs schools.

The story of Manassas Park's transformation from a low-performing educational backwater to an outstanding school system illustrates the importance of salary enhancement (Duke, 2008). When Tom DeBolt took over as superintendent of Manassas Park City Schools in 1995, teacher salaries ranked 42nd out of 133 school systems in Virginia. It was not unusual for a quarter of the teaching force to turn over each year, as Manassas Park teachers found better paying jobs in neighboring northern Virginia school divisions. By 2006, DeBolt could boast that teachers in Manassas Park were the fourth highest paid teachers in Virginia. Realizing that Manassas Park could not become a "world class" school system without great teachers, he made teacher recruitment and retention a top priority. To fund his efforts, he negotiated a revenue sharing agreement with the city council that guaranteed 57 percent of annual local revenues would flow to the school system.

DeBolt realized that competitive salaries were necessary, but insufficient alone to ensure that teachers were retained. He took other measures to make certain that working conditions were appealing. Every school building included attractive work spaces where teachers could plan and collaborate with colleagues. When teachers received tenure, they were acknowledged at a public reception. Knowing that teachers and students benefitted from relatively low teacher-student ratios, DeBolt saw to it that the elementary school ratio was lowered from 1:14 to 1:12. At the secondary level the ratio was reduced from 1:17.7 to 1:13. Tenured teachers qualified for a generous tuition reimbursement allotment so that they could earn graduate credits. All of these changes were effected in one of the poorest school systems in Virginia, evidence of what a capable leader can do when he makes up his mind to generate community-wide support for a worthy cause.

KEEPING TEACHERS FOCUSED

All organizations, school districts included, must take steps to ensure that employees remain committed to and focused on their mission. To do so means grappling with a variety of factors including ambiguity, distractions, and self-interest.

The most obvious manifestation of ambiguity, of course, is when individuals are unsure about the organization's mission. Uncertainty can arise because leaders do a poor job communicating the mission or because the organization is trying to accomplish too many things. Organization theorists use the term *goal displacement* to characterize situations where the original mission is supplanted by more immediate and less client-centered aims. Some critics of public education argue that the primary mission of public schools has become the employment of teachers and administrators, not the education of young people.

McCaskey (1982, p. 5) identified a number of other sources of organizational ambiguity, including the nature of problems on which to focus energy, the origins of these problems, and the roles and responsibilities of those charged with addressing the problems. While McCaskey goes on to suggest that ambiguity is not always undesirable, he recognized that uncertainty must be managed carefully, lest valuable time and resources be wasted.

Keeping focused on the mission also is difficult when people are confronted with an unending series of distractions. Jackson (2008) suggests that this problem is ubiquitous in contemporary society, and she places much of the blame on technology. Driving an automobile while chatting on a cell phone, of course, is quite a different distraction from trying to plan an engaging lesson while thinking about what to prepare for dinner and how to get one's daughter to soccer practice. The fact remains that life has grown ever more complex. Attention is becoming a scarce commodity. The likelihood of performing a given task successfully is reduced when individuals are unable to focus.

A third reason why concentrating on matters of mission cannot be assumed involves self-interest. When an employee calls in sick to have a "mental health" day, self-interest is at work. This is not to suggest that self-interest is necessarily a bad thing. It is, in fact, essential to survival. Problems can arise, however, when self-interest consistently interferes with efforts to achieve organizational objectives.

To ensure that people stay focused for the most part on the mission, school districts, along with most other organizations, rely on four basic measures: (1) supervision, (2) evaluation, (3) sanctions, and (4) rewards.

Supervision

Direct supervision of teachers typically is the responsibility of school-based administrators. Principals and assistant principals are expected to conduct periodic observations of teachers in order to assess performance and provide constructive feedback. Depending on local policy, observations may be announced or unannounced, brief "walk-throughs" or lesson-long sessions. Formal observations may be preceded by a pre-observation conference and followed by a post-observation conference. Conferences constitute opportunities for school administrators and teachers to share information, discuss instructional issues, and explore possible improvements.

District leaders must decide whether or not to supplement school-based supervision with supervision by central office personnel. In some cases, for example, content specialists and instructional supervisors may be called on to supplement observations by school administrators. When teachers are expected to implement a district-mandated program or instructional model, central office personnel often are enlisted to conduct observations in order to ensure proper implementation. External consultants also may be tapped for supervisory purposes when a program has been purchased from a private provider. Another reason for supplementing school-based supervision involves teachers who have been placed on a plan of assistance. These individuals may have a central office resource person assigned to help them improve in identified areas of concern.

Evaluation

Information gathered during observations constitutes one type of data for use in the evaluation of teachers. Other types of data can include student achievement data, teacher portfolios, student work samples, and student evaluations. The categories of data that can be used to evaluate teachers usually is a matter addressed by district personnel policy. Where collective bargaining is in effect, teacher evaluation policy is typically negotiated.

Two important considerations for district leaders concern the purpose and structure of teacher evaluation.

Evaluation can be designed to promote professional growth and to ensure accountability. When accountability is the primary focus, teacher evaluation policy must address a set of questions: "Accountable to whom, for what, in what manner and under what circumstances?" (Wagner, 1989, p. 1) Should teachers, for example, be held accountable for meeting the specifications in their job descriptions? Complying with district rules and regulations? Demonstrating various performance standards? Seeing that students attain designated levels of achievement? Each focus for accountability gives rise to additional questions regarding acceptable evidence and how it is to be gathered.

In many school districts, the work of teaching is spelled out in job descriptions, teacher evaluation guidelines, and contracts. Confusion can arise, however, when these sources are not in alignment. It is not unusual, for instance, to have job descriptions that were developed separately from teacher evaluation guidelines. Both may not reflect the language in the latest teacher contract. District leaders should make certain that job descriptions, teacher evaluation guidelines, and contracts reflect a common set of expectations for teachers.

A second important purpose of teacher evaluation is the promotion of ongoing professional growth and instructional improvement. It is difficult to imagine fulfilling the mission of any school district without the continuous development of teachers. In the 1980s district leaders began to acknowledge that accountability-based teacher evaluation might not be especially useful in promoting continued development for the majority of competent, veteran teachers (Duke, 1995, p. 6). Many teachers complained that being evaluated annually using the same set of basic performance standards had become a meaningless ritual. They expressed a desire for a different approach to evaluation, one that permitted teachers to set growth goals based on their individual assignments and idiosyncratic needs.

Recognizing that the traditional or "unitary" teacher evaluation system was not serving the needs of all teachers, some district leaders began to explore differentiated evaluation systems (Duke & Canady, 1991, pp. 116–119). The Beaverton, Oregon, school system, for example, distinguished between the standards to be used in evaluating beginning teachers and those applied to tenured teachers. A plan backed by the teachers union in Toledo, Ohio, called for peer evaluation of beginning teachers.

A strong case can be made that school districts can benefit from a teacher evaluation system separated into three strands. The first strand is intended to satisfy the accountability purpose. Put differently, this strand provides the public assurance that teachers have met basic performance standards rooted in research on best practice. All non-tenured teachers and teachers new to the school system are subject to Strand 1 evaluation. So, too, are tenured veteran teachers, but not on a yearly basis. Once teachers have demonstrated competence based on the district performance standards, they should not have to be checked every year. To do so is to squander valuable administrator and teacher time. It should be sufficient to cycle highly qualified teachers through Strand 1 evaluation once every three or four years.

Strand 2 evaluation is designed to promote ongoing professional growth based on goals negotiated between individual teachers and their principals. Tenured teachers with a track record of success on Strand 1 evaluations participate in Strand 2 evaluation for three out of every four years. Having three years to work on a growth goal encourages teachers to undertake challenging goals. District leaders, of course, need to set aside resources to underwrite teachers' efforts to accomplish their goals. One can envision teachers tackling longitudinal action research projects, new course development, and the acquisition of additional credentials as part of their Strand 2 evaluation cycle.

Strand 3 evaluation focuses on teachers who fail to demonstrate an acceptable level of performance on one or more of the district's performance standards. Teachers in Strand 3 are placed on a plan of assistance, which can be drafted by a principal or an individual appointed by the central office. Some districts form a committee consisting of administrators and teacher union representatives in order to develop and monitor plans of assistance. Failure to satisfy the requirements of a plan of assistance can lead to a recommendation to terminate employment.

Regardless of whether district leaders opt for a unitary or a differentiated teacher evaluation system, it is essential that the system identify weak teachers. Critics of teacher evaluation often fault principals, rather than the evaluation systems themselves, for failing to conduct rigorous evaluations. One study of more than 15,000 teachers and 1,300 administrators across four states and 12 school districts found that more than nine in 10 tenured teachers met local performance standards on their most recent evaluation (Sawchuk, June 10, 2009, p. 6). Skeptical observers wonder how so many teachers can receive satisfactory evaluations when thousands of schools and millions of students are under-performing.

Recent years have witnessed growing concerns over chronically low-performing schools. Partial responsibility for these schools' inadequate performance must be assumed by the faculty. The fact that significant numbers of teachers in these schools might be struggling has led some district leaders to take the radical step of requiring all teachers in low-performing schools to re-apply for their jobs. This process serves as the prelude to initiating a "school turnaround" process (Gewertz, 2009, p. 1). It enables a new principal, or "turnaround specialist," to handpick their faculty, thereby ensuring that their efforts are backed up by a capable and supportive faculty.

When district leaders endorse measures such as having all teachers, even those with seniority, re-apply for their jobs, it suggests that even "insiders" doubt the validity of many teacher evaluations. Since the evaluation of teachers takes up a substantial amount of administrative time, it is essential that district leaders do everything they can to develop and maintain credible teacher evaluation systems that reliably identify areas where teachers need to improve and that protect students from teachers who perennially fail to promote effective learning.

Rewards and Sanctions

Two other measures used by organizations to keep people focused on the mission are rewards and sanctions. Sometimes rewards and sanctions are administered at the discretion of individual leaders. A principal gives a valued teacher a desirable schedule or an attractive classroom. A weak teacher is not allowed to continue teaching a course in which students have to take a state test at the end of the year. In other cases, rewards and sanctions are formalized in contracts and board policy. One measure that has received considerable attention in recent years is pay-for-performance.

Pay-for-performance compensation schemes can take several forms. In Lamesa, Texas, all teachers and administrators in a school are rewarded if designated performance targets are achieved (Terry, 2008). The performance targets include passing rates on state standardized tests, student attendance, and graduation rate. Houston, Texas, also adopted a pay-for-performance plan, but its plan includes both campus-wide awards and bonuses for individuals and departments (Terry, 2008). Instead of basing awards exclusively on end-of-the-year state tests, Houston's plan focuses on value-added and student growth over the course of a year.

Pay-for-performance plans in Denver, Minneapolis, and Toledo provide incentive pay to teachers based not only on student outcomes, but also on teacher knowledge and skill and the taking on of additional responsibilities. Teacher unions played key roles in the development of these plans.

Whether pay-for-performance is effective in boosting student achievement is a hotly debated topic. A report on plans in Lamesa, Houston, Dallas, and Austin, Texas, concluded that incentive pay had resulted in "higher test scores, higher state accountability rankings, improved teacher morale, and lower teacher turnover" (Terry, 2008, p. 3). Researchers meeting at a national conference on performance incentives in education, however, indicated that the positive effects of most incentive pay plans had been relatively small (Honawar, 2008).

If pay-for-performance plans are to be successful, it is likely that certain conditions will need to be met. Slotnik (2009, p. 32), for example, warns that district leaders should not regard incentive pay strictly as a financial reform. "It must be tied directly to the educational mission of a district," he contends, "and must focus on how a school system thinks and behaves—specifically in the areas of student learning, teacher support and rewards, and institutional culture" (p. 32). Pay-for-performance also must have broad community support and be based on metrics that are credible and that can be objectively measured.

Interest in pay-for-performance has led some district leaders to question some seemingly "sacred" assumptions associated with school staffing and compensation for teachers. The principle of seniority, for example, was challenged in Charlotte-Mecklenburg, North Carolina, when veteran teachers with low performance on evaluations were released in order for less experienced teachers to be retained (Sawchuk, June 17, 2009). Elsewhere district leaders are re-examining tenure. In Washington, D.C., Superintendent Michelle Rhee offered to raise teacher salaries substantially in return for abandonment of the tenure system. The long-accepted practice of increasing pay for teachers with Master's degrees also is under scrutiny. Doubting that Master's degrees necessarily lead to more effective teaching, some researchers suggest that the money that has been used to compensate teachers for advanced degrees might better be used to fund pay-for-performance plans (Sawchuk, July 21, 2009).

EFFECTIVE LEADERS FOR EVERY SCHOOL

If there is one individual on whose shoulders rests the success of every school, it is the building principal. Research has linked school leadership with student achievement and teacher effectiveness (Hallinger & Heck, 1998; Leithwood, Louis, Anderson, & Wahlstrom, 2004; Robinson, Lloyd, & Rowe, 2008). Earlier in this chapter the central role of principals in teacher satisfaction and retention also was noted. Given the linchpin role of the school principal, district leaders should regard as one of their highest priorities the identification and development of top quality principals.

Here again, however, district leaders face another challenge. The long lines of candidates that used to seek school leadership positions are dwindling in many places, especially high-poverty urban and rural areas. Fewer educators want to be high school principals in particular. Superintendents no longer can afford to wait for talented candidates to beat a path to the central office. They must take the initiative if schools are to get the leaders they need. That is why Philadelphia's Campaign for Human Capital, described in the beginning of this chapter, also included provision for the creation of the Academy of Leadership in Philadelphia Schools (ALPS), an organization dedicated to preservice training for prospective principals as well as inservice training for incumbent school administrators.

To ensure capable leadership for schools, district leaders should undertake two broad sets of activities. The first set focuses on the establishment of formal processes for identifying and developing promising candidates for school principalships. The second set involves providing principals with the support they need to provide their schools with effective leadership.

Leader Identification and Development

Finding talented school leaders is a complex process consisting of at least three distinct components. First, a pool of promising candidates must be identified. Candidates then need to be assessed according to standards and criteria of importance to the particular school system. Finally, top candidates need to be matched with schools. To be done correctly, each of these components should be planned carefully and conducted in a systematic manner.

Consider the development of an applicant pool. Districts typically advertise for applicants. Human resource personnel also may contact university-based principal preparation programs for recommendations of promising graduates. In addition, district leaders may initiate programs for identifying promising candidates from within the school system. When Arne Duncan was CEO of Chicago Public Schools, he also looked beyond traditional sources of applicants to organizations such as the Academy for Urban School Leadership and New Leaders for New Schools (Duncan, 2009). These groups seek school leaders outside of public education. In developing a pool of leader prospects, district leaders should strive for a diverse representation of individuals.

Screening the applicant pool is the second step. This process may entail individual and panel interviews as well as participation in a formal assessment center. Sometimes commercial interview protocols may be employed. When a district sets up its own leader development program, participants can be assigned leadership responsibilities or placed in internships where they can be observed and assessed on-the-job. When screening individuals from outside the school district, it is desirable to interview persons in the candidates' work setting.

Screening should be guided by an understanding of the particular challenges involved in a specific principalship. While most principal preparation programs and credential criteria are based on a generic model of school leadership, district leaders understand that schools can be vastly different and, therefore, require vastly different types of leadership. Duke (2010) has offered a differentiated perspective on school leadership that recognizes the distinct challenges involved in such circumstances as preventing school decline, turning around a chronically low-performing school, sustaining school improvement beyond initial turnaround, and implementing an innovative school design. Realizing that schools require different leadership means that district leaders must devote time and energy to ensuring that screened candidates are a good match for their schools.

The selection of a new principal does not conclude the work of district leaders. Especially when principals are new to the school system and new to the role of principal, systematic efforts should be made to socialize individuals to district norms and expectations. In small districts, a mentor may be assigned these responsibilities. Larger districts that hire a number of new principals each year often set up formal induction classes and new leader institutes. Leithwood, Begley, and Cousins (1994, p. 160) stress the value of several socialization activities for new principals, including exposure to effective role models, having a mentor, and opportunities to interact with peers. Hart (1993, p. 280) cautions district leaders not to leave principal socialization to chance.

Internships and assistant principalships afford excellent opportunities to begin the socialization process. It is important, however, for these assignments to cover a wide range of responsibilities for which principals ultimately are accountable. Some school systems, for example, rotate assistant principals through several administrative roles before appointing them to a principalship. An individual might serve as a dean of students, an athletic director, and an assistant principal for curriculum and instruction to be prepared for a high school principalship.

It is necessary for district leaders to build their expectations for principals into the evaluation criteria used to assess principals' performance. One study of principal evaluation criteria found that superintendents place great emphasis on student management (discipline), communication skills, personal conduct, and loyalty (Duke & Stiggins, 1985). In recent years, however, superintendents have begun to place greater stress on student achievement and school improvement.

Leader Support

The second major challenge associated with school leadership is making certain that principals get the support they need to run their schools effectively. Without such support, principals, like teachers, are likely to move on, often with dire consequences for their schools and communities. District support for principals can take a variety of forms.

Consider the case of a principal who is placed in a chronically low-performing school and charged with turning it around in short order. To demonstrate that she can get things done and thereby inspire confidence in her staff, the new principal must achieve a few "quick wins" (Duke, 2010). Perhaps the school needs new textbooks, a new coat of paint, or an additional reading specialist. Whatever the case, the principal depends on school district leaders to cut through the red tape and get the needed approvals as expeditiously as possible. When the Southern Regional Education Board compared the most-improved high schools and the least-improved high schools in its "High Schools That Work" program, it found that principals in the most-improved schools felt more supported and empowered by the central office than their counterparts in the least-improved schools (Bottoms & Fry, 2009). The latter group of principals complained that district leaders were unwilling to delegate authority over the reform process to them.

One of the most frequently heard criticisms of district-school relations by principals is that they are given too much responsibility and too little authority. Principals who cannot be trusted to exercise authority should be replaced. It is not the job of district leaders to micro-manage schools. Effective school leadership requires that principals have authority over hiring, assigning staff, resource allocation, program coordination, and school-community relations. Bottoms and Fry (2009, p. vii) conclude that the "district leadership challenge is to move from oversight, from holding principals accountable at arms length, to providing the capacity-building support that true district-school partnerships require."

To be able to perform their responsibilities as effectively and efficiently as possible, principals need ongoing professional development. Large districts often operate leadership academies that provide regular opportunities for principals to receive advanced training, learn about new state and district policies, and network with each other. Small districts can benefit from professional development partnerships with other small districts, professional associations, and universities. One of the most comprehensive approaches to the professional development of principals was launched by New York City District No. 2 in 2003 (Bottoms & Fry, 2009, p. 33). It consisted of monthly conferences on instructional initiatives, support groups for principals that focused on sharing problems, a "buddy system" to provide mentoring for new principals, inter-school visitations by principals, and individualized coaching in which central office supervisors conducted "walkthroughs" with principals.

Even with extensive professional development for principals, there is no disputing the fact that the job of leading a school is difficult. In an effort to provide on-site support to principals, some district leaders have embraced the idea of hiring school administration managers (SAMS). SAMS are expected to relieve principals of many routine managerial responsibilities so that they can focus on instructional leadership and school improvement. A SAM, for example, might schedule a principal's classroom observations and coaching sessions, supervise non-instructional staff, coordinate the ordering of supplies, and serve as the first contact for student discipline and parent communications (Holland, 2008). An alternative to the SAM involves school leadership by co-principals. This arrangement allows responsibilities to be divided in a manner that balances workloads and taps individual strengths.

EXECUTIVE CONCLUSION

The key ingredient in high-performing school systems is the professionals who teach in and lead schools. District leaders cannot assume that highly qualified teachers and principals will be available to fill positions when current staff members retire or resign. Many school systems, especially those in high-poverty urban and rural locations, struggle to find personnel. The problem is especially acute when it comes to minority teachers and teachers of certain subjects, such as mathematics and English as a Second Language.

District leaders must anticipate staffing challenges and take proactive steps to recruit a talented and diverse pool of educators. Such steps can include contacting prospects while they are still in college and offering signing bonuses and other incentives. The human resource challenge does not end when talented teachers are hired. Retaining teachers requires that district leaders attend to the quality of work life for new hires, provide continuing support and professional development, and offer competitive compensation. Creating opportunities for teachers to participate in professional learning communities and undertake leadership responsibilities also have proven to be effective strategies for improving teacher retention.

Another challenge for district leaders involves ensuring that teachers stay focused on their mission, namely student learning and instructional improvement. The measures that are employed typically include supervision, evaluation, rewards, and sanctions. Pay-for-performance has attracted considerable attention in recent years, but its role in raising student achievement and improving instruction has yet to be proven. Working closely with teacher organizations, district leaders are taking a close look at a variety of once taboo subjects, including peer evaluation and the elimination of tenure and seniority.

District leaders cannot provide the leadership for individual schools. They must rely on capable principals. Research indicates that the effectiveness of a school is highly dependent on the quality of its principal. The recruitment, selection, and support of principals are among the most important functions of district leaders. Provisions must be made for the ongoing development of principals and seeing that they have the resources to accomplish their goals. To make certain that principals have adequate time to devote to instructional leadership, some school systems are exploring alternative arrangements, including co-principalships and school administration managers.

NOTE

1. Material for this vignette was based on information in "The Three R's Retention, Recruitment, and Renewal: A Blueprint for Action." Philadelphia: The School District of Philadelphia, Office of Recruitment and Retention, 2003; and D. Thomas & A. Modupe. (2004). *The Campaign for Human Capital at the School District of Philadelphia.* Cambridge, MA: Public Education Leadership Project at Harvard University. Additional information was downloaded from the website for the National Center for Alternative Certification: www.teach-now.org/newsdisp.cfm?newsid=23

REFERENCES

Barnes, G., Crowe, E., & Schaefer, B. (2003). *The Cost of Teacher Turnover in Fve School Districts: A Pilot Study.* Washington, D.C.: National Commission on Teaching and America's Future.

Bolman, L.G., & Deal, T.E. (1997). *Reframing Organizations,* second edition. San Francisco: Jossey-Bass.

Bottoms, G., & Fry, B. (2009). *The District Leadership Challenge.* Atlanta: Southern Regional Education Board.

Coburn, C.E., & Russell, J.L. (2008). District policy and teachers' social networks. *Educational Evaluation and Policy Analysis,* 30(3), 203–235.

Council of the Great City Schools. (2000). *The Urban Teacher Challenge: Teacher Demand and Supply in the Great City Schools.* Belmont, MA: Recruiting New Teachers/urban Teacher Collaborative.

Darling-Hammond, L. (1997). *The Right to Learn.* San Francisco: Jossey-Bass.

Duke, D.L. (2010). *Differentiating School Leadership: Facing the Challenges of Practice.* Thousand Oaks, CA: Corwin.

Duke, D.L. (2008). *The Little School System That Could: Transforming a City School District.* Albany: State University of new York Press.

Duke, D.L. (2005). *Education Empire: The Evolution of an Excellent Suburban School System.* Albany: State University of New York Press.

Duke, D.L. (1995). The move to reform teacher evaluation. In D.L. Duke (ed.), *Teacher Evaluation Policy.* Albany: State University of New York Press, 1–11.

Duke, D.L., & Canady, R.L. (1991). *School Policy*. New York: McGaw-Hill.

Duke, D.L., & Stiggins, R.J. (1985). Evaluating the performance of principals. *Educational Administration Quarterly*, 21(4), 71–98.

Duncan, A. (June 17, 2009). Start over. *Education Week*, p.36.

Gewertz, C. (July 21, 2009). Duncan's call for school turnarounds sparks debate. *Education Week*, p.1.

Grossman, P., Thompson, C.S., & Valencia, S.W. (2002). Focusing the concerns of new teachers: the district as teacher educator. In A.M. Hightower, M.S. Knapp, J.A. Marsh, & M.W. McLaughlin (eds.), *School Districts and Instructional Renewal*. New York: Teachers College Press, 129.142.

Hallilnger, P., & Heck, R.H. (1998). Exploring the principal's contribution to school effectiveness: 1980–1995. *School Effectiveness and School Improvement*, 9(1), 157–191.

Hanushek, E., Kain, J., & Rivkin, S. (2004). Why public schools lose teachers. *Journal of Human Resources*, 39(3), 326–354.

Hart, A.W. (1993). *Principal Succession*. Albany: State University of New York Press.

Holland, H. (2008). *Out of the Office and Into the Classroom*. Seattle: Center for the Study of Teaching and Policy, University of Washington.

Honawar, V. (March 12, 2008). Performance-pay studies show few achievement gains. *Education Week*, p. 7.

Ingersoll, R.M. (2003). Is there really a teacher shortage? Center for the Study of Teaching and Policy. Accessed from http://depts.washington.edu/ctpmail/PDFs/shortage-R1-09-2003.pdf

Ingersoll, R.M. (2003). *Who Controls Teachers' Work?* Cambridge, MA: Harvard University Press.

Ingersoll, R.M. (2001). Teacher turnover and teacher shortages: an organizational analysis. *American Educational Research Journal*, 38(3), 499–534.

Jackson, M. (2008). *Distracted*. Amherst, NY: Prometheus Books.

Jacob, B.A. (2007). The challenges of staffing urban schools with effective teachers. *The Future of Children*, 17(1), 129–153.

Johnson, S.M., Berg, J.H., & Donaldson, M.L. (2005). *Who Stays in Teaching and Why*. Cambridge, MA: Harvard Graduate School of Education, Project on the Next Generation of Teachers.

Lankford, H., Loeb, S., & Wyckoff, J. (2002). Teacher sorting and the plight of urban schools: a descriptive analysis. *Educational Evaluation and Policy Analysis*, 24(1), 37–62.

Leithwood, K., Begley, P.T., & Cousins, J.B. (1994). *Developing Expert Leadership for Future Schools*. London: Falmer.

Leithwood, K., Louis, K.S., Anderson, S., & Wahlstrom, K. (2004). *How Leadership Influences Student Learning*. New York: The Wallace Foundation.

Luekens, M.T., Lyter, D.M., Fox, E.E., & Chandler, K. (2004). *Teacher Attrition and Mobility: Results from the Teacher Follow-Up Survey, 2000–2001*. Washington, D.C.: National Center for Education Statistics.

Mayrowetz, D. (2008). Making sense of distributed leadership: exploring the multiple usages of the concept in the field. *Educational Administration Quarterly*, 44(3), 424–435.

McCaskey, M.B. (1982). *The Executive Challenge*. Boston: Pitman.

Meier, K.J., & Juenke, E.G. (2005). Electoral structure and the quality of representation on school boards. In W.G. Howell (ed.), *Besieged: School Boards and the Future of Education Politics*. Washington, D.C.: Brookings Institution Press, 199–227.

Monk, D.H. (2007). Recruiting and retaining high-quality teachers in rural areas. *Future of Children*, 17(1), 155–174.

Murnane, R.J., & Steele, J.L. (2007). What is the problem? The challenge of providing effective teachers for all students. *Future of Children*, 17(1), 15–43.

National Center for Education Statistics. (2006). Characteristics of schools, districts, teachers, principals, and school libraries in the United States, 2003–2004, Schools and Staffing Survey, Report 2006-313. Washington, D.C.: U.S. Department of Education.

Olson, L. (January 10, 2008). Human resources a weak spot. *Quality Counts/Education Week*, 12–19.

Paynter, J.L. (2003). The motivational profiles of teachers. Doctoral dissertation, The Johns Hopkins University.

Robinson, V.M.J., Lloyd, C.A., & Rowe, K.J. (2008). The impact of leadership on student outcomes: an analysis of the differential effects of leadership types. *Educational Administration Quarterly*, 44(5), 635–674.

Sawchuk, S. (June 10, 2009). Grade inflation seen in evaluations of teachers, regardless of system. *Education Week*, 6.

Sawchuk, S. (June 17, 2009). N.C. district lets go of veteran teachers, but keeps TFA hires. *Education Week*, 10.

Sawchuk, S. (December 10, 2008). Out-of-field teaching more common in poor schools. *Education Week*, 6.

Slotnik, W.J. (July 15, 2009). Get performance pay right. *Education Week*, 32, 26.

Stotko, E.M., Ingram, R., & Beaty-O'Ferrall, M.E. (2007). Promising strategies for attracting and retaining successful urban teachers. *Urban Education*, 42(1), 30–51.

Snipes, J., & Horwitz, A. (2007). *Recruiting and Retaining Effective Teachers in Urban Schools. Research Brief.* Washington, D.C.: The Council of the Great City Schools.

Terry, B.D. (2008). *Paying for Results: Examining Incentive Pay in Texas Schools.* Austin: Texas Public Policy Foundation.

Thomas, D., & Modupe, A. (2004). *The Campaign for Human Capital at the School District of Philadelphia.* Cambridge, MA: Public Education Leadership Project at Harvard University.

Thomas-Lester, A. (July 4, 2009). Number of black male teachers belies their influence. *The Washington Post*, B-1, B-4.

Wagner, R.B. (1989). *Accountability in Education: A Philosophical Inquiry.* New York: Routledge.

3
Fundamental Challenges

9

THE CHALLENGES OF CHANGE

TURNING AROUND AN ENTIRE SCHOOL SYSTEM[1]

Business-as-usual was not on the minds of North Carolina's Charlotte-Mecklenburg School Board when they hired Eric Smith to assume leadership of the nation's 26th largest school system in 1996. The district needed a change agent, someone with the vision and political skills to address a variety of pressing issues. No issue was more urgent, though, than the substantial achievement gap between African American and white students. Only four of every ten African American students were reading at or above grade level. Math performance reflected a similar statistic.

At the time Smith came to Charlotte-Mecklenburg, the district enrolled 100,000 students in 135 schools. The racial composition of the student population consisted of 48 percent white, 43 percent African American, 4 percent Hispanic, and 5 percent other groups. Approximately 38 percent of the students were eligible for free or reduced price lunch.

Beginning in 1959 with the consolidation of the Charlotte city school system and the Mecklenburg County school system, district leaders had made a variety of efforts to promote educational equity. Perhaps the most controversial measure involved busing students in order to achieve racial balance in schools. Despite these efforts, Eric Smith found a school system in which schools were not racially balanced. One report indicated that African American students did not have access to the same educational opportunities as white students. Schools with large percentages of African American students tended to be inferior facilities staffed by less experienced teachers.

To address these issues, Smith and his school board adopted a number of initiatives. None was more important, however, than a pair of measures that targeted low-performing schools for added resources.

The Equity-Plus and A-Plus programs enabled low-performing schools, most of which were predominantly African American, to reduce class sizes and focus on teacher professional development. The schools also qualified for educational specialists in reading and mathematics and after-school tutors for struggling students. Principals were given additional authority through site-based budgeting so that they could hire part-time literacy staff to work with students whose performance in language arts was below grade level.

To address the problem of inexperienced teachers in low-performing schools, Smith and the school board adopted several initiatives. Teachers who agreed to remain at an Equity-Plus or A-Plus school for three years received a bonus. Bonuses also were awarded when schools hit specific performance targets. Veteran teachers with skills in areas of critical need qualified to have their base salaries increased if they consented to teach at a low-performing school.

Smith's vision for Charlotte-Mecklenburg did not stop with the achievement of educational equity, however. He was committed to promoting across-the-board excellence. Toward that end, he zeroed in on middle school course offerings. Careful review of data on student course assignments revealed that relatively few African American students were enrolled in algebra and other college preparatory courses. He realized that their placement in so-called "basic" courses in middle school would increase the likelihood of similar assignments in high school, thereby limiting their chances of being exposed to challenging subject matter.

Over the objections of many Charlotte-Mecklenburg educators, Smith ordered counselors to re-assign African American middle schoolers to advanced courses in mathematics and other subjects. When teachers eventually realized that these students were capable of handling more challenging material, they applauded Smith's bold mid-year move.

Smith then set his sights on high school. If his mantra of "high expectations for all students" were to have any meaning, the number of African American students enrolled in Advanced Placement and International Baccalaureate courses had to increase dramatically. Smith let it be known that he expected every high school student to take at least one AP or IB course.

✳✳✳✳✳

Change is a curious thing. At times it appears that the only constant in the world is change. But then there is that nagging expression from the French—"The more things change, the more things remain the same."

Prior to Eric Smith's arrival, many changes had been implemented in order to promote educational equity in Charlotte-Mecklenburg. Despite these efforts, African American students still lagged far behind their white peers. The schools in which they predominated were less well staffed and had less adequate facilities than did the predominantly white schools. Smith understood that simply adopting a high-minded mission statement and adding some new programs were unlikely alone to produce meaningful changes. Basic patterns of behavior, such as student course-taking, had to be altered. How resources were allocated and for what purpose had to be re-examined. There were no shortcuts to fundamental educational change.

THE RESTLESS CONTEXTS OF PUBLIC EDUCATION

No sooner had Eric Smith assumed the superintendency than white parents in Charlotte-Mecklenburg sued to stop race-based policies in the district. If they prevailed, it would mean overturning the 1969 *Swann* decision, which had led to court-ordered busing in the interests of district-wide desegregation. District leaders fought to preserve their prerogatives under *Swann*, but they ultimately lost the case. A new student assignment plan that permitted greater parental choice was instituted and the ability of district leaders to address desegregation issues was drastically reduced.

The point of this example is to illustrate what every seasoned school district leader already knows. They do not exercise much control over the contexts in which public education takes place. These contexts account for everything from legal decisions and legislative mandates to economic changes and cultural shifts. Even the weather can be a factor. Just consider the impact of Hurricane Katrina on public education in the New Orleans area.

In the immediate aftermath of the disastrous storm, schools in and around New Orleans ceased to operate. Some were damaged so much that they could not re-open. When other schools eventually re-opened, their enrollments were decimated. The post-Katrina diaspora resulted in the departure of educators as well as students. Displaced students caused enrollments elsewhere, especially Baton Rouge and Houston, to swell.

When some residents eventually returned to New Orleans, they discovered that major changes had occurred in public education. Faced with a crisis in public services, including education, the State of Louisiana, with the help of federal disaster relief funding, stepped in. Prior to Katrina, many of New Orleans' lowest performing schools had been reorganized into the Recovery School District. Paul Vallas, former CEO of Chicago Public Schools and the Public Schools of Philadelphia, was hired to tackle the job of rebuilding the schools and raising the level of student achievement. The New Orleans Parish school system continued to exist as a public entity, but with only a handful of schools. Other public schools were allowed to convert to charter schools and hire their own teachers and administrators. Overnight, New Orleans became home to one of the largest concentrations of charter schools in the United States.

Opinions vary as to the impact of all the changes wrought by Hurricane Katrina. Some observers believe that the storm created an opportunity for the state to introduce sweeping reforms in an area long plagued by poor public schools and corruption. Others worry that the new arrangements are too complex and that the spread of charter schools will siphon off the most able students, leaving the public schools to accommodate large concentrations of struggling students. Those who understand change, of course, recognize the potential of every reform to produce unanticipated and sometimes negative outcomes.

Preceding chapters already have noted a variety of external impetuses to educational change besides the weather. School district leaders have been compelled to respond to demographic changes, court decisions, and new laws. To this list can be added economic fluctuations, technological developments, and social and cultural changes. With each external impetus to educational change comes debate over the potential impact on schools and school districts. The public, it appears, is intensely interested in any development that might change public education.

A good example concerns school choice. The push for school choice did not originate with public education leaders. Many credit the economist, Milton Friedman, with initiating the campaign for greater choice in schooling (Henig, 1994). Friedman argued that any restriction of market forces in education was harmful to the interests of parents and students. This argument was embraced by conservatives, but they were not alone in supporting more school choice. In the 1970s liberals started to link school choice with educational equity (Miron, Welner, Hinchey, & Molnar, 2008). They noted that well-to-do parents long had enjoyed the benefits of choice when it came to their children's education. Why shouldn't less affluent parents, they asked, be extended the same options?

Subsequent decades have witnessed the development of various voucher schemes and charter school bills. School choice was built into the No Child Left Behind Act. When a school repeatedly fails to make adequate yearly progress, parents are accorded the right to transfer their children to a more successful public school.

Pressure for more school choice clearly can pose a dilemma for school district leaders. Should they support choice and risk losing students to charter schools and nonpublic schools that accept vouchers? Should they resist choice and incur the anger of parents and special interest groups? Should they co-opt the idea of school choice and develop within-district options? Each course of action obviously entails potential costs and benefits. The challenge for district leaders is to weigh the costs and benefits of choice options and arrive at a decision that serves the best interests of young people.

Facing the challenge of change is especially difficult when the change involves a reduction in the resources available to district leaders. Snipes and Casserly (2004) have noted that the uncertainty of funding along with evolving state accountability systems and local politics are three major sources of change for large urban school systems. Any district leader who was in California following the passage of Proposition 13 in 1978 is well aware of how reduced resources can serve as an impetus to change. Prompted by a so-called "taxpayers revolt," Proposition 13 limited the ability of school districts to increase the tax rate on local property. Since a substantial portion of school funding was derived from property taxes, the impact was immediate and far-reaching. Many California school systems had to cut their budgets by 10 percent or more for several years in a row.

Accounts (Duke, Hallinger, Kuntz, & Robinson, 1981; Duke & Meckel, 1980) of the actions taken in California school districts indicate that such substantial cuts could not help but impact teaching and learning. Teachers had to be released, thereby increasing class sizes and reducing the number of courses available to students. Seniority rules meant that veteran teachers could "bump" less experienced teachers even if they lacked appropriate credentials. Some school systems reduced or eliminated guidance counselors and other non-teaching personnel. Special programs, many of which targeted struggling students, had to be curtailed or shut down entirely. Under such dire circumstances, district leaders must make every effort to prevent budget cuts form sending schools into a "downward spiral" where each new round of reductions accelerates the pace of decline (Duke, 2008b).

The availability of resources also can be adversely affected by a downturn in the economy. Such a downturn began in 2007 when a combination of financial crises involving homeowners, banks, and other financial institutions set into motion a major recession. Unable to pay on their mortgages, many people were forced to leave their homes, depriving school systems of revenue and causing major shifts in enrollments. Only the distribution of so-called "stimulus funds" by the federal government in 2009 prevented major lay-offs by school districts across the United States. As it was, many district leaders had to come up with substantial cost-saving measures to weather the financial storm.

Yet another impetus to educational change that can be traced to the economic sector is globalization. Times have changed since the end of World War II when U.S. business stood alone as the dominant force in the world economy. Spurred on by technological advances, contemporary corporations know no boundaries. Friedman's (2005) declaration that "the world is flat" captures the new reality, one characterized by a more level global playing field on which industrialized and developing nations are increasingly able to challenge U.S. economic dominance. The competitive edge enjoyed by these nations is attributed in part to the quality of their school systems and their high level of academic achievement. It is predictable, of course, that U.S. schools would be exhorted to raise their own standards and produce a more competitive workforce.

Turbulent is a word that is used to describe the environment in which district leaders work (Leithwood, 1995, p. 317). The term captures the fact that external developments can develop with little warning and upset the "best laid" plans of educators. Since there is no evidence that the environment in which public schools function will become less turbulent in the future, it is incumbent on school district leaders to do whatever they can to anticipate new developments. When Diamond (2005) analyzed the reasons why entire societies collapse, he concluded that two key reasons involved failure to anticipate problems and failure to recognize problems after they had surfaced. These reasons are also likely to help account for variations in the effectiveness of school systems. Some district leaders manage to stay abreast of developing circumstances that might threaten the performance of their school systems. Others appear surprised and unprepared when faced with change.

District leaders who make it their business to anticipate demographic, legal, legislative, social, cultural, economic, and technological change may not be able to control such change, but they at least can reduce the potential negative impact of change on the educational process. What's more, district leaders do not have to settle for always reacting and responding to change. There are many opportunities for district leaders to function as initiators of change. In order to do so, they should be able to answer the following questions.

The Challenges of Change

1. Why can organizational change be so difficult to achieve?

2. What can district leaders do to increase the likelihood of successful organizational change?

3. What is needed to sustain successful organizational change over time?

THE IMPORTANCE OF DEVELOPING PEOPLE

When a change in district leadership occurs, it is not uncommon for a new superintendent or a new school board to announce a reorganization. While making adjustments to school district structure, roles, and reporting relationships can serve important symbolic purposes, such moves are unlikely to make much of a substantive difference unless the individuals affected by the moves make appropriate changes. These changes can entail the acquisition of new skills, the development of new routines, the abandonment of dysfunctional beliefs and attitudes, and the cultivation of new understandings.

To say that change constitutes a challenge for many adults is to point out the obvious. Witness how many adults struggle to quit smoking, alter spending habits, and lose weight. Even when people understand that such behaviors are dangerous, they still have difficulty changing them. Some behavioral problems, of course, have physiological roots. Simply making up one's mind to change may be insufficient to overcome the problem. In other cases, however, people's beliefs and behaviors are closely linked. It is difficult to change one without changing the other.

District leaders who have tried to initiate new policies, programs, processes, and practices probably have encountered some degree of resistance to change. The first challenge of change, therefore, involves understanding the variety of reasons why people resist change and what can be done to address these reasons. In some cases, of course, the causes of resistance may be so deep-seated that they require therapeutic intervention. This section will not focus on such causes. Instead, we shall examine several sources of resistance that district leaders may be able to address successfully by undertaking well-designed staff development and constructive supervision. These sources of resistance include fear of failure, fear of success, routines, complacency, heightened anxiety, and lack of awareness.

Before discussing these sources of resistance as they might apply to district personnel, it is important to point out that they also can apply to district leaders themselves. While this section focuses primarily on obstacles to change encountered by district leaders, district leaders should remember that they, too, may be seen as impediments in the road to reform (Snipes, Doolittle, & Herlihy, 2002, p. 60).

Fear of Failure

There are few obstacles to individual change greater than fear of failure. Ironically, many people who fear failure have experienced considerable success in their lives. Dweck (2006) refers to these individuals as having a "fixed mindset." A fixed mindset is characterized by a desire to look capable and intelligent. This desire, which often derives from early experiences of success, leads people to become increasingly cautious and to avoid challenges out of fear that they might mishandle them and appear incompetent. Over time, they amplify on proven capabilities and neglect to grow in new directions and acquire new skills. People with a fixed mindset, according to Dweck, tend to ignore useful feedback if they perceive it to be critical. They also feel threatened by others' success. Fixed mindset people often plateau early in their careers and fail to realize their potential.

Dweck (2006) contrasts the fixed mindset with the growth mindset. Those blessed with a growth mindset are committed to their own development and improvement. They consequently seek new challenges, regarding them as opportunities for growth, not failure. They learn from mistakes and solicit feedback on their performance. Constructive criticism does not devastate them. Unlike those with a fixed mindset, growth mindset people are not threatened by others' success. They instead are inspired by it. These qualities enable those with a growth mindset to continue developing and improving.

The origins of fear of failure are complicated. Frequently, it is not failure itself that people fear, but the perceived consequences of failure (Duke, 2004, pp. 127–128). A veteran educator, for example, may perceive that failure to master new technology will result in the loss of respect from fellow educators. Rather than take the risk of tackling technology and failing, he does not even try, relying instead on traditional practices and all the while criticizing new technology.

Fear of Success

Fear of success functions in much the same way as fear of failure. People fear success because of the perceived consequences of success, not success itself (Duke, 2004, p. 128). This fear leads them to avoid situations where they might acquire greater expertise or distinguish themselves.

Fear of success can be traced to a variety of impetuses. In some cases, for instance, educators may believe that any effort on their part to embrace reforms and acquire new skills and knowledge is likely to incur the displeasure of their colleagues. Payne (2008, p. 196) has observed that this phenomenon often characterizes low-performing schools. In these "demoralized environments," individual teachers grow reluctant to put forth a concerted effort to improve. Their reason is disturbing. If a teacher actually succeeds in improving and this improvement benefits her students, her success casts her fellow teachers in a negative light. Observers begin to question the causes of low performance and point accusing fingers at the faculty. As long as no teacher is succeeding, however, the reasons for low student achievement can be shifted to factors beyond the teachers' control—poverty, lack of parental involvement, inadequate resources, and the like. If one teacher manages to overcome these obstacles, though, the spotlight moves to the teaching staff. The social pressure to resist change in low-performing schools understandably can be substantial.

Another reason why educators resist success is the likelihood that it will result in more work. Teachers who manage to achieve miracles with a couple of struggling students may be assigned a lot of struggling students. Principals who achieve success in a challenging school may be assigned to an even more challenging school. An educator who comes up with an innovative idea may be assigned to head up a committee to develop the idea, thereby increasing his workload. The disincentives associated with success are part of the folklore of public schools.

Routines

Many educators devote considerable time early in their careers to developing routines for handling predictable tasks and challenges. Those who fail to develop routines, in fact, often are regarded as ineffective. They confront recurring situations as if they were encountered for the first time. Their inconsistency gives rise to confusion.

After many years, veteran educators probably have developed dozens of routines. Their routines, however, can constitute a major impediment to change. We sometimes speak of these individuals as having settled into a "comfort zone" (Duke, 1993). Any proposal for change is perceived as a threat to their contentment. This fact probably helps to explain why some teachers, even ones in low-performing schools, are inclined to resist change. Bridges (2004) points out that change invariably occasions a sense of loss, even when people realize that change is necessary. Feelings of loss can be traced in part to the fact that people have invested considerable energy in making their circumstances as comfortable as possible. Any risk of upsetting well-established routines and dislodging them from their comfort zones is bound to be greeted with reluctance and even resistance. As Senge (1990, p. 88) has written, "Resistance to change is neither capricious nor mysterious. It almost always arises from threats to traditional norms and ways of doing things."

Complacency

While some people fear success, others embrace it. They are convinced that what they are doing is right. Consequently there is no reason to change. When the faculty of a school is poised on the cutting edge of complacency, they tend to discount new challenges. Faced with a changing student population, for example, they insist that how they have taught for years is the appropriate way to teach newcomers. They point to the track records of their past students. If the newcomers fail to perform, it must be their problem.

One problem with complacency is that it is often unjustified. High levels of student achievement could have more to do with the fact that students come from well-to-do homes with parents who stress the importance of academic success than with the quality of instruction. Even when teachers rightfully take credit for student achievement, they should not assume that their practices cannot be improved upon or that how they have always taught necessarily will succeed as they grow older and encounter new groups of students.

District leaders in high-performing school districts have an especially great challenge when it comes to promoting reform. Superintendent Ceil Chavez discovered this when she launched Directions 2000 in Littleton, Colorado. The bold initiative aimed to prepare students for the 21st century workplace by introducing a set of ambitious performance-based graduation requirements (Bradley, 1994; Duke, 2004, pp. 1–4). No longer would it be good enough just to pass courses. The new arrangements called for students to demonstrate their ability to apply what they had learned across 19 "performance areas" ranging from ethics and personal growth to mathematics and communications. Many parents and some teachers challenged Directions 2000 on the grounds that Littleton schools already were doing a fine job of educating young people. Why, they questioned, should the district embark on a new and risky initiative, one that could jeopardize graduation for a number of students and greatly increase teachers' workloads?

Heightened Anxiety

Change can be stressful. New initiatives invariably entail more meetings, more planning, more training—in short, more work. Many educators already feel they lack sufficient time to accomplish everything they should do under normal circumstances. Introducing new initiatives threatens to eat into scarce time, thereby increasing pressure on individuals and raising their level of anxiety.

The problem can be chronic in low-performing school systems where the pressure for improvement is virtually continuous. Educators in struggling schools today also must confront the possibility that their schools will be closed or reconstituted if they fail to improve. Their forebears rarely had to deal with such dire consequences. A study of urban school districts (Snipes et al., 2002, p. 62) found that many educators "reported that the continual pressures [of improvement] took a toll on their emotions and threatened to take the joy out of being educators and working with children."

Lack of Awareness

Resistance to change can result from lack of awareness of the need for change and how one figures into plans for change. Educators who never come into contact with struggling students, for example, may never appreciate how badly change is needed. This was the case at West Linn High School (Oregon) in the early 1980s. Newly appointed principal Dick Sagor was concerned that too much attention was focused on the students taking college preparatory courses. Roughly half of West Linn's students, however, did not go on to college. Sagor believed that the quality of the courses these students took could be greatly improved. The challenge was convincing teachers who never taught low-level courses of the need for change.

BOOSTING THE ODDS OF SUCCESSFUL CHANGE

One key to understanding change is realizing that it is a process, not an event (Hall & Hord, 2001). Scholars have offered various models of the change process. Some models pertain to change in individuals, others to organizational change, and still others to change in large systems. Of particular relevance to school district leaders are models of organizational change. While the number of stages in the organizational change process vary somewhat across experts, most models include at least four elements: (1) a phase during which a determination is made that change is needed, (2) a phase when the nature or design of the change is decided, (3) a phase when plans for effecting the change are made, and (4) a phase when the change is actually put into operation (Duke, 2004, pp. 28–30). These phases are referred to as discovery, design, development, and implementation.

Organizational change, of course, may not always conform exactly to this model. Sometimes phases of the change process are omitted, repeated, or experienced in a different order. The value of a model derives from its capacity to facilitate reflection and analysis. For present purposes, for example, it is instructive to realize that resistance to change can arise during any one of the four phases of the change process. Let us examine each phase in order to see what actions district leaders can take to increase the odds of successful change.

Discovery

The discovery phase, as indicated earlier, represents that part of the change process when a decision is made regarding the need for change. The need for change may involve matters of mission, organizational structure, personnel, policies, programs, procedures, and practices. It is often the case that change is necessitated as a result of a discrepancy between desired and actual outcomes. Under certain circumstances, however, the need for change can result from a consideration of new possibilities. Sometimes the change process ends at the discovery phase because no need for change is determined.

A variety of conditions can give rise to a need for change. District leaders may determine that sufficient progress toward achieving district and school goals is not being made. One or more stakeholder groups may be dissatisfied with educational outcomes. Educational benefits may not be shared by all groups of students, or certain practices and policies may be found to benefit (or harm) certain student groups more than others. Educational practices may not comply with board-adopted policies or state laws. A need for change also can result from new research, technological innovation, and shifting conditions external to schools. Sometimes the acquisition of new resources or the loss of existing resources can occasion change.

In the preceding section, an example of resistance to change at West Linn High School was provided. The teachers of college preparatory courses were unaware of problems in non-college preparatory courses. To help build awareness and therefore promote the discovery of a need for change, Principal Dick Sagor went to his superintendent, Dea Cox, and asked for funds to hire 20 substitute teachers. His intention was to have 20 teachers spend a day shadowing 20 students who were not in the college preparatory track. Cox supported Sagor's plan, and Sagor proceeded to ask for teacher volunteers. He had no problem getting enough volunteers. Each teacher met with their assigned student to explain what they intended to do. Then each teacher spent the day sitting with the student through every class as well as during lunch. The result of this "day in the life of a student" experience was to raise faculty awareness of the boring nature of instruction in non-college preparatory courses and to sensitize them to the need to make sweeping improvements.

One key element in discovering whether a need for change exists, therefore, is getting to know what school is really like for stakeholders. Students, of course, are not the only stakeholders. District leaders need to understand how teachers and other staff members feel about their work. Needs assessment surveys sometimes are used to identify areas for improvement, but they are not always helpful. Individuals are unlikely to recommend changes if they are unaware of better options. To maximize the value of needs assessments, it may be necessary to begin by raising awareness of new developments and promising alternatives.

Another approach to discovering whether a need for change exists involves a careful analysis of student achievement data. Disaggregating standardized test results by student sub-group, for example, can reveal gaps in achievement between sub-groups that require the adoption of special interventions. When large numbers of students in various sub-groups miss the same items on tests, inadequate instruction or instructional materials may be to blame.

The challenges associated with the discovery phase of the change process do not end with the identification of one or more areas in need of change. Care must be taken not to mis-label a need for change. Attributing low performance in a school to inadequate leadership, for example, could conceal the fact that there is little alignment between the content of state standardized tests and district curriculum guidelines. The effectiveness of change efforts hinges on the accuracy of diagnoses of problematic conditions.

District leaders also must be careful not to identify too many areas in need of change. An over-abundance of targets for change can overwhelm a district's capacity to support change and discourage district personnel. The ability of district leaders to focus change efforts on a relatively short list of high priorities is invaluable.

The change process invariably involves a political component. District leaders not only must specify a need for change, they must justify it. The possibility therefore arises for problems associated with explaining why particular changes are necessary. Some stakeholders may not be swayed by particular explanations. Arguing that middle school class sizes need to be increased in order to reduce primary class sizes, for instance, is unlikely to be received well by middle school teachers and parents of middle school students. The ability to articulate clear and persuasive justifications for change is as important as the ability to accurately identify needs for change.

Design

The second phase of the change process involves agreeing on the nature of the changes to be implemented. District leaders often prefer to "design" their own changes, but in some cases, new programs, practices, and processes may be adopted or adapted from existing designs. To increase the likelihood of choosing or developing a good design, district leaders should consider a variety of possibilities. All too often, though, leaders opt for the first attractive design they encounter. This is not a good approach to buying a home or an automobile, and it is not a good way to go about choosing a new program, process, or practice.

When engaging in the creation or adoption of a design related to the instructional process, district leaders can benefit from considering the following characteristics of a good design (Duke, 2003).

A Good Design for Instructional Change:

1. Addresses legitimate educational needs

2. Reflects a clear understanding of how people learn

3. Is supported by research and professional judgment

4. Takes into account local conditions

5. Enables educational needs to be addressed without adversely affecting any particular group of learners

6. Enables educational needs to be addressed as efficiently as possible without sacrificing effectiveness

---

Where chronically low-performing schools are involved, it is not uncommon for the justification of a particular design for improvement to be based on the fact that things could not get any worse. Regrettably, the history of educational change provides evidence that things always can get worse. Students in struggling schools are not guinea pigs on whom should be tried any new idea. It is up to district leaders to see that students are not subjected to untested and unproven designs.

Educators sometimes have been criticized for addressing change in a piecemeal fashion. Such an approach, critics claim, focuses on symptoms not root causes of problems and ensures that no meaningful improvement will be achieved. The answer supposedly is comprehensive change. This was the course taken by John Fryer (see Chapter 6) when he became superintendent in Duval County.

Harvard researchers Childress, Elmore, and Grossman (2006) support Fryer's approach, taking the position that it is unrealistic to expect individual schools in a large district to mount effective improvement efforts. "Achieving excellence on a broad scale," they contend, "requires a districtwide strategy for improving instruction in the classroom and an organization that can implement it" (p. 55). They go on to point out that only the district office is positioned to spread best practices, develop leadership capabilities at all levels, create information systems to monitor student achievement, and hold people accountable for results. The researchers acknowledge, though, that getting all schools in a large district to execute a new design consistently remains a major challenge for district leaders.

One classification scheme for large scale designs comes from a Rand study of New American Schools, a national program supported by public and corporate money to promote sweeping reform (Bodilly, 1996, pp. 297–298). Large scale designs are divided into three categories: core designs, comprehensive designs, and systemic designs. The categories are distinguished by the number and type of design elements and the number of partners involved in developing the design. Core designs, such as Expeditionary Learning and Roots and Wings, focus on school partnerships and changes associated with such central matters as curriculum, instruction, standards, and assessment. Comprehensive designs involve additional elements, such as integrated youth services, new forms of school governance, and staffing changes. Community Learning Centers exemplify this type of design. Systemic designs, such as the National Alliance for Restructuring Education, call for changes in all design elements as well as widespread collaboration. Systemic designs typically extend beyond individual schools to encompass entire school districts.

Research on the desirability of large scale designs for change has been mixed. Muncey and McQuillan (1996, pp. 157–158) studied change efforts related to the Coalition of Essential Schools and concluded that comprehensive change was more likely to "take root and endure" than more modest initiatives. On the other hand, Lee (2001, p. 75), in a study of high school reform, determined that "the simultaneous implementation of many restructuring reforms…did not increase either effectiveness or equity." Research on so-called "whole-school reform" raises questions regarding the wisdom of trying to scale up changes that have proven effective in a particular school or district (Viadero, 2001). Schlechty (2001) argues that the nature of contemporary educational challenges demands that the appropriate unit for change be the school district, not individual schools. School-initiated reforms, he points out, easily can be neutralized by an unsupportive district central office.

Development

The third phase of the change process involves developing plans for implementing changes. Reforms that are implemented immediately after the design process often struggle because too little attention is devoted to planning the implementation process. District leaders increase the likelihood of successful change when they set aside time and resources for the development of an implementation plan.

An implementation plan is "a structured sequence of specific steps for achieving a particular design for change" (Duke, 2004, p. 138). Let us say the design involves developing a districtwide initiative to get eighth graders to take Algebra I. The implementation plan for this initiative is rooted in an "implementation strategy," which is defined as "an overall approach to achieving change in a particular setting at a particular time" (Duke, 2004, p. 138). It is pointless to develop an implementation plan without considering the context in which change is to occur. Context has a bearing on such critical matters as resources for change and resistance to change. In the example above, district leaders decided on an implementation strategy that called for piloting the eighth grade Algebra I initiative in one middle school that was receptive to the reform. This strategy was chosen because it entailed relatively little additional funding at a time when money was tight and because it provided an opportunity to "work out the kinks" before going to scale. Piloting the initiative at a receptive middle school also maximized the likelihood of successful implementation. The odds of achieving successful implementation are greatly reduced when the initial implementers are unreceptive to change.

District leaders can choose from a variety of implementation strategies. Besides piloting a new design, they can opt for a sequenced implementation in which a new design is introduced in segments, rather than all at once. Another strategy involves starting with voluntary participation in order to fine tune a new design and generate support for eventual scaling up. When resistance to a new design is encountered, the strategy of choice may entail either postponing implementation until conditions are more favorable or delaying the consequences of the new design until people have learned about and adjusted to it. The latter strategy characterized the implementation of high-stakes testing in many states. The results of the first few administrations of new state tests were not used to determine student promotions, thereby giving teachers and parents an opportunity to gear up for new accountability measures.

Once an implementation strategy has been selected, district leaders can focus on the specific elements of an implementation plan. Bullard and Taylor (1993, p. 284) identify six basic elements: (1) goal statements, (2) activities designed to achieve the goals, (3) personnel responsibilities associated with each activity, (4) necessary resources and materials, (5) timelines and/or checkpoints for assessing progress, and (6) summative evaluation provisions to determine whether implementation was successful.

A number of school districts have adopted versions of the Balanced Scorecard to help in guiding the process of implementing change (Archer, 2007; Kaplan & Norton, 1996). Balanced Scorecards identify measurable objectives, timelines, benchmarks for assessing progress, specific strategies for implementing new measures, and individuals responsible for seeing that strategies are undertaken and monitored. This approach to change relies heavily on project management, a process used throughout the business world, but only recently employed by school systems. The implementation of a new program, policy, or practice is treated as a "project" and assigned a "project manager," who in turn appoints a "project team." The project team is held accountable through the use of a Balanced Scorecard, which specifies implementation benchmarks that need to be attained by certain dates and a system for regularly reporting progress.

The most important component of almost every implementation plan is the provision for staff development and inservice training. It is hard to imagine implementing a new design without enhancing the skills and knowledge of the implementers. Pasmore and Fagans (1992, p. 391) put it like this: "There can be no sustained organizational development without individual development and that individual development is predicated upon the creation of an organizational context in which…people can experience, reflect, experiment, and learn." One-shot workshops and inspirational speakers won't do it. Sound implementation plans provide for ongoing training and staff development.

A good illustration of the elements of a sound implementation plan are provided by Payne (2008, pp. 185–186) in *So Much Reform, So Little Change*. He considers the provisions that a school system should have in place if it wants to reduce the amount of didactic instruction in mathematics and increase student inquiry and problem-solving. The resulting list of implementation "musts" includes five full days of pre-implementation training for teachers and at least half that for principals, a minimum of five more days of training during the regular school year, a common planning period each week so that teachers can plan and discuss math lessons, and bi-weekly interactions between teachers and a highly trained math coach.

Implementation

The goal of implementation is to see that an agreed-upon design is implemented as faithfully and productively as possible. Veteran district leaders are likely to realize that such implementation never can be assumed. Even when great care is exercised during the preceding phases of the change process, problems still can arise late in the process and derail implementation. Among these problems are uncertainty, conflict, and disappointment.

Before a new initiative is launched, people may think they are clear about the nature of the proposed change and what it is supposed to accomplish. Once actual implementation begins, though, clarity often is displaced by uncertainty. Questions arise about the impact of the new design on cherished routines and longstanding relationships. It is not unusual when these concerns surface for some former advocates of change to reconsider their support. Others may continue to insist on moving ahead. The result can be a deep division among those expected to implement the new design. Division in turn can lead to rancor and conflict, causing additional people to question the wisdom of change.

Even if the implementation phase goes relatively smoothly at first, some people may become disappointed with the results. Reforms that were promised to yield impressive results fail to live up to expectations. Implementers who thought that their work would become easier are surprised to learn that they have much more to do and less time in which to do it. Then there is the constant possibility that circumstances will change. School districts do not exist in a vacuum, inured to the effects of environmental shifts. Resources that were counted on to fund implementation can dry up. Political support for change can evaporate. Turnover in key staff positions can deplete the ranks of committed implementers.

There are no insurance policies that district leaders can purchase to underwrite implementation, but that does not mean there is nothing that can be done to increase the likelihood of successful implementation. First of all, district leaders may need to acknowledge that some of the criticism that surfaces once implementation has begun is well-founded. There is no law that forbids adjustments being made in a design for change once it leaves the drawing board. This is precisely why piloting a new design can be a useful implementation strategy.

By making certain that implementation is accompanied by ongoing staff development, district leaders provide opportunities for questions and concerns to be addressed as implementers receive the training they need. Sustained staff development also ensures that newcomers receive the training necessary to support the new design.

There is some evidence to suggest that the likelihood of successful implementation of a particular reform is reduced when new reforms are added to the agenda for change (Elmore, Peterson, & McCarthey, 1996; Kanter, 1988). People have a limited capacity for change. Too much change can result in loss of focus, inadequate attention to detail, reform fatigue, and burn-out. District leaders can increase the chances of successful change by ensuring implementers that they will not be expected to undertake additional reforms until they have had a chance to implement the reform at hand.

KEYS TO SUSTAINED CHANGE

As noted earlier, change must be understood as a process, not an event. As such, change does not end with implementation. Every new design can be modified, undermined, ignored, or superseded. Fullan (2007, p. 225) writes of the "plateau effect," where initial improvements from a reform initiative level off over time. Such a result can lead to diminished commitment to the reform and eventual reversion to previous practice. Sometimes the problem involves premature celebration. Implementers are so pleased with initial results that they believe the main work of change has been accomplished. The resulting reduction in effort leads to slippage and disappointment. The message is clear—change cannot be assumed. Like a healthy relationship, sustained improvement requires continued attention and effort.

A lot more is known about how to introduce new policies, programs, practices, and processes than about how to make sure they continue to be effective over time. Still, there is a small but growing body of knowledge regarding the keys to sustaining change. Much of this literature concerns capacity building. Evans (1996, pp. 119–144) identified six components of a school's capacity to support and sustain change. They included: (1) a structure to promote professional activity, (2) sufficient trust and consensus to maintain supportive constituencies, (3) a tradition of successful innovation, (4) a sense of urgency regarding change, (5) the financial wherewithal to underwrite reform, and (6) an organizational culture that values constructive change.

Drawing on various work, including that of Evans (1996), Duke (2004, pp. 174–178) identified six components of an organization's capacity to sustain change. The components include: (1) the mobilization of broad-based support for change, (2) a continuing emphasis on the benefits of change, (3) maintenance of a facilitative organizational structure, (4) secure funding, (5) judicious recruitment, and (6) ongoing monitoring of progress. District leaders who are able to see that these components are in place stand a reasonably good chance of fostering lasting change.

Broad-Based Support

All change has a political component. Whenever a reform is proposed, some groups may be perceived to benefit more than others. It is the responsibility of district leaders to address such perceptions, allay or correct fears of inequities, and build a strong and diverse base of support for reform. Even after a reform has been implemented, leaders must continue to nurture and maintain this base of support. Berman and McLaughlin

(1978) were among the first researchers to connect the long-term fate of reform to the continued mobilization of support by stakeholders. A longitudinal study of restructuring in one school district captures the challenge of ensuring continued support for change (Brouillette, 1996, p. 214):

> Cottonwood administrators involved in the restructuring effort repeatedly mentioned frustrations arising out of the continuing need to explain to new groups of parents the rationale behind building- and district-level policies that had been extensively discussed with stakeholders before they were adopted. The mobility of families, the continual arrival of new cohorts of students at each grade level, the number of parents who paid attention to communications from the schools only when emotion-laden issues were involved, meant that site-based decisions and policies had to be continually reexplained.

Focus on Benefits

A substantial proportion of change initiatives are justified on the basis of improved teaching and learning. Following implementation, however, questions may arise regarding the intended impact of reform. When improvements are relatively small in comparison with the required investment of time and energy, support for change can waver. Support also can erode when implementers encounter unanticipated negative by-products of reform. Math performance, for example, may decline because a new reading initiative doubles the time for literacy instruction at the expense of mathematics instruction.

District leaders must not assume that those who initially support reform will continue to regard reform as beneficial. A key component of the capacity to sustain change involves reminding implementers and other stakeholders of why change was needed in the first place and keeping them apprised of encouraging outcomes. When legitimate questions about the value of change arise, they should not be ignored or discounted. Leaders need to remain sufficiently flexible to be able to make adjustments in new designs when evidence merits them.

A Facilitative Structure

Educational change occurs within an organizational context. Chapter 4 noted many of the challenges associated with the organizational structure of school districts. Features of this structure can undermine or facilitate change. Consider a concrete example. District leaders launch an initiative to equip regular classroom teachers with the skills to provide struggling students with targeted interventions to address academic problems. The training goes reasonably well, but no adjustments are made to the processes by which teachers are supervised and evaluated. As a result, principals fail to reinforce the expectation that regular education teachers will assist struggling students. Teachers are not held accountable for implementing targeted interventions. Within a few months, teachers revert to the previous practice of referring struggling students to specialists. The initiative is deemed a failure.

Change that targets one aspect of district operations invariably influences and is influenced by other aspects of district operations. Senge's (1990) insistence that change leaders think "systemically" recognizes the interconnectedness of organizational functions. District leaders committed to sustaining change must understand the direct and indirect impacts of new designs on organizational units. They should consider how district policies, regulations, staffing arrangements, calendars, schedules, evaluation procedures, and reporting relationships can facilitate or subvert change. The ultimate goal is to have all aspects of district organization aligned with and supporting change initiatives.

Secure Funding

While the need for resources may be greatest before and during the early stages of implementation, new initiatives typically require continuing financial support (Berman & McLaughlin, 1978; Knapp, 1997). Staff development may be needed on an ongoing basis, especially for newly hired personnel. Instructional materials and equipment may have to be replaced or upgraded. Based on what is learned during the initial period of implementation, adjustments that call for modifications to school schedules and improvements in facilities may be required.

To ensure adequate resources to support change over the long haul, district leaders sometimes create a line item in the annual budget to cover anticipated expenses for particular reforms. A more ambitious strategy may be needed, however, when district leaders set out to transform an entire school system. Some district leaders establish school district foundations to acquire funds outside the tax base in order to support major reform initiatives. When Superintendent Tom DeBolt (see Chapter 2) took on the challenge of transforming Manassas Park City Schools in Virginia, he had to negotiate a revenue sharing agreement with the city council (Duke, 2008a). The agreement ensured the school system would receive 57 percent of local revenues each year. These funds allowed DeBolt to implement a variety of new programs, offer competitive salaries, and support the replacement of deteriorating facilities.

Judicious Recruitment

Sustaining change depends on the availability of professional personnel who understand the need for change and possess the skills to fine tune reforms as the years go by. Chapter 8 indicated that district leaders should never take staffing for granted. Proactive steps are required to ensure that capable staff are recruited, recognized and retained. When key personnel resign or retire, district leaders must search for replacements who are committed to the reforms that have been implemented.

The first line of defense against the erosion of change initiatives is an organizational culture that values change in general and the new initiative in particular. The key to such an organizational culture, in turn, is a staff that embraces continuous improvement and supports new programs and practices. The Fairfax County, Virginia, school system has been blessed for decades with such a districtwide culture, and this fact helps explain why Fairfax has been able to maintain a very high level of performance. A 50-year organizational history of Fairfax County Public Schools concluded that its culture "embraces the belief that everybody and everything can get better" (Duke, 2005, p. 167).

Ongoing Evaluation

Earlier it was noted that uncertainty regarding the impact of a new design can reduce the likelihood that the new design will be sustained. The antidote to uncertainty is continuous monitoring of new initiatives coupled with periodic formative evaluation. By checking to see whether reforms are having the desired effect, district leaders can intervene when necessary to make mid-course corrections and adjustments.

The prospect of evaluation, of course, can induce considerable anxiety. Implementers often worry that premature evaluation will sink a reform before it has had a chance to prove itself. The answer is to focus more on formative than summative evaluation and make formative evaluation a routine process. When personnel expect to receive regular feedback on the implementation and consequences of change initiatives, they are less likely to be threatened by and discount evaluation data.

EXECUTIVE CONCLUSION

Few things are more fundamental to school district leaders' success than an understanding of change. One important realization is that the context in which public education takes place is far from stable. Leaders who embark on a course of change must do so with the knowledge that the environment is also likely to change at the same time. School districts are subject to shifts in demographics, politics, and the economy. New laws, mandates, and court decisions can intrude on the process of educational change. Ignoring these environmental changes places district reforms at risk.

Achieving meaningful change is unlikely unless changes occur with district personnel. Every change initiative, however, is sure to result in some resistance to change from the very people expected to implement change. Part of understanding change involves comprehending the reasons why some people resist change. Possible reasons include fear of failure, fear of success, reliance on routines, complacency, heightened anxiety, and lack of awareness.

There is much that district leaders can do to increase the chances for successful change. By breaking down the change process into phases, leaders can pinpoint problems that can arise along the road to reform and take appropriate precautions. Strategies that have proven useful include stakeholder involvement in identifying a need for change and designing new programs, processes, and practices; the development of strategies and plans to guide the implementation of reforms; and the provision of adequate staff development for all individuals engaged in the implementation process.

District leaders' responsibilities for change do not end with implementation. To ensure that changes are sustained, leaders must continue to play a central role in the change process. This role entails mobilizing continued support for reform, regularly pointing out the benefits of reform, maintaining a facilitative organizational structure, ensuring adequate funding, making certain that change efforts are properly staffed, and closely monitoring the impact of change.

NOTE

1. Much of the material for the opening vignette was gathered from a case study of Charlotte-Mecklenburg School District in J. Snipes, F. Doolittle, and C. Herlihy. (2002). *Foundations for Success.* Washington, D.C.: The Council of the Great City Schools.

REFERENCES

Archer, J. (February 21, 2007). Districts tracking goals with "Balanced Scorecards." *Education Week*, 10.

Berman, P., & McLaughlin, M. (1978). *Federal Programs Supporting Educational Change: Vol. VIII, Implementing and Sustaining Innovations.* Santa Monica, CA: Rand Corporation.

Bodilly, S. (1996). Lessons learned. In S. Stringfield, S. Ross, & L. Smith (eds.), *Bold Plans for School Restructuring.* Mahway, NJ: Erlbaum, 289–324.

Bradley, A. (June 1, 1994). Requiem for a reform. *Education Week*, 21–24.

Bridges, W. (2004). *Transitions.* Cambridge, MA: DaCapo Press.

Brouillette, L. (1996). *A Geology of School Reform.* Albany: State University of New York Press.

Bullard, P., & Taylor, B.O. (1993). *Making School Reform Happen.* Needham Heights, MA: Allyn and Bacon.

Childress, S., Elmore, R., & Grossman, A. (2006). How to manage urban school districts. *Harvard Business Review*, 84(11), 55–68.

Diamond, J. (2005). *Collapse.* New York: Viking.

Duke, D.L. (2008a). *The Little School System That Could: Transforming a City School System.* Albany: State University of New York Press.

Duke, D.L. (2008b). Understanding school decline. *International Studies in Educational Administration*, 36(2), 46–65.

Duke, D.L. (2005). *Education Empire: The Evolution of an Excellent Suburban School System.* Albany: State University of New York Press.

Duke, D.L. (2004). *The Challenge of Educational Change.* Boston: Pearson.

Duke, D.L. (2003). Principles of good educational design. Charlottesville, VA: Thomas Jefferson Center for Educational Design.

Duke, D.L. (1993). Removing barriers to professional growth. *Phi Delta Kappan*, 74(9), 702–704, 710–712.

Duke, D.L., Hallinger, P., Kuntz, J., & Robinson, T. (1981). Responses to retrenchment in California schools. *Action in Teacher Education*, 3(2/3), 49–66.

Duke, D.L., & Meckel, A.M. (1980). The slow death of a public high school. *Phi Delta Kappan*, 61(10), 674–677.

Dweck, C.S. (2006). *Mindset: The New Psychology of Success.* New York: Ballantine Books.

Elmore, R.F., Peterson, P.L., & McCarthey, S.J. (1996). *Restructuring in the Classroom.* San Francisco: Jossey-Bass.

Evans, R. (1996). *The Human Side of School Change.* San Francisco: Jossey-Bass.

Friedman, T.L. (2005). *The World Is Flat.* New York: Farrar, Straus and Giroux.

Fullan, N. (207). *The New Meaning of Educational Change,* fourth edition. New York: Teachers College Press.

Hall, G.E., & Hord, S.M. (2001). *Implementing Change.* Boston: Allyn and Bacon.

Henig, J.R. (1994). *Rethinking School Choice.* Princeton, NJ: Princeton University Press.

Kanter, R.M. (1988). When a thousand flowers bloom: structural, collective, and social conditions for innovation in organizations. In B.M. Staw & L.L. Cummings (eds.), *Research in Organizational Behavior*, vol. 10, Greenwich, CT: JAI Press, 169–211.

Kaplan, R.S., & Norton, D.P. (1996). Using the Balanced Scorecard as a strategic management system. *Harvard Business Review*, reprint no. 96107.

Knapp, M.S. (1997). Between systemic reforms and the mathematics and science classroom: the dynamics of innovation, implementation, and professional learning. *Review of Educational Research*, 67(2), 227–266.

Lee, V.E. (2001). *Restructuring High Schools for Equity and Excellence.* New York: Teachers College Press.

Leithwood, K. (1995). Toward a more comprehensive appreciation of effective school district leadership. In K. Leithwood (ed.), *Effective School District Leadership.* Albany: State University of New York Press, 315–340.

Miron, G., Welner, K.G., Hinchey, P.H., & Molnar, A. (2008). *School Choice: Evidence and Recommendations.* East Lansing, MI: Great Lakes Center for Education Research and Practice.

Muncey, D.E., & McQuillan, P.J. (1996). *Reform and Resistance in Schools and Classrooms.* New Haven, CT: Yale University Press.

Pasmore, W.A., & Fagans, M.R. (1992). Participation, individual development, and organizational change: a review and synthesis. *Journal of Management*, 18(2), 375–397.

Payne, C.M. (2008). *So Much Reform, So Little Change.* Cambridge, MA: Harvard Education Press.

Schlechty, P.C. (2001). Assessing district capacity. In *The Jossey-Bass Reader on School Reform*. San Francisco: Jossey-Bass, 361–381.

Senge, P.M. (1990). *The Fifth Discipline*. New York: Doubleday Currency.

Slavin, R.E. (1998). Sand, bricks, and seeds: school change strategies and readiness for reform. In A. Hargreaves, A. Lieberman, M. Fullan, & D. Hopkins (eds.), *International Handbook of Educational Change*. Dordrecht, The Netherlands: Kluwer, 1299–1313.

Snipes, J.C., & Casserly, M.D. (2004). Urban school systems and education reform: key lessons from a case study of large urban school systems. *Journal of Education for Students Placed at Risk*, 9(2), 127–141.

Snipes, J.C., Doolittle, F., & Herlihy, C. (2002). *Foundations for Success*. Washington, D.C.: Council of the Great City Schools.

Swann v. Charlotte-Mecklenburg Board of Education, 402 U.S. 1 (1971).

Viadero, D. (November 7, 2001). Whole-school projects show mixed results. *Education Week*, 1, 24–25.

10
THE CHALLENGES OF LEADING AND LEADERSHIP

LEADERSHIP FOR THE LONG HAUL[1]

When Tom Payzant took office as the superintendent of the Boston Public Schools (BPS) on October 1, 1995, he understood that years of low performance, political struggles, and public criticism could not be corrected overnight. Payzant also understood that he would not face the challenges of improving BPS alone. Boston's mayor, Thomas Menino, had pledged his support. Payzant was the first superintendent to assume leadership since the school system came under mayoral control.

Thinking strategically had been a hallmark of Payzant's leadership prior to coming to Boston. Soon after he arrived, he articulated his administration's vision and theory of action in a five-year reform plan entitled *Focus on Children*. His approach would not be limited to turning around the lowest performing schools. Payzant insisted that every school in BPS be improved. This enormous task would be accomplished by focusing on five "actions."

First, clear expectations for what all students should learn needed to be specified. At the time few large districts had undertaken such an initiative. Second, a uniformly rigorous curriculum had to be developed to replace the hodgepodge of programs in place across the district. Creating a set of common expectations regarding instructional practices constituted the third element of Payzant's theory of action. The last two elements involved comprehensive professional development for Boston teachers and the implementation of formative and summative assessments to enable district leaders to track progress.

When Payzant eventually stepped down after 11 years of leadership, much of his agenda for change had been implemented and student achievement had risen substantially. To ensure the success of his plan, Payzant had spent time in every Boston public school getting to know its special needs and staff strengths and weaknesses. This knowledge allowed him to develop district policies and practices to support the improvement of classroom instruction. Part of the infrastructure of central office support was a Web-based system for examining student data by school and by classroom. The data management system was updated on a daily basis and used to drive decision making.

Payzant realized that large scale school improvement would require an army of talented teachers and administrators. He consequently targeted the human resources department for upgrading. The result was a more efficient operation that meant principals no longer had to scramble to fill positions after the beginning of school.

In a step intended to eliminate the bureaucratic "silos" that separated related services and inhibited collaboration, Payzant merged the special education department and the student support services team into a single unit. This move had the effect of reducing the number of referrals to special education and out-of-school placements for students with disabilities.

In an effort to overcome communications problems between the central office and schools, Payzant appointed principals to his superintendent's leadership team. Not only did this move symbolize his high regard for the role principals play in district improvement, but it enabled him to monitor closely school-based concerns. Payzant also streamlined the supervision system for principals by having each principal report directly to one of three deputy superintendents.

Knowing that meaningful change in BPS depended upon community support and involvement, Payzant created the role of deputy superintendent for family and community engagement. One of the responsibilities associated with this new position involved the development of partnerships between BPS and various public and private organizations in the Boston area. For his part, Payzant met regularly with a group of community leaders to learn about their hopes for the school system as well as their concerns.

One of the most frequently voiced concerns from parents and the community involved the need for more choices for secondary students. Payzant set to work developing a portfolio of high school options, ranging from small schools and theme schools to schools that required entrance exams.

✷✷✷✷✷

Few can dispute the fact that Tom Payzant exercised the leadership that Boston Public Schools needed to reverse years of decline. During the course of his 11 years at the helm of BPS, he addressed almost all of the challenges discussed in the preceding chapters of this book. How then can his leadership best be described? He clearly was a problem solver who identified and successfully addressed a number of longstanding issues that had held back Boston Public Schools. Problem solvers focus on eliminating problems. Payzant, however, did not stop with eliminating problems. He was a creator as well, designing improved organizational structures for supporting teaching and learning. Add to his leadership portfolio the skills of a master politician, a coalition builder, and a visionary, and it becomes apparent that leadership can be a very complex phenomenon to try and understand.

THINKING ABOUT LEADERSHIP

Fundamental to meeting the challenges of leading a school district is reflecting on the nature of leadership. This topic has been saved for last because, in many ways, it is the most daunting of all challenges. So much has been written about leaders and leadership that one can find support for just about any position. As a consequence, confusion often trumps clarity when discussions of leadership occur. Perhaps it is best therefore to begin this section by trying to understand what leadership is not.

Leadership, first of all, is not a role. One individual may occupy the role of leader (superintendent, school board chair, division head, and so forth) and yet not be perceived to manifest leadership. Another individual may fill a relatively low-level organizational role and yet be widely credited with exercising leadership. This book has focused on school district leaders, individuals who occupy top-level, formal leader roles in school systems. It is important to distinguish between these roles and the phenomenon of leadership. This book is entitled *The Challenges of School District Leadership*, not *The Challenges of School District Leaders*, because it is leadership rather than a particular job title that, in the final analysis, enables the various challenges to be addressed effectively. It is highly desirable, of course, for the individuals who occupy top-level leader roles to manifest leadership.

It is unlikely, though, that any leader will manifest leadership at all times. A substantial part of being a leader involves managing the organization. This observation leads to a second assertion about what leadership is not. Leadership is not management. The exact nature of the difference between the two varies with the observer. In the military a distinction is often drawn between the management of things and the leadership of people. With a touch of unintended irony, President Richard M. Nixon, in his book *Leaders* (1982), maintained that management involves "doing the thing right" while leadership calls for "doing the right thing." The former entails following procedures and observing rules and regulations. The latter, however, carries a moral imperative. Under certain circumstances, leadership may require that procedures, rules, and regulations be set aside in order to do the right thing.

Burns (2003, p. 2) insists that leadership is an inherently moral enterprise. "Bad" leadership is an oxymoron. To speak of "good" leadership, in other words, is to risk redundancy. When people use the term *leadership*, after all, they generally do not associate it with lack of direction, disorder, incompetence, and ineffectiveness. Leadership invariably is related in some way to uncommon achievement and desirable outcomes. Perhaps this explains why the term *leadership* tends to be used more in the past tense than the present tense (Duke, 1986). People expect to see results before they credit someone with leadership.

We have considered what leadership is not. So what is leadership? Clearly the term is full of complexity. Otherwise why would experts insist on adding adjectives to it? Over the years leadership has been modified by such adjectives as charismatic, democratic, differentiated, distributed, resonant, situational, transactional, transformational, and visionary. District leaders are exhorted to exercise change leadership, cultural leadership, instructional leadership, and symbolic leadership. Despite the plethora of leadership concepts, university-based programs to prepare district leaders tend to be guided by a highly generalized notion of leadership. This notion usually is rooted in a set of skills and functions that must be mastered in order to fulfill the role of an education executive.

The focus of leader preparation programs on skills and functions reflects the egalitarian nature of U.S. society. It is consistent with prevailing values to believe that anyone can be a district leader as long as they acquire the appropriate skills and understand how to perform the necessary functions. This belief contrasts with the traditional notion that leadership depends on the possession of certain key traits (Northouse, 2007, pp. 15–38). Those who are not endowed with these traits presumably stand little chance of exercising leadership.

While it is not politically correct these days to publicly associate leadership too closely with specific traits, many people privately believe that leadership is a function of such trait-like qualities as intelligence, self-confidence, determination, integrity, and sociability. These qualities tend to be stable and enduring. Those who lack them therefore are unlikely to develop them through coaching and instruction.

Closely related to trait-based notions of leadership is the concept of *fit* (Duke, 1986, pp. 17–18). Fit concerns the perceived relationship between leaders and the settings in which they are expected to lead. Fit also can refer to the extent to which leaders conform to the expectations of the times in which they live. "A continuing interaction," according to Duke (1986, p. 17), "takes place between the leader, his followers, and the culture in which they exist." So, while a leader attempts to influence what followers think and do, followers are simultaneously trying to influence what the leader thinks and does.

Fit obviously is a controversial concept because it can be used to justify discriminatory selection processes for leaders. This is especially true when candidates are rejected because of their race, ethnicity, gender, age, or other factors beyond their control. Nonetheless there is no denying the fact that some leaders seem to be a better fit with their setting and times than other leaders.

The notion of differentiated leadership (Duke, 2010) is not subject to the legal and ethical shortcomings of fit. Based in part on the work of contingency theorists and advocates of situational leadership (Northouse, 2007), the idea of differentiated leadership is straightforward: different circumstances are likely to require different priorities, theories of action, and ways of leading. In *Differentiating School Leadership* (Duke, 2010), examples are provided to show how effective leadership can vary depending on whether a principal is faced with preventing school decline, turning around a chronically low-performing school, sustaining school improvements over time, or developing a non-traditional school from scratch. It is likely that district leadership can be similarly differentiated.

All leaders, it is safe to assume, have more to do than time available to do it. So, too, do the professionals working with them. Under such circumstances, focus is absolutely essential. If there is one function universally associated with leadership, it involves direction. In the presence of leadership, people sense where they need to go and how they can get there. If direction is a key to leadership, then focus is a key to direction. People cannot move in all directions at once. Given limited time and resources—and time and resources are always limited—leaders must know how to discern what must be done from what might be done and be able to convey this information in a sufficiently convincing way to win the commitment of those they lead.

With regard to school district leadership, it is reasonable to expect that a superintendent with a large number of low-performing schools will choose to focus on a different set of priorities than a superintendent charged by her school board with moving the district from "good to great." Leading a large urban district that is welcoming large numbers of newcomers from abroad likely will call for a different focus than leading a small rural district with a highly stable population. The universal leadership challenge, of course, is to identify what to focus on.

While a district leader's focus of attention depends on such factors as the district's track record of performance, financial condition, size, and demographics, there is one constant to which all district leaders must attend. Every superintendent is a leader of leaders. He or she has an obligation to do everything possible to develop the capacity of others for leadership. Fulfilling this obligation, of course, necessitates understanding leadership. It is hard to promote leadership in others if one is confused about what leadership is and is not.

Leadership, in the final analysis, is an interaction between a leader and a group of followers (Burns, 1978). The interaction is intended to accomplish a set of purposes that is unlikely to be accomplished in the absence of leadership. Leadership is what enables followers to understand and commit to what must be done to accomplish these purposes. This book has discussed a variety of challenges that frequently must be addressed by district leaders and those they lead in the course of accomplishing the purposes of the district.

The remainder of this chapter considers three questions on which every district leader should reflect as they grapple with the challenges of leadership. Being able to answer these questions should help district leaders assess their own performance and cultivate leadership in others.

The Challenges of Leading and Leadership

1. What makes school district leadership so challenging?

2. How can district leaders undermine their own effectiveness?

3. What is required to sustain success as a district leader?

KNOWING WHERE THE LANDMINES LURK

Previous chapters have described a variety of challenges facing school district leaders, and there are dozens more that could be discussed. It is tempting to contend that these challenges are what have made the job of leading school districts so daunting. This contention, however, would only be partially correct. There is no question, of course, that matters of competing priorities, changing demographics, governance, district organization, accountability, instructional improvement, school safety, staffing, and change can be demanding and difficult. To a great extent, however, district leaders expect to confront these challenges. They go with the territory, so to speak. It is the unexpected obstacles that often turn out to be greater sources of angst for district leaders than the challenges themselves. Every district leader traverses territory dotted with landmines. At any moment seemingly innocuous issues can blow up and threaten the effectiveness and even the tenure of a leader. And those are just the innocuous issues! The major controversies can even take a toll on a leader's health and well-being. There is a reason why Blumberg's (1985) path-breaking book on school superintendents was sub-titled *Living with Conflict*. Bennis (1989) entitled one of his leadership books *Why Leaders Can't Lead: The Unconscious Conspiracy Continues*, and while he was not writing specifically about school district leaders, his title easily could apply to the experiences of many superintendents. Bennis argued that a collection of forces ranging from distrust of authority to organizational inertia conspire to prevent leaders from taking charge and making changes.

When Blumberg (1985) interviewed superintendents in the early 1980s for his book, he uncovered a variety of sources of frustration. Superintendents complained about how long it took to make decisions, even relatively minor ones. The popular image of the decisive leader stepping into the breach and making the critical decision required to save the day rarely applies to district leaders. By the time stakeholder groups have been consulted and deliberations have taken place at various levels, months and perhaps years may have passed. Whatever initial enthusiasm existed regarding a particular course of action is likely to have evaporated.

Blumberg's (1985) superintendents expressed concern over "loneliness at the top." Some were wary of friendships with those they supervised. Others were never sure whom they could trust. Superintendents realized that people often told them what they thought they wanted to hear in the hopes of currying favor. When major problems arose, however, superintendents frequently felt as if they stood alone. Support was hard to come by at these times.

Another concern involved the frequency of situations in which superintendents felt that they were compelled to compromise their values. One superintendent spoke about concealing information in an effort to avoid conflict. Another related how he had sided with school personnel instead of parents, though he really believed that the parents were right.

Several superintendents poignantly noted that they had made so many compromises over the years that they wondered whether they held true to any values.

There are no indications that the job of leading school districts has gotten any less frustrating since Blumberg's interviews were conducted in 1985. Contemporary district leaders are still called upon to make compromises and trade-offs. They frequently are faced with deciding between what is ethically correct, what is politically expedient, and what is educationally effective. They are expected to uphold the Constitution and the rule of law, but in some cases they question the benefit to society of certain laws. The law, for example, may require a superintendent to spend large sums of money for private school tuition for severely disabled students who are unlikely ever to function on their own. The superintendent knows that the funds required for these services reduce the funds available to help other students who are not protected by law.

The increasingly political nature of leading a district has been pointed out at various places in the preceding chapters. Few district leaders sought careers in education because they loved politics and enjoyed conflict. Yet the world in which they must function is characterized by special interest groups, lobbying, campaigning, threats, and personal attacks. Hess (1999) observed that superintendents and school boards are frequently caught up in an enervating process he calls *policy churn*. Policy churn involves political factions that continually promote pet reforms in order to please their supporters. Once they have taken credit for the reforms, they move on to new reforms. District leaders are left to fend for themselves and try to sustain the reforms.

The disappearance of stable coalitions in American society has been noted by observers (Janowitz, 1978). This development affects district leaders as much as it does elected politicians. Superintendents in many locations are uncertain about whom they can count on. This week's ally may become next week's adversary. As a result, district leaders must devote considerable time and energy to the mobilization of support, not just for new initiatives and annual budgets, but also for themselves. The high turnover rate for superintendents in the United States suggests that the battle to win such support is frequently lost.

There is another aspect of leading school districts that generates considerable anxiety and stress for many leaders. Put simply, it is often difficult for leaders to determine whether they are making much of a difference. This problem exists for anyone who is far removed from the "chalkface." Should district leaders judge their effectiveness in terms of goal achievement? If so, who deserves more credit, the leader who sets modest goals and always achieves them or the leader who sets ambitious goals and just misses? Or what about the satisfaction of customers? Customer satisfaction clearly is important, but what of customers who have relatively low expectations for their schools? Or unreasonably high expectations?

District leaders serve at the pleasure of the school board. Is it therefore a sufficient indicator of effectiveness to have earned the support of board members? What if board support comes at the expense of support from teachers and principals? Some district leaders seem to feel that they have performed well if they comply with rules and regulations, live within their budgets, and manage to avoid controversy. Does such a cautious conception of effectiveness constitute leadership?

Each leader must answer these questions for himself or herself. One thing is certain, though. Regardless of how district leaders judge their effectiveness, when they are successful, credit should be given to others in the school system. Leaders who try to take all the credit for accomplishments rarely enjoy much support or popularity. When things do not go well, on the other hand, it is expected that leaders will assume full responsibility. Such is the burden of leadership.

Of all the reasons why leading a school district can be so challenging, though, perhaps none is greater than the variety of ways by which district leaders can undermine their own effectiveness and sabotage their leadership. It is to these self-inflicted wounds that we now turn.

HOW LEADERS UNDERMINE THEIR LEADERSHIP

One of the fastest growing medical specializations is iatrogenic medicine. This field is devoted to understanding and correcting problems *caused* by physicians. Stories abound of physicians who made an incorrect diagnosis, ignored a patient's valid complaint, or prescribed the wrong treatment. A comparable specialization that focuses on problems created by leaders in the act of leading may not be a bad idea, given the variety of ways that leaders can undermine their effectiveness. Awareness of these self-inflicted problems can help district leaders avoid shooting themselves in the foot. Among these problems are relying on false necessity, downplaying bad news, enabling groupthink, dealing ineffectively with data, succumbing to distractions, neglecting to follow up and follow through, and failing to learn from mistakes. Let us take a closer look at each of these leader lapses.

Relying on False Necessity

The parable of the shepherd who cried "Wolf!" once too often comes to mind when thinking about the dangers of false necessity. Leaders who rely on false necessity to rally followers elevate every concern to the level of an emergency. Such action eventually can cause followers to disregard a leader's exhortations. Their ability to distinguish between a true crisis and a contrived crisis is compromised.

A similar price can be paid when leaders declare every goal to be a high priority. The point has already been made. When everything is a high priority, nothing is a high priority. The primary purpose of establishing priorities is to provide guidance to people on how to allocate scarce time and resources. When every goal is a high priority, people are left to decide for themselves where to focus effort.

Why leaders may be tempted to rely on false necessity and over-prioritization is understandable. Leaders operate, as noted earlier, in a political world. Not to designate some interest group's pet problem as a crisis or a high priority is to risk criticism and conflict. Rather than incur the wrath of patrons of the arts, for example, a district leader may decide to declare arts education to be as high a priority as science education. Or every time funds for special education are threatened, a crisis is declared. While such decisions may be "playing it safe" politically, they hardly represent leadership. Leadership is associated with the courage to make tough and often unpopular decisions, decisions that place the good of the entire community above the welfare of any particular component of the community.

Downplaying Bad News

While some leaders seem prone to exaggerate problems, others head in the opposite direction, preferring to minimize the importance of concerns. They invest considerable energy in putting a positive "spin" on even the most troubling information. "When people are scared to draw attention to unwelcome information," according to Finkelstein (2003, p. 177), "it's a slippery slope to becoming involved in cover-ups."

The author is familiar with a superintendent, for instance, who lost her job because she tried to cast depressing student achievement results in a positive light. Instead of comparing her district's test scores with those in comparable school systems, an approach that would have revealed serious deficits in her district's achievement, she insisted that students in her district were making steady gains. As it turned out, any gains that were made were attributable to a small group of very high-performing students. When the performance of these students was set aside, test scores in virtually every subject and grade-level had declined dramatically.

Besides the ethical concerns associated with misleading people by downplaying and misrepresenting negative information, such a strategy ultimately can backfire. When the public has been led to believe that everything is going well, they are likely to feel angry and betrayed when things get so bad that they can no longer be plausibly denied. To make matters worse, efforts to enlist help from the community at this point are likely to fall on deaf ears. Asking for support after pretending that everything was fine cannot help but raise questions about a leader's credibility.

Leadership depends on transparency. District leaders must accept the fact that the public has a right to know how the public schools are doing. This policy of openness goes for all aspects of district operations, from how well students are achieving relative to other districts to how public funds are being spent. Only in a few areas such as personnel matters must leaders observe confidentiality.

When superintendents like John Fryer and Tom Payzant took over, they did not pretend that things were better than they were. Nor did they suggest that the situation was hopeless. It is part of the art of leadership to convey an honest assessment of how much needs to be done without implying that it is undoable. Launching any improvement initiative when people lack a clear understanding of the current situation is risky at best and foolhardy at worst.

Enabling Groupthink

One reason why some leaders tend to downplay bad news is their tacit tolerance for *groupthink*, a phenomenon defined as "a collective pattern of defensive avoidance" (Janis & Mann, 1977, p. 129). Most leaders typically rely on a group of trusted advisors or a leadership team of some kind to assist them in the process of making non-routine decisions. Groupthink is the term coined to characterize these high-level groups when group members are more concerned about group cohesion and maintaining their own standing in the eyes of the leader than they are in making sound decisions.

Janis and Mann (1977, p. 130) identified a variety of indicators that groupthink is at work. One sign is that the group screens out warning signals and discounts information that could cast leaders in a negative light. Outside criticism typically is met with excuses. One can imagine, for example, a superintendent's leadership team reacting to declining student achievement by denying responsibility and instead complaining about lack of adequate resources and parental support. When groupthink is at work, group members anticipate what the leader wants and support this position rather than challenging it, even when they have serious misgivings about the course they believe the leader has chosen. Conformity and denial are the hallmarks of groupthink.

It is not hard to understand why leaders who enable groupthink to characterize their advisory groups can run into problems. To deal effectively with challenges, a leader must be aware of the challenges and must have access to open and honest information about what can be done to address them. When a leader's closet advisors withhold information that might upset the leader, refuse to point out weaknesses in the leader's reasoning, and parrot the position they guess is favored by the leader, they increase the likelihood of eventual disaster. This was precisely the fate of President Richard M. Nixon when members of his inner circle concealed crucial information regarding the American public's concerns over the Watergate scandal.

There is much that leaders can do to avoid groupthink. According to Janis and Mann (1977, pp. 179–180), leaders should keep their positions to themselves until they have heard from all their advisors. Doubts and misgivings should be encouraged and even rewarded. Leaders can designate one group member to play the role of devil's advocate to make sure that prevailing beliefs and preferences are challenged. Leaders also should be careful about assuming that silence constitutes consensus. It is always a good idea to have each group member vocalize their feelings about a particular position or decision. Leadership teams and advisory groups that routinely "rubber stamp" the desires of the leader probably should be reconstituted.

Dealing Ineffectively with Data

Pick up any book on contemporary organizational leadership and it is likely to include an exhortation for leaders to see that as much performance-related data as possible is collected and analyzed. Data-driven decision making is the mantra of today's leader, and school district leaders are no exception. As Chapter 5 of this volume suggests, district leaders are awash in all kinds of data related to student achievement, school outcomes, teacher qualifications, and the like.

Wagner (2002) offers a reminder, however, that data is no better than the mindset that a leader brings to its analysis. A leader, for example, may tend to over-generalize based on preliminary findings or give too much weight to information gathered relatively early in the decision-making process. How leaders interpret data is likely to be influenced by their prior experience, experience which may be limited to a particular locale or type of organization. A superintendent who has worked only in "right to work" states where public employees are not allowed to collectively bargain may have difficulty, for example, making sense of data on teaching performance in a district with a powerful teachers union that participates in collective bargaining.

Wagner (2002, p. 47) points out that leaders are likely to discover what they expect to discover when they analyze data. Leaders develop *causal stories* (Stone, 1989) to explain why things happen in a particular way. They may believe, for example, that the cause of the achievement gap between black students and white students is due to socioeconomic differences. This belief can lead them to disregard data on high-performing, high-poverty schools.

One of Wagner's (2002, pp. 47–48) most disturbing findings concerns how some leaders process information. Once these leaders form an opinion, they are unlikely to change it, no matter how much new and contradictory information is introduced. Whether this dogged defense results from fear of appearing equivocal is unclear, but such disregard for data can lead to dreadful consequences.

Paying too much attention to real time data also can result in problems for leaders. Senge (1990) warns leaders not to ignore trend data. "Learning to see slow, gradual processes," he points out, "requires slowing down our frenetic pace and paying attention to the subtle as well as the dramatic" (p. 23). The decline or improvement of a school district is not necessarily a linear process. Data from a given year may bring false hopes or occasion premature pessimism. Leaders should look at data over a number of years and across all organizational units before drawing conclusions.

To further reduce the likelihood of ineffective data interpretation and analysis, leaders are advised to seek input from knowledgeable individuals who possess different experiences, causal stories, and perspectives. When the focus of concern is problems internal to the organization, it is advisable to solicit impressions from those who are closest to the problems. Leaders typically are far removed from front-line problems. Their efforts to make sense of data can be distorted unless they hear from individuals "in the trenches."

Succumbing to Distractions

Focus is a key to leadership. Maintaining focus on priorities is not so simple, however, given the ceaseless parade of distractions that intrude on every leader's agenda. When Deborah Jewell-Sherman became superintendent of Richmond Public Schools, she understood that the only hope for turning around her chronically low-performing school system was to initiate a laser-like focus on literacy and instructional improvement. No sooner had she taken office, however, than budget problems necessitated curtailing some bus runs. Parents reacted angrily. Then problems arose with her special education office, and the state insisted on immediate action to correct compliance issues. A flap over the use of metal detectors in schools required considerable attention. Richmond's mayor, against the wishes of the school system and his own city council, sought to move the school system offices out of city hall. The fact that Jewell-Sherman was able to deal with these matters without losing focus is testimony to her effectiveness under fire.

Many leaders, however, are not as skilled as Jewell-Sherman. They allow themselves to be caught up in petty squabbles and diverted from priorities. Those they lead begin to lose their sense of direction and question whether anyone is in charge. Consider the many plans that are carefully developed during the summer when schools are out of session. In all too many cases, the plans are backburnered by November, set aside because of more immediate (though less strategic) concerns.

Distractions obviously are not going to disappear. District leaders must learn to attend to distractions without allowing themselves or those they lead to forget about district priorities. Processes like the Balanced Scorecard and project management (discussed in Chapter 9) have proven useful for keeping district personnel focused on accomplishing high-priority goals.

Neglecting to Follow Up and Follow Through

No one disputes the fact that district leaders are very busy people. The pressures of a packed schedule can lead to various self-inflicted problems if a leader is not careful. One such problem is failure to follow up in order to determine if directions have been understood and acted upon. Successful leaders do not assume anything. They realize that those to whom they give directions also are busy. There is always a possibility that a subordinate misunderstood what the leader wanted or failed to appreciate the urgency of the expectation. While every leader must delegate responsibilities (failure to delegate constitutes another way that leaders can undermine their effectiveness), it is essential that they periodically check to see that their wishes have been carried out. When subordinates know that leaders routinely follow up, they are much more likely to get things right the first time.

Just as it is important for leaders to be able to count on subordinates to carry out their directives, it is important for subordinates and patrons to be able to count on leaders to follow through on their commitments. Follow through is a key to trust, and trust is an essential ingredient in leadership. Leaders can get into trouble, for example, when they meet with personnel and patrons to learn about their concerns and then fail to address the concerns. People expect that their expressions of concern will lead to action. Of what value is it to elicit concerns and then do nothing to improve conditions? When leaders fail to deliver on their explicit and implicit promises, they jeopardize their credibility.

Failing to Learn from Mistakes

Every leader, no matter how competent and conscientious, makes mistakes. The greatest mistake that any leader can make, however, is failing to learn from their mistakes. Argyris (1991) examined successful professionals and concluded that their strengths can beget weakness. Most individuals who rise to the position of leader are bound to have succeeded at many things they tried. It is likely, in fact, that they have relatively little experience with failure. "And because they have rarely failed," Argyris observes, "they have never learned how to learn from failure" (p. 100). When things go wrong, those who lack much experience with failure often become defensive and search for excuses. By denying their own contribution to problems, these individuals increase the likelihood that the problems will recur.

Each of the self-inflicted problems mentioned in this section can become an opportunity for leader learning and growth. All that is required is the right mindset, one that is oriented more to improvement than appearing smart. When leaders possess a *growth mindset* (Dweck, 2006), they are more likely to inspire an organizational culture of openness. Finkelstein (2003, p. 277) characterizes such a culture thusly:

> Openness means fighting the natural tendency to cover up unfavorable or distasteful information. It requires leaders to set the standard for learning from mistakes—an unnatural act in many organizations. Leaders who are unable or unwilling to build a culture of openness create organizations that almost choose not to learn.

SUSTAINING SUCCESS AS A DISTRICT LEADER

It is tempting to argue that the key to sustained success as a district leader is either the avoidance of self-inflicted problems or the ability to learn enough from reflecting on self-inflicted problems to ensure that they are not repeated. There is, however, more to sustained success that these important elements.

In a search for similes to capture what leading a school district is like, a three-ring circus comes to mind. So much is going on simultaneously under the big tent that at any moment things can get out of hand. A wild animal might escape. A trapeze artist could fall. It is up to the ringmaster to see that everything runs smoothly and, if disaster strikes, to ensure that people do not panic.

A superintendent shares many of the responsibilities of a ringmaster. At the same time, superintendents are also like circus tightrope walkers. It is on this particular simile that we shall focus as we consider the keys to sustained success for district leaders.

A tightrope walker's greatest asset is a keen sense of balance. Without a sense of balance, a tightrope walker's career is likely to be a short one. So it is as well with leaders of school districts. Effective district leaders understand the importance of balanced leadership. They also appreciate the fact that maintaining balance can be very challenging. Leaders are pushed and pulled in various directions. Moving too far in any one direction can be risky.

It is important to bear in mind that maintaining balance is not the same as sitting on the fence. Fence-sitting is the curse of the cautious. It characterizes those who avoid taking a stand. Leadership is not about playing it safe and dodging controversy and conflict. Nor is leadership about taking unnecessary risks and acting impulsively.

Balance applies to many aspects of school district leadership. Let us conclude this book by considering several examples of the need for balance.

Mission and Vision

According to Blankstein (2004, p. 77), a mission statement reminds us of why we exist, while a vision statement describes what we can become. A school district's mission constitutes a commitment to the public. It is squarely focused on the here and now, a guarantee that district personnel (1) understand what students need in order to become productive adult citizens and (2) are prepared to address these needs.

A school district's vision is fixed on the future. It represents an acknowledgement by district leaders that we live in an ever-changing world and that we have an opportunity, indeed an obligation, to shape the future in ways that will make the world a better place in which to live.

Dwelling exclusively on matters of mission can lead to several potentially undesirable outcomes. First, attending to the here and now can increase the likelihood that tomorrow will be a lot like today. This outcome may be fine in a world that never changes, but it is hardly helpful when change is a constant. Second, concentrating on the mission and ignoring the vision ensures that when changes occur, those committed only to the mission will have had no hand in shaping the changes.

Problems also can result from focusing exclusively on vision. Long distance airline pilots refrain from looking too long at a cloudless horizon because they can develop a kind of temporary blindness that prevents them from reading their instrument panel. Leaders who over-concentrate on the future, in similar fashion, may trip and stumble over day-to-day challenges.

Effective district leadership calls for a balance of attention to mission and vision. Leaders need to make certain that they do whatever is necessary to accomplish the district mission, while anticipating future educational needs. Both mission statements and statements of vision must be living documents that are reviewed and adjusted as circumstances change. Perhaps the best mission statement is one that includes provisions for the continuous monitoring of emerging trends and their possible implications for education. In other words, the mission statement acknowledges the value of vision.

Continuity and Change

Many experts on leadership cast leaders in the role of change agents. While understandable, this view neglects the importance, under certain circumstances, of organizational continuity. Chapter 9 suggests that too much intentional change at one time can be self-defeating. People lose a sense of direction and, in trying to attend to multiple reforms, often ensure that no reform is implemented appropriately. Though it seems ironic, effective change depends, to a significant degree, on a measure of stability. Continuity, in other words, constitutes a desirable condition for change.

Stability is typically associated with routines. Routines are important elements in organizational effectiveness. If personnel fail to develop standard operating procedures for handling predictable problems, the organization is likely to suffer. The longer routines are in place, however, the more they can contribute to inertia. As Kouzes and Posner (1987, p. 47) put it, "Routines...can be the enemies of change." They go on to acknowledge, however, that routines "are among those things we can't live with and we can't live without" (p. 48). The critical issue for leaders, they contend, is neither the implementation of routines or no routines, but *which* routines. Leaders who balance their appreciation for routines with a recognition of the limitations of routines are able to determine when particular routines are no longer functional and need to be changed.

Blumberg's (1985, p. 208) interviews with superintendents led him to conclude that leading a school district required both behaving "in ways that maintain the organization as a system with minimally disruptive conflict" and behaving "in ways that change the character and substance of educational life in the system." Knowing when and what to change and when and what to preserve, of course, boils down to a matter of judgment. And it is judgment, a cognitive dimension of leading, that turns out to be one of the most fundamental components of leadership.

Creativity and Caution

Successful leaders are always scanning the environment for promising new ideas. On occasion, they even come up with their own original ideas. The gifts of creativity and imagination can be invaluable assets for leaders, especially when they are faced with unprecedented challenges and novel situations (Duke, 1986). Tom Payzant exemplified creativity and imagination when he took over the superintendency of Boston Public Schools. His efforts to reinvent the human resources department, combine the special education and student support services units, and place principals on his central office leadership team demonstrated his willingness to challenge convention and experiment with new and better ways of doing things.

Payzant also knew where to draw the line on innovation. Students in low-performing schools are not laboratory subjects on whom any new "cure" can be tried. A commitment to consider reforms has to be balanced against an insistence on credible evidence that the reforms are likely to benefit teaching and learning. District leaders have an obligation to protect students from hucksters peddling untested and unproven panaceas. They also are expected to protect taxpayers from wasteful and unnecessary expenditures. Since school districts are rarely blessed with in-house research and development units of the kind found in the private sector, district leaders often must rely on published educational research and third-party evaluations to guide their reform efforts. When relevant research and evaluation data are unavailable, district leaders should lobby government, universities, and foundations to support systematic investigation of matters of practical significance.

Control and Support

School boards and superintendents ultimately are responsible for everything that goes on in a school district. The weighty burden of such responsibility can cause district leaders to concentrate on controlling every aspect of district operations. When control becomes too heavy-handed, however, initiative and accountability on the part of subordinates can be undermined and trust can evaporate. District leaders cannot run a school system on their own. Leadership is needed at every level. With this *distributed* leadership must go a certain measure of autonomy and a good deal of central office support.

Some school districts have swung 180 degrees from a top-down control orientation to extensive school-based management. Hargreaves and Fink (2006, p. 103) warn that distributing greater authority to school-based leaders is not automatically a prescription for success. When Deborah Jewell-Sherman took the helm of Richmond Public Schools and launched a district-wide campaign to improve student literacy, she first had to curtail the authority of school principals. Principals had been allowed under previous administrations to choose whatever reading program they wanted. As a result, there were almost as many reading programs as there were schools. Many of the programs had not proven to be effective. The proliferation of different programs inhibited the provision of district-wide professional development on literacy instruction.

Fairfax County Public Schools, as has been noted before, is considered to be one of the nation's best school systems. One key to its success has been the ability of district leaders over the years to maintain balance in the distribution of authority (Duke, 2005, p. 169). A measure of school-based management has enabled Fairfax principals and their staffs to customize many offerings and allocate resources in ways that respond to local needs. At the same time, the central office has developed its capacity for setting standards and monitoring school performance. By maintaining close and constructive relations between the central office and the schools, Fairfax leaders have achieved a productive balance between control and support.

Balanced Perspectives

Among the definitions of *perspective* in the *Microsoft Encarta College Dictionary* (2001, p. 1084) are the following:

- a particular evaluation of a situation or facts, especially from one person's point of view
- a measured or objective assessment of a situation, giving all elements their comparative importance
- the appearance of objects to an observer allowing for the effect of their distance from an observer

An important dimension of leadership is a leader's perspective. As the above definitions suggest, however, perspective is a complex concept. Perspective constitutes a point of view regarding some situation or body of factual information, but it also connotes an effort to make certain that the point of view is an objective one based on a careful assessment of the relevant elements. The third definition implies that this point of view may be affected by the distance between the observer and the observed.

Heifetz and Linsky (2002) capture the complexity of perspective by referring to the view from the balcony and the view from the dance floor. When leaders are in the midst of action, in other words when they are on the dance floor, it is necessary at times to gain perspective by ascending to the balcony. Only by doing so will they be able to appreciate the ebb and flow of activities and detect patterns of activity over time.

Leaders must be careful, however, not to spend too much time on the balcony. To do so is to risk losing touch with the dancers on the dance floor. Heifetz and Linsky (2002, p. 73) recommend that leaders regularly move back and forth from the dance floor to the balcony. Only in this way can they be assured of a reasonably balanced perspective on organizational operations.

A slightly different take on the notion of balanced perspective was offered by Schein (1985) in his analysis of leadership and organizational culture. The introduction to this book discussed Schein's view that all leaders are compelled to grapple on a continuing basis with two overarching challenges—internal integration and external adaptation. Internal integration is necessary to keep personnel focused on the organization's mission. When people are allowed to advance their personal interests and disregard the need for cooperation and team work, the organization suffers. External adaptation refers to the requirement for every organization to adjust to its environment. An organization that is continually at odds with its neighbors is unlikely to succeed.

From time to time, the need to concentrate on internal integration may be greater than the need to concentrate on external adaptation, or vice versa. No leader, though, can afford to ignore either challenge. Leaders must maintain a balanced perspective that takes into account both the internal needs of the organization and the expectations of the environment. Leithwood (1995, p. 322) recognized the necessity of this balanced perspective when he concluded that every superintendent must attend to five areas of concern—"the community, the elected school board, the school district itself, mandates from national and...state governments, and general social trends."

A Final Qualifying Comment

As crucial to leadership as is the need for balance, it would be a mistake to overlook the power of passion. When it comes to the welfare of young people, balance must give way to whole-hearted and unambiguous advocacy. Balance, in other words, is only valuable to the extent that it enables district leaders to create and sustain the conditions needed to serve the interests of students. Educators frequently talk about the readiness of children for school, but the more important consideration is whether schools are ready for children. It is the responsibility of district leaders to see that they are.

EXECUTIVE CONCLUSION

There is no matter more fundamental to the leadership of school districts than an understanding of leadership and what it means to lead. An individual who occupies the role of a district leader also must realize that a significant portion of the job involves managerial responsibilities. Leadership constitutes an interaction between a leader and subordinates to accomplish a set of purposes that could not be accomplished otherwise. Leadership provides the direction and inspires the commitment necessary to get the job done.

A variety of factors conspire to make school district leadership especially challenging. Besides the "routine" challenges discussed in previous chapters, district leaders must contend with the unexpected. They can never be sure, for example, that their directives will be carried out as they intended or that their decisions will be implemented as hoped. Then there are the personal challenges associated with isolation and compromised values. The highly politicized nature of district leadership can take a heavy toll and interfere with leaders' efforts to promote educational equity and excellence.

District leaders can contribute to their problems through actions over which they exercise some control. Examples of self-inflicted problems include relying on false necessity, downplaying bad news, enabling groupthink, dealing ineffectively with data, succumbing to distractions, neglecting to follow up and follow through, and, perhaps worst of all, failing to learn from mistakes.

There is much that district leaders can do to sustain successful leadership. A key to long-term effectiveness is the ability to maintain a sense of balance with regard to such perennial issues as mission and vision, continuity and change, creativity and caution, and control and support. There is also great benefit in a balanced perspective on leading, one that enables a leader to understand what is going on at ground level as well as to see the "big picture." To these examples of balance must be added one more ingredient for successful district leadership—a passionate commitment always to act in the best interests of young people.

NOTE

1. Much of the information on Tom Payzant's tenure as Boston's superintendent was derived from S.P. Reville (ed.), *A Decade of Urban School Reform*. Cambridge, MA: Harvard Education Press, 2007.

REFERENCES

Argyris, C. (1991). Teaching smart people how to learn. *Harvard Business Review*, 69(4), 99–109.

Bennis, W. (1989). *Why Leaders Can't Lead: The Unconscious Conspiracy Continues*. San Francisco: Jossey-Bass.

Blankstein, A.M. (2004). *Failure Is Not an Option*. Thousand Oaks, CA: Corwin.

Blumberg, A. (1985). *The School Superintendent: Living with Conflict*. New York: Teachers College Press.

Burns, J.M. (1978). *Leadership*. New York: Harper & Row.

Burns, M.J. (2003). *Transforming Leadership*. New York: Atlantic Monthly Press.

Duke, D.L. (2010). *Differentiating School Leadership*. Thousand Oaks, CA: Corwin.

Duke, D.L. (2005). *Education Empire: The Evolution of an Excellent Suburban School System*. Albany: State University of New York Press.

Duke, D.L. (1986). The aesthetics of leadership. *Educational Administration Quarterly*, 22(1), 7–27.

Dweck, C.S. (2006). *Mindset: The New Psychology of Success*. New York: Ballantine Books.

Finkelstein, S. (2003). *Why Smart Executives Fail*. New York: Portfolio.

Hargreaves, A., & Fink, D. (2006). *Sustainable Leadership*. San Francisco: Jossey-Bass.

Heifetz, R.A., & Linsky, M. (2002). *Leadership on the Line*. Boston: Harvard Business School Press.

Hess, F.M. (1999). *Spinning Wheels: The Politics of Urban School Reform*. Washington, D.C.: Brookings Institution.

Janis, I.L., & Mann, L. (1977). *Decision Making*. New York: The Free Press.

Janowitz, M. (1978). *The Last Half-Century*. Chicago: University of Chicago Press.

Kouzes, J.M., & Posner, B.Z. (1987). *The Leadership Challenge*. San Francisco: Joseey-Bass.

Leithwood, K. (1995). Toward a more comprehensive appreciation of effective school district leadership. In K. Leithwood (ed.), *Effective School District Leadership*. Albany: State University of New York Press, 315–340.

Microsoft Encarta College Dictionary. (2001). New York: St. Martin's Press.

Nixon, R.M. (1982). *Leaders*. New York: Warner Books.

Northouse, P.G. (2007). *Leadership: Theory and Practice*, fourth edition. Thousand Oaks, CA: Sage.

Reville, S.P. (ed.). (2007). *A Decade of Urban School Reform*. Cambridge, MA: Harvard Education Press.

Schein, E.H. (1985). *Organizational Culture and Leadership*. San Francisco: Jossey-Bass.

Senge, P.M. (1990). *The Fifth Discipline*. New York: Doubleday Currency.

Stone, D. (1989). Causal stories and the formation of policy agendas. *Political Science Quarterly*, 104(2), 281–300.

Wagner, R.K. (2002). Smart people doing dumb things. In R.J. Sternberg (ed.), *Why Smart People Can Be So Stupid*. New Haven, CT: Yale University Press, 42–63.

INDEX